DATE DUE

Shell Shock

Shell Shock

Traumatic Neurosis and the British Soldiers of the First World War

Peter Leese
Senior Lecturer in Social and Cultural History,
Jagiellonian University
Kraków, Poland

First published 2002 by
PALGRAVE MACMILLAN
Houndmills, Basingstoke, Hampshire RG21 6XS and
175 Fifth Avenue, New York, N. Y. 10010
Companies and representatives throughout the world

PALGRAVE MACMILLAN is the global academic imprint of the Palgrave Macmillan division of St. Martin's Press, LLC and of Palgrave Macmillan Ltd. Macmillan® is a registered trademark in the United States, United Kingdom and other countries. Palgrave is a registered trademark in the European Union and other countries.

ISBN 0–333–96926–X

This book is printed on paper suitable for recycling and made from fully managed and sustained forest sources.

A catalogue record for this book is available from the British Library.

Library of Congress Cataloging-in-Publication Data
Leese, Peter.
    Shell shock: traumatic neurosis and the British soldiers of the First World War/by Peter Leese.
        p. cm.
    Includes bibliographical references and index.
    ISBN 0–333–96926–X (cloth)
        1. War neuroses—Great Britain—History—20th century. 2. World War, 1914–1918—Psychological aspects. 3. World War, 1914–1918—Medical care—Great Britain. I. Title

    RC550
    616.85′212′0094109041—dc21
                                                                    2002022412

10   9   8   7   6   5   4   3   2   1
11   10   09   08   07   06   05   04   03   02

Printed and bound in Great Britain by
Antony Rowe Ltd, Chippenham and Eastbourne

for Lydia Ellen Fletcher (1908–1999)
and
Gordon William Leese (1931–2000)

Contents

Preface and Acknowledgements

I first thought of an inquiry into the lives of the war-traumatized soldiers of 1914–18 as an MA student at the University of Warwick in 1983 studying the cultural history of Western Europe. The notion struck me then, and I still hold by the idea, that to speak about a modern age it is necessary to investigate not only changes in artistic expression or artillery tactics, but also shifts in thinking and feeling that were poorly articulated or never consciously formulated, expressed in changing bodily gestures and patterns of behaviour and distributed among a mass population. From the beginning then, the idea of a study of the war-traumatized soldiers of the Great War seemed an ideal vehicle for a study of what it meant to live a life in the modern age, of how historical changes registered in mental states, which had personal, bodily and cultural implications. My intention has been, therefore, to scrutinize some aspects of the lives of ordinary men who were altered by their extraordinary labours during the war: their healers, supporters and chastisers; their feelings, thoughts and bodies, all changed drastically by combat; their stories of illness, treatment and, sometimes, renewal. Looking back to 1983, I am now able, as well, to discern some of the sources of my attraction to the 1914–18 generation and to recognize that the impetus for this study has its roots not only in intellectual curiosity, but also in family history.

My family, like most British families of the twentieth century, has been touched by the events of 1914–18. My maternal great-grandfather, Frank Fletcher Sr, born in 1880, worked as a stevedore at the Surrey Docks in East London, and after joining the 51st Argyle and Sutherland Highlanders he participated, as a corporal, in the Great War. What precisely happened to him remains unclear. The only letter we have related to his war service, presumably written in March 1915, though it is dated '5.3.14', is headed '7897 Corp F. Fletcher, Arg and Suth Highlanders, No 5 Group British Interned Prisoners, Scheveningen, Holland'. One of Frank's sons-in-law, who still survives, aged 81, became a conscientious objector during the Second World War not, as I might have expected from my nonconformist upbringing, on religious grounds, but simply because he had seen the damage inflicted by the Great War on his parents' generation, and he refused to kill.

I was educated at a Manchester comprehensive school in the 1970s and, like many children of my own and earlier generations, I was given the poems of Wilfred Owen to read. Although I did not know about my great-grandfather at that time, Owen's work deeply impressed me, and 'Dulce Et Decorum Est' became a part of the way I have come to understand the world around me as well as a part of the way I understand myself. It was Owen too who helped reinforce in me that sceptical view of authority that has seeped into the British temperament. I became more fully aware of this outlook in myself when, in the early 1990s, I first encountered Polish society, which in some respects has a stronger sense of authority, hierarchy and deference, and a quite different view of war and patriotism. These are not in any way extraordinary snippets from the history of a British family, but they are clues that show some of the ways in which the Great War runs right through the social history of twentieth-century Britain.

Beyond this personal inheritance I have also incurred many professional debts of gratitude during the writing of this study. For leading me to the idea of a study of shell shock I have Volker Berghahn to thank. For reading, commenting and suggesting many improvements I am grateful to Bernard Waites, without whose support, encouragement and hospitality over many years this book would not have existed. For key appearances and probing questions at several critical occasions my thanks also to Jay Winter. I have benefited from discussion with many others closely and distantly involved in this subject, including Alan Costall, Paul Lerner, Mark Micale, Gerry Oram and Ben Shephard. Similarly both staff and students at the Jagiellonian University have listened patiently and discussed intelligently as I have worked on this book.

My thanks also to the librarians and archivists of the British Library, the British Red Cross Archive, the Cambridge University Library War Collection, the Oxford English Faculty Library, the Oxfordshire District Health Authority Archive and the Public Record Office. The Peter Liddle Archive kindly granted me access to their records. The staff at the Cassel Hospital gave me all the help they could and a space to examine their registers and files; the National Hospital at Queen Square did the same. I am grateful to them both for permission to quote from their records, and to the Wellcome Library for the History and Understanding of Medicine for allowing me to use the Royal Army Medical Corps Muniment Collection. Sir Islay Campbell of Succoth allowed me access to and permission to use passages from the records of Lennel Convalescent Home. For permission to quote from family papers deposited at the Imperial War Museum I thank Felix Gameson (Gameson Papers), H. Sturdy (Sturdy Papers) and James Crerar (Crerar Papers).

Parts of Chapter 5 were published as ' "Why Are They not Cured?": British Shell Shock Treatment during the Great War', in M. Micale and P. Lerner, eds., *Traumatic Pasts: History, Psychiatry and Trauma in the Modern Age, 1860–1930* (Cambridge University Press, 2001). Similarly, a draft of Chapter 8 appeared as 'Problems Returning Home: The Experience of British Psychological Casualties during the Great War', *The Historical Journal*, XL (1997). These are reprinted here with the permission of Cambridge University Press. Parts of Chapter 10 appear in 'The Memory and Mythology of the Great War in Contemporary Britain', in K. Kujawińska-Courtney and R. Machnikowski, eds., *The Role of Britain in the Modern World* (Łódz University Press, 1999). My thanks to the editors.

My special thanks go to Elżbieta Wójcik-Leese and to Tomasz Adam Wójcik-Leese for their irreplaceable companionship and encouragement.

P.J.L.
Kraków

1
Introduction

At the Battle of the Marne in September 1914, soldiers began to circulate strange tales: a group of men had been discovered in the front line, standing on duty, alert, ready for action, but no longer alive. 'Every normal attitude of life was imitated by these men,' reported *The Times History of the War* (1916), elaborating on the story two years later, 'their bodies were found posing in all manner of positions, and the illusion was so complete that often the living would speak to the dead before realising the true state of affairs.'[1] From such rumours came the impression that the huge firepower of the newly mechanized artillery could lead to virtually undetectable brain damage from the impact of microscopic mortar fragments. Taken up by both military leaders and civilian observers, this persistent idea led in turn to a new term used by soldiers in the trenches as early as November and December 1914 and by many doctors in France and Britain throughout the war when referring to brain injury. It was no coincidence that a splintering 'shell' was now connected to an obliterating 'shock'. 'Shock' was associated with both individual and collective military action as far back as the sixteenth century, particularly with the collision between warring opponents; by the nineteenth century its meaning was connected too with the technology of war and the medical disorders of peace, nervousness and emotional strain as well as the collapse of the circulatory system.[2] If the implicit association with the nervous system and with the anguish of war was not intended in the first use of 'shell shock', front line soldiers quickly made it.

As a genesis story for the naming of shell shock, the Marne incident is suitably mythic, but it obscures a more complex history of medical knowledge, industrial technology and urban modernity as they interact to create an early twentieth-century epidemic of hysteria. The German

1

sociologist Georg Simmel observed the conditions for this confluence in 1903. Industrial technology, he thought, had transformed human experience: speed, noise and nervous tension were now the defining characteristics of city life, which had a new quality of 'calculative exactness' observable in the timekeeping of the office commuter, the finger strokes of the typing secretary and the time and motion measurements of the scientific shop floor manager.[3] What Simmel failed to note, however, was the consequent need to withdraw from everyday life. If varieties of mental distress were not in themselves any reason to leave the routines and restraints of the ordinary world, physical disorder did sanction the sick role: it made an escape route. Mental pressures were accordingly manifest in varied physical symptoms, among them fits, faints and paralyses. These symptoms constitute an idiom of suffering and sickness: a physical style for expressing inner pain, which was bound in time and culture.[4] The new style of mental sickness was discussed in the court, the clinic and the officers' mess: insurance legislators began to make employers liable for workplace stress injuries and owners liable for traumatic railway accidents; doctors began to examine the effects of fatigue and strain on work performance. Similarly, as they used more accurate and powerful transportation systems and shells, generals were faced with reports on unfamiliar battlefield injuries. The soldiers' hysteria of the First World War can best be seen, then, as a part of a wider craze that took off in Western Europe and America in the 1870s and responded to the stresses and anxieties of urban industrial society. With its intensified version of industrial labouring, and with types of sickness, injury and mutilation all its own, the First World War further refined this style of hysteria and thereby made a particular idiom of traumatic neurosis. By dint of this common background, traumatic neurosis was often analysed, regulated and treated in the 1880s and 1890s in ways that would become familiar to any shell-shocked soldier from the Western Front.

With the naming of shell shock came the organization of bureaucratic structures, medical literature and viewpoints that could serve both patriotic and dissenting causes. Doctors began to investigate and write papers, and to talk to each other about symptoms and ways to counter the damage. Generals began to think about the implications of the mental breakdown of troops, and how it might be discouraged or prevented. Soldiers began to talk too, telling each other what they had seen or heard, and in some cases experiencing shell shock for themselves. Public and politicians also became involved as concerned relatives discovered more; Members of Parliament tried to protect men from the asylum and the death penalty, to promote the efficiency of the war effort and exploit their populist cause. Medics brought to shell shock their training and experience as asylum and Army doctors; soldiers brought their own strong opinions on madness, cowardice and loyalty to their comrades, all tempered by an intimate acquaintance with the rumour, mutilation and death found in the trenches. Unwillingly, and often unsuccessfully, doctor and patient tried to come to some mutual understanding of the startling physicality and range of symptoms that described the hysterias of war. These symptoms included withered, trembling arms, paralysed hands, stumbling gaits, tics, tremors and shakes, as well as numbed muteness, palpitations, sweaty hallucinations and nightmares, all of which might constitute the outward signs of mental distress.

As the hostilities ended, the implications of wartime traumatic neurosis began gradually to filter through to civilian society. War neurotic ex-servicemen came to symbolize the struggle for the rights of all former soldiers: by promoting their cause, campaigners hoped to establish that the generals had wrongly sanctioned execution, to ensure that proper treatment and care were available as long as they were needed. In popular memory the shell-shocked soldier now becomes a wretched figure, no better off than a blinded or paralysed veteran begging on a street corner. To the Ministry of Pensions the war neurotic ex-serviceman was a financial burden; to the War Office he was a clue to future tactics and the preservation of manpower resources; to the postwar doctor who specialized in work-related conditions his arrival marked the beginning of a more sophisticated form of industrial psychology. Made from the stories of soldiers, from the wartime image of heroes who sacrificed their sanity, and from the growing sense of disenchantment after the Armistice and between the wars, the war-traumatized neurotics of 1914–18 gradually became associated with a particular view of the war. In popular imagination and memory as well as in the creations of the literary elite, shell shock changed its meanings to suit the preoccupations of British society through the twentieth century.

To understand these histories of traumatic neurosis in the First World War – how it came into being, how it was experienced and negotiated, and how it is remembered – is to understand how a mental condition is culturally shaped. One of the purposes of this study is to understand this process; another is to investigate the condition and fate of a particular group of war-damaged British soldiers who fought in the Great War. To further these objectives I have organized what follows around three themes: 'Discoveries', 'Wartime' and 'Legacies', with most attention paid to the war years. My argument is that shell shock defines for the first time, both qualitatively and quantitatively, a modern condition that becomes all too familiar through the twentieth century: mass trauma. Shell shock is modern because surrounding it are scientific and bureaucratic procedures designed to manage human emotions and behaviour and direct them towards mass, state-controlled activity, in this instance, making war. As I have tried to show, this parallels wider processes that took place in civilian society before and after the First World War. Within these totalizing procedures, however, I want to stress the role of agency by concentrating on personal experience: the ways in which both patients and doctors made shell shock after their own image, sometimes negotiating common meanings, sometimes resisting the soldierly and disciplinary medical roles they were expected to play.

Part I, 'Discoveries', is concerned with the continuity of the worker's experience through peace and war, and with related technology and bureaucratic practices. In Chapter 2, 'Shocking Modernity: Hysteria, Technology and Warfare', I describe how the soldier of the Great War was an industrial worker of sorts, and how he was subject to the same pressures, in an intensified form, that shaped traumatic neurosis before 1914. In peace or in war, the worker calculates the relationship between authority and danger, while the bureaucrat and the medic calculate the arithmetic of disability and compensation. There are limits to the parallels between peace and wartime work. At a certain point the sheer mass of weapons technology begins to make the Great War experientially unique for its participants. Although this is not a military history of the war, it is necessary to understand something of how it was fought, and particularly how participants experienced combat, in order to comprehend the trauma it inflicted as well as the ways soldiers could avoid such damage. The discovery of shell shock is also to be found in the relationship between doctor and patient, and the social setting in which both tried to understand and react to these new conditions. Chapter 3, 'Casualties: On the Western Front', thus explores the ways in which the Army and the medical community responded to the challenge of shell shock, how the ethos and organization of Army Medical Services affected its ability to deal with the condition, and how this compares to the response of the French and German Armies. This is a study of British soldiers, but comparison allows other points of reference to establish in what ways the British experience of wartime traumatic neurosis was shaped and bound by its culture.

Part II, 'Wartime', examines the front line and Home Front, and the experience of trauma in both the other ranks and the officer ranks.

Chapter 4, 'Enlistment: Army Policy, Politics and the Press', argues that civilians and state representatives alike viewed war neurotic servicemen with profound ambivalence. Among members of the public, giving donations to a shell shock treatment centre made it possible to support the war effort without imagining bodily destruction; it was the cause too of several public appeals and newspaper campaigns that sought to prevent wrongful executions or asylum incarceration, and ensure the proper treatment and care for men who had sacrificed their nerves and their minds to the war effort. Despite all this apparent support, shell-shocked soldiers were tainted by the condition's association with insanity, cowardice and malingering. These associations were strongest within the military, where discipline and medicine made few concessions to mental disorder, viewing it as a threat to manpower and morale that had to be neutralized. This affected both the management and treatment of soldiers-patients. Chapter 5, 'Treatment: On the Home Front', thus describes the arrangements for cures, and compares the British, French and German approaches. I also explore in some detail two of the major schools of treatment practice: disciplinary, as represented by the Queen Square Hospital, and analytic treatment, as used particularly at Maghull. These represent, though, only a part of the soldiers' hospital experience. Chapter 6, 'Patients: The Other Ranks', and Chapter 7, 'Patients: The Officer Ranks', examine various sets of case notes as well as hospital journals, diaries and letters to learn more about how shell shock hospitals functioned in practice, how patients were treated and how men interpreted their own sickness experience. Maghull and Craiglockhart are used as case studies on hospital organization, ethos and military–medical relations, but non-specialist hospitals treated a large proportion of shell-shocked soldiers, especially from the other ranks, and an analysis of case notes provides a way to understand a form of treatment that I would characterize as 'benign neglect'.

Part III, 'Legacies', explores the post-combat experience of war neurotics and the place that shell shock has taken within British culture through the twentieth century. Chapter 8, 'Demobilization: On Returning Home', discusses the problems men encountered as they returned to civilian society. There was continued political debate on veterans' rights and pensions policy, and this makes it possible to see war neurotic ex-servicemen as one section of the much larger group of all returning veterans, many of whom faced the same problems as traumatized returnees. In the early postwar years Sir John Collie, whose career and thinking are examined in some detail here, was most responsible for the formation and implementation of pension and treatment policy.

Chapter 9, 'Veterans: War Neurotic Ex-Servicemen', explores the points of contact between individual and state: the bureaucratic procedures and structures within which men were placed, and especially the working of the pension assessment, or Special Medical Board system. A close examination of individual pension records provides a picture of the degree of disablement men continued to suffer after the Armistice, and shows how unstable the conditions of war neurotic ex-servicemen were. This chapter also attempts to reconstruct the life patterns of such men through the 1920s and 1930s: their failed and successful efforts to reintegrate back into civilian society, their tendency to relapse during times of economic or personal hardship, their exclusion from state institutions with the passage of time.

Chapter 10, 'Recall: The Great War in the Twentieth Century', asks why traumatic neurosis, uniquely, has taken such an important role in the British cultural memory of the Great War. Recollection is viewed here as a malleable source that cannot be relied on to reveal historical truth, but still provides an invaluable insight into how individuals and societies conceive and shape their identities through their relationship with the past.[5] In this chapter I note that the two world wars hold a pre-eminent place in modern British memory, and argue that the coincidence of Britain's attempt to redefine its place in the world following the fall of the Berlin Wall in 1989 and the anniversary cycle of fifty years following the Second World War is only one example of how past and present are used to define each other. Concepts of popular memory also help to explain the personal meaning of public history in recent historical thinking. In this sense the persistence of a popular memory of shell shock forms a part of the wider mythology of the war – a story of betrayal and sacrifice that continues to resonate into the 1990s with the long-running campaign to pardon the executed soldiers of 1914–18, many of whom, it is now assumed, were suffering post-traumatic stress disorder.[6]

The sources and research process for this study require a word of explanation. Piecing together the making of shell shock has, through its many meandering turns, been both frustrating and fascinating. Only exceptionally do the sources give a direct, personal experience of war trauma; hospital records and medical case notes, where they survive, are among the most oblique and faceless of sources; sometimes access to records was denied on ground of medical confidentiality. Among the wider mass of letters, diaries and memoirs that recall the war, accounts of shell shock are only a part of any story: they are to be found in fragments, comments, and habitually retold anecdotes based on a ritualized form of shorthand that bears little relation to the wider experiences of war. Still, remote as they are in time and sentiment, these sources contain some of the most vivid accounts of the war's effect on the mind. My first reading of Hiram Sturdy's manuscript at the Imperial War Museum was especially memorable. After months of sifting evidence, reading this mordant, bitter commentary, with its dramatic, hand-drawn illustrations showed me, almost for the first time, the awful experience of the war, and the reality of wartime traumatization. The extraordinary hospital training films recovered in the 1990s, which put me face to face with the twisted gaits and tic-ridden faces of the men I had studied for so many years, were similarly illuminating.[7]

Researching hospitalization and hospital life in France and the UK provided different challenges: personal accounts were useful, but soldiers were usually incapable of taking notes or writing letters. Hospital magazines provided a way around this problem because patients were relatively unguarded in personal statements when addressing their peers. The *Gazette of the 3rd London Hospital*, the *Springfield War Hospital Gazette*, and the *Craigleith Chronicle* were all invaluable; *The Hydra*, Craiglockhart's magazine, uniquely documents life in an officers' specialist hospital. Similarly, the huge clinical literature shows how doctors tried to understand and treat traumatized soldiers, but professional medical dialogue and written accounts of treatment are no guide to what happened in the consulting room.

Medical case sheets provided a way out of this impasse, but presented their own difficulty: every set of notes seemed to imply something different about the nature of medical practice, the medical gaze and the role of patient records within the hospital regime. Despite their faults, such sources contain a wealth of insight into medical practice and perspective in a way that published medical texts cannot, as I hope this study shows. The Queen Square case notes provide a remarkable opportunity to observe and understand the workings of a specialist hospital for nervous and mental disorders, revealing especially that there are no simple divisions between 'good' and 'bad' practice. Chapter 5 argues that Yealland's work at Queen Square is an overused example of treatment, and an unrepresentative one. Working at the Queen Square Institute of Neurology Library where the hospital records are preserved, as well as at the Cassel, was in itself immensely helpful. Seeing the rooms where soldiers were treated, walking the same corridors, gave me another view of their experience. A final set of wartime medical case notes came from the Lennel Convalescent Home for Officers in Scotland. The Lennel papers are the only notes devoted exclusively to the treatment of officers, and so give a unique insight into the differences and similarities of officer and other rank experience. Their limitation is that as a private convalescent home, doctors kept a bureaucratic log rather than a day-by-day record, and again, without a comparable set of institutional records for an other ranks hospital, it remains difficult to identify what aspects of the Lennel notes were merely idiosyncratic and what were common practice.

Hospital admission and discharge registers were useful because, while medical records were often destroyed or inaccessible, these records were frequently kept, so the Ashurst War Hospital registers, the partial Lennel registers and the Yearly Statistics and Reports of the Cassel Hospital for Nervous Diseases all provided otherwise inaccessible data on hospital regime and patient profile. Tracing patients from hospital registers back to the front line was time-consuming but revealing, and the most useful in this respect were the Craiglockhart registers, which are examined in Chapter 7. Likewise, Ministry of Pensions records, used in conjunction with soldiers' pension documents, provided the bulk of information on the after-effects of traumatic neurosis: the treatment network system, reviews of cases and treatments, discussions on veterans' grievances and accusations of malingering. The mass of detail to be found in soldiers' personal pension documents is only touched on here to gather details of claimants' histories, life-stories and symptoms. Veterans' experience was, however, invariably interpreted and edited according to the doctors' interests, thus making it all the harder to understand and piece together the lives of war neurotic ex-servicemen.

Readers will note from these comments on sources that I have quoted extensively from medical notes: from Queen Square in Chapter 5; from non-specialist war hospitals throughout Britain in Chapter 6; from Lennel convalescent home in Chapter 7; and from the Ministry of Pensions files in Chapter 9. My purpose in doing so is to escape from the use of shell shock as a cultural metaphor, to focus on the relationship between medic and patient, wherever possible in their institutional and broader social context, and to give a realistic picture of the nature and variety of one idiom of traumatic neurosis. A complete recovery of the clinical encounters between therapist and patient is impossible. My ideal sources, two diaries, one by a patient and one by a doctor, recording and reflecting on the nature of their clinical encounter, simply do not exist. What might be reconstructed though are parts of that dialogue, especially through doctors' medical records, as well as the institutional and intellectual framework within which the therapeutic encounter took place. The sections of this study where I quote extensively from medical records are my attempt to re-create these encounters – to show a fraction of the bargaining that such meetings surely entailed, and so to recover something of the means by which an historically bound mental condition came into being. The use of medical records also raises a more practical issue of medical confidentiality. My rule throughout this study is to use only initials to identify individual soldiers, and false initials whenever I have been asked that soldiers should remain entirely anonymous. Some soldiers are named, but only when their identity is already clearly in the public domain. Two related issues of definition remain to be addressed: the number of casualties affected by wartime traumatic neurosis and the nature of their condition.

Even with the knowledge that we now have, the number of British shell shock cases is very difficult to estimate accurately. The official statistics are notoriously unreliable, chiefly because of the limitations placed on doctors by Army medical policy and the lack of standardized diagnostic techniques. Diagnosis was, in any case, difficult under the best of circumstances. As a result, many psychological casualties are omitted from the official count: traumatic symptoms were often dismissed by medics, and in many instances re-diagnosed later. The most notable instances are 'fits' diagnosed as epilepsy, and confusion over the aetiology of what came to be known as 'Soldier's Heart'.[8] What also emerges from a close scrutiny of medical notes is that many of the men who were diagnosed during the war as shell shock cases were mentally deficient, with disabling mental handicap or learning and behavioural difficulties.[9] According to one estimate this group may have constituted around 13 per cent of all those diagnosed as shell shock cases, but while some of these men might have been deliberately misdiagnosed because this was the only way to remove them from active combat, it remains impossible to say what proportion of mental defectives were also cases of traumatic neurosis.[10] Another cause of misdiagnosis and a proportion of 'invisible' cases was the practice on the part of some medical officers not to give an official recorded diagnosis to officers; other officers avoided doctors altogether and got transfers away from the Front or even back home with the aid of higher-ranking comrades. Finally, in their work during and after the war, Ministry of Pensions medics frequently limited the definition of shell shock for reasons of medical judgement and financial pressure.

The earliest volume dealing with shell shock statistics was the *Medical Diseases of War*, Volume 2 (1923), which gives figures for a total number of cases amounting to 80,000 or 2 per cent of all soldiers injured.[11] Given the variable basis of definitions of shell shock and the loss of records in the second half of the war, these are the least reliable statistics. The figures in the *History of the Great War Based on Official Statistics*, Volume 7, *Medical Services, Casualties and Medical Statistics* (1931) also invite caution, based as they are on the narrow definition of shell shock used by the Ministry of Pensions. In listing causes of disability amongst British pensioners from the Great War, the figure amounts to 58,402 cases, or 6.8 per cent of all soldiers receiving a pension.[12] According to recent studies, 200,000 is a reliable estimate of the number of troops suffering psychological disorders in both the French and German Armies, though in the case of France, where the mobilization was largest, this represents a smaller proportion of the total fighting force.[13] The true British figure is probably closer to the numbers in France and Germany. Sir John Collie, who was closely involved in the treatment of shell shock throughout the war and in the work of the Ministry of Pensions, and who would certainly have preferred to give the lowest figure he could, claimed that around 200,000 soldiers were discharged from active service due to various mental disorders. His estimate is by far the most credible.[14]

One idiom of the sickness experienced by British soldiers during the Great War, and which they might well have referred to as 'shell shock', would today be called 'post-traumatic stress disorder'. My understanding of shell shock is, as Allan Young has persuasively argued, that it was one of a group of hysterical conditions 'glued together by the practices, technologies, and narratives with which it is diagnosed, treated and represented'.[15] There is nothing universal here. Post-traumatic stress disorder, like shell shock before it, is the product of historical conditions: of the particular institutions where patients are treated, of the preconceptions brought by those who treated it and those who suffered it. In this study shell shock is seen as a malleable, subjective state: muscles, vocal cords and limbs respond to the soldier's distressed mind, but that same distressed mind absorbs too the sympathy of comrade and relative, the outrage of editor and MP, the censure of officer and pension doctor. My intention is not to imply that shell shock was an imaginary condition, nor to diminish its importance, but to take it seriously as a means to further our understanding and interpretation of the human experience of industrial labour, of the Great War and of cultural change in British society. My particular focus is shell shock as it was experienced, because at the centre of all pasts is individual human understanding: a synthetic, subjective knowledge that encapsulates from one point of view the social and political pressures, the intellectual climate and the cultural mood of a particular time and place. The place is Britain, the time is the modern age of the late nineteenth and early twentieth centuries, the subject is the industrial worker traumatized by war. What follows, therefore, is an exploration of the forces that caused shell shock, the attitudes that shaped it and the cultural echo that follows it.

Part I
Discoveries

2
Shocking Modernity: Hysteria, Technology and Warfare

Technology and traumatic neurosis

The proper starting point for the study of traumatic neurosis during the Great War is the mid- and late nineteenth century. It is at this time that nervous disorders resembling those that became so prominent between 1914 and 1918 began to appear in the workplace, at the site of the train crash and on the battlefield. It is at this time that employers, politicians and generals started to notice traumatic neurosis. Medics did the same as they encountered these new forms of hysteria, and usually their clinical gaze was coloured by the requirements of morality, money and manpower. To understand what was later called shell shock then, it is necessary to appreciate something of the technological and medical developments in Europe and America in the decades before the Great War, of their relationship to Western Front warfare and the processes of psychic self-protection those workers on the shop floor and in the trenches had to develop to survive the shocks and rattles of modern industrial labour.

The closest experience to trench warfare before winter 1914 in civilian society was to be found in the wreckage of a railway accident. Both the trench and the locomotive carriage were confined spaces in which the occupant was at the mercy of external events; the surrounding environment could be only passively observed as sight and sound were severely obstructed; the impact of collision could not be anticipated or avoided, only experienced.[1] By the late 1850s trains were beginning to speed up, and with the new expansion of the track system across Europe came 'engineer's malady' and a batch of other conditions associated with the jars and jolts of steam engine transportation. E.A. Duchese investigated these conditions in *On the Railroads and Their Influence on the Health of Engineers and Firemen* (1857) and in a London pamphlet on

The Influence of Railway Travel on Public Health (1862). Most prominent of all was the work of John Eric Erichsen in *Concussion of the Spine, Nervous Shocks and Other Obscure Injuries of the Nervous System* (1882).[2] The issue was legal as well as medical because where there was 'injury to the nervous system' a doctor often gave evidence against a railway company. Erichsen's work became a standard reference in both legal and medical literature as claims against rail companies increased, promoting the view that unseen and undetected molecular changes in the nervous system, brain and spine were responsible for paralysis, tremors or the loss of senses such as sight and hearing. However, Erichsen's views were soon challenged by Herbert Page, a surgeon to the London and North-West Railway, and author *Injuries of the...Spinal Cord without Apparent Mechanical Lesion* (1885), who argued that injuries such as paralysis, loss of hearing or sight, or mutism often occurred where no evidence existed for concussion of the spine or other shocks.[3] The explanation of *Injuries of the...Spinal Cord* was that psychological trauma was the source of these symptoms, and this view soon attracted a vocal group of supporters within the medical community.[4] Through the 1880s, for example, Page found support from J.J. Putnam, writing in the *Boston Medical and Surgical Journal*, who argued that railway accident cases displayed both neurotic and hysterical symptoms.[5]

In the 1880s, G.M. Beard also began writing on the wider psychological effects of modern industrial living. Beard identified a novel outbreak of new nervous disorders. In *American Nervousness* (1881) and *Sexual Neurasthenia* (1884), he suggested that an increasingly competitive business-oriented society, and the luxuries and vices of urban living, had given rise to an epidemic of fretfulness, tension and depression.[6] 'Beard's malady' became a common diagnosis in the 1880s associated with the new concept of fatigue, although some medics remained sceptical of the wearing effect of modern technology and mechanical collision.[7] These conditions resemble shell shock in that they were grab-bags of symptoms that constituted sickness without observable lesion, and required the disentanglement of complicated psychological and physical causes. Similarly, Silas Wier Mitchell faced an unexpectedly large number of nerve and shock cases while working as a medic during the American Civil War. In response, he developed the standard cure for the most common nervous complaint of the age, neurasthenia: seclusion, massage, electricity and immobility, together with restricted diet. The diagnostic label and the cure associated with it were widely adopted by medics in both Europe and America, becoming a standard, inexpensive, if ineffective treatment for shell shock.[8]

These early indications that the modern age contained within it the 'pathogenic' source of mental disorder took on new urgency as state welfare and compensation systems adapted to the changed conditions of industrial labour. In Britain, as elsewhere, welfare provision schemes were weighted against neurasthenia and other new disorders such as work-related traumatic neuroses; even when the idea of damages resulting from 'sudden terror or mental shock' gained a foothold in theory, as in *Mayne's Treatise on Damages* (1899), it was not widely embraced in practice.[9] The Employer's Liability Act (1880), the Workmen's Compensation Acts (1897, 1901, 1906), and the National Health Insurance Act (1911) all made employers liable if their workers were injured or incapacitated beyond a minimum period, and it was the compensation system itself, state officials and employers came to believe, that was responsible for increased absences and consequent increased costs. The Workmen's Compensation Act of 1906 seemed to provide convincing evidence. The Act extended employer liability, and over the next six years, the number of workplace insurance accident claims increased from 326,701 to 472,408.[10] Similarly, specialists in the detection of malingering noted that, between 1908 and 1913, when the number of employees and fatal accidents remained steady, the accident rate rose by 44 per cent and compensation payments by 62 per cent.[11] In military and civilian practice, the medical eye was cast with an increasingly sceptical gaze wherever there was traumatic collision of man and machine, wherever there was a calculable financial consequence attached to a chosen diagnosis.

Hysteria, a complex of elusive conditions, also preoccupied the medical community at this time, and its fate, too, was tied to moral, financial and employment issues of the day.[12] There was widespread disagreement about hysteria. Some saw it as merely a cluster of subjective associations on the part of doctor and patient, others as an objective, measurable disease like any other. There was more agreement on the variety of emotional and physical symptoms associated with the diagnosis. Quick, successive changes in mood or activity, fits, fainting, vomiting, choking, sobbing, paralysis or excessive laughter were some of the symptoms that might prompt this diagnosis, and though there was some medical debate on male hysteria in both England and France towards the end of the nineteenth century, it was still a condition most widely associated with women.[13] Within the British medical tradition doctors from the 1870s to the Great War saw the diagnosis and treatment of neurasthenia and hysteria, and its association with women, as the management of a measurable disease. Practitioners such as George Savage,

George Blandford and Thomas Clouston saw themselves as empirically-minded 'nerve specialists'. By temperament they were suspicious and derisive of continental practice and theory, favoured hereditary, organic and environmental explanations, and attached to neurasthenia and hysteria the taint of moral failure.[14]

The career of Sir George Savage (1842–1921) is an exemplary case study, not least because he went on to treat shell-shocked patients during the war. The author of *Insanity and Allied Neuroses* (1884), which ran to a fourth edition in 1907, he had a successful society practice, but despite writing a well-known and popular textbook, his career was very different from that of more academically-minded specialists with wider interests in anthropology, physiology and social psychology.[15] Savage edited the *Journal of Mental Science*, which published research on heredity and organic medicine, and was widely read by practitioners of psychological medicine. When required, Sir George and his like-minded contemporaries would explain hysteria by reference to hereditary defect or to the biological and social crisis of puberty, but they were often uneasy about or hostile to the very idea of hysteria because the vagaries of the condition made it difficult to classify and analyse. Savage certainly felt on firmer ground with neurasthenia, which he described in 1907 as an attention-seeking, neurotic condition that might result in loss of voice or limb paralysis.[16] Moreover, where there was no organic explanation available to the medic, mental conditions were usually interpreted as the consequence of character defect, which justified the intense physical and emotional pressure used to treat both hysteria and neurasthenia.[17]

At Salpetrière, outside Paris, from the 1870s until his death in 1893, Jean-Martin Charcot took an entirely different approach when he turned his attention to traumatic hysteria.[18] For Charcot this was as real as an organic condition (although it was not organic), it affected men as much as women, it had no moral stigma and its symptoms were unconscious in origin. Like so many other doctors of the 1880s, Charcot was faced with hysteria cases related to work compensation claims and railway accidents, but unlike most of his contemporaries in Britain or Germany, he did not moralize. Charcot's theories were, however, cast aside between 1893 and 1914, in favour of Joseph Babinski's view that hysteria was a non-disease. Babinski, like many British doctors, believed that whatever parts of hysteria biology could not explain found their questionable origin in the patient's psyche.[19] This suggestibility on the part of the patient was correctable by persuasion; therefore hysteria should be re-named 'pithiatism': curable by persuasion. Treatment was the process of establishing moral ascendancy for the doctor, moral culpability for the patient.[20] In Germany, Herbert Oppenheim also worked on traumatic neurosis through the 1880s, producing a study, published in 1889 and revised in 1892, of various cases related to rail crashes and factory accidents. The author acknowledged in his published findings both the physical effects that a crash or accident might have on the nervous system and the nervous trauma of such an event.[21] Just as in Britain, the increase in compensation claims that followed the recognition of traumatic neuroses by the Imperial Insurance Office in 1889 led a number of medics and politicians to the belief that policies stimulated claims.[22] The response in both countries was a widespread rejection of traumatic neurosis as a diagnostic category and the stigmatization of traumatic hysteria because mental health signified patriotism, duty and national well-being. Oppenheim held a minority view within the German medical community however, and his opponents finally prevailed during the Great War.[23] Throughout 1914–18 the stark diagnostic choice was between traumatic neurosis, which gave pension rights, yet allegedly cost the nation dearly in both its finances and its moral and mental health, and traumatic hysteria, which yielded no compensation but usually ended in return to employment. So, between 1890, when Oppenheim was first attacked at the Berlin Medical Congress as a rare advocate of traumatic neurosis, and the outbreak of the Great War, hysteria lost ground to rival concepts of mental illness, especially the psychotic and pathologic. Military medicine responded in like manner to the new mechanical and chemical technologies as their implications for the conduct of modern combat were played out in the military conflicts between the American Civil War and the outbreak of the Great War.

The second Industrial Revolution in particular reversed the existing view of military technology, so that whereas to earlier generations a weapon was seasoned by age, by the late nineteenth century the newest gun or artillery piece signalled tactical advantage. Technological obsolescence now became a chronic feature of industrial development. The gigantic new corporations, Krupp in Germany, and Vickers in Britain, magnified the size, power and number of all kinds of weapons, including artillery, battle cruisers and aircraft.[24] Consequently, each successive generation of armies became capable of destroying the next, technologies replaced themselves over shorter periods through the nineteenth century and, by 1914–18, weapons development had reached a state of constant innovation. A machine gun in the First World War had the same firepower as a Napoleonic battalion; artillery range increased by a factor of ten or more in the same period, and with it came the new, exacting mathematics of trajectory.[25] Military leaders were not always pleased to observe these changes, however. Count Helmuth von Moltke, for instance, German general and chief of staff 1906–14, regretted that extended troop movements and increasingly powerful weapons now forced armies to disappear below the line of visibility.

The American Civil War (1861–65) first uncovered the face of modern industrial combat, with its soldier-citizens, its large-scale train move-ment of troops and resources, and its long, dispersed fronts during Sherman's march south. The volume of participants, firepower and set-piece confrontations was also new: 48 large-scale engagements; 359,528 Union and about 385,000 Confederate soldiers killed; and allegedly 20.8 per 1,000 discharged for limb paralysis.[26] Similarly, the impact of new weapons systems is apparent in the large offensives and high casualty rates of the Russo-Japanese war (1904–5), the establishment of forward treatment centres, the train evacuation of 2,000 soldiers as psychiatric cases from Manchuria to Russia, and the discovery of men 'suffering from confusion and terror and deep-seated delusion'.[27] The increasingly marginal role of cavalry in Sudan (1898), the Boer War (1899–1902) and at the start of the Great War only hinted that warfare was changing into a race for technological advantage. Changed military strategy was one consequence of industrial innovation, another was rising populations: together they gave the potential for mass mobilization, destruction and psychological traumatization.[28]

The mental casualties of the American Civil War and the Russo-Japanese War were said to suffer 'nostalgia', 'paralysis' or 'insanity'. These diagnostic categories stressed the organic and hereditary, and so such men were seen not as part of a new pattern of sickness, but as isolated instances to be discharged as unfit for military service.[29] Some doctors, however, were able to discern a few of the warning signs. In 1910, Captain L.R. Richards of the American Medical Corps argued that large-scale mechanized warfare was likely to produce a high proportion of mental casualties in any future conflict. 'The tremendous endurance, bodily and mental, required for the days of fighting over increasingly large areas,' Richards argued, 'and the mysterious and widely destructive effects of modern artillery fire will test men as they have never been tested before. We can surely count, then, on a larger percentage of mental diseases ... in a future war.'[30] Similarly, two Royal Army Medical Corps doctors, observing the Serbo-Bulgarian War of 1913, noted con-cussion-like symptoms in 350 out of 5,000 wounded soldiers passing through one dressing station, and were also alerted to the potentially damaging mental effects of modern combat.[31]

Compensation, liability and injury-related calculation were of little consequence to the Army before the age of mass conscription, but they became important in the civilian workplace at around the same time as rail accidents began to generate a new medical literature. The 'railway spine' debate also raised interest in the detection of malingering, a condition of concern to both civilian and wartime employers, and long studied by military doctors. Not surprisingly, therefore, the earliest use of the term malingering related to fitness for military duty: in 1795, it was defined as 'a military term for one who under pretence of sickness evades duty'.[32] H. Gavin's *On Feigning and Factitious Diseases Chiefly in Soldiers and Seamen* (1843) defines fitness as the ability to work.[33] Subtitled *On the Means Used to Simulate or Produce Them and on the Best Modes of Discovering Impostors*, Gavin's study codifies a much older military tradition and sets out a modern view of work-related fitness; in effect, Gavin provided a self-contained reference system which let doctors test sceptically the alleged disease or disorder.

Gavin also gave particulars of a scale of pensions and compensation payments at fixed rates which allowed any medic to calculate the relevant degree of disability and the related sum of money. However, before making any such calculation doctors were duty-bound to question, if not disbelieve. By the time of the Boer War, little had changed. The Royal Army Medical Corps (RAMC), formed as a new division in 1898, was keen to establish its military rather than its scientific credentials within a system of health care designed 'to root out malingerers and penalize the victim of venereal disease'.[34] Consequently, the treatment of mental conditions was passed over by Gavin and ignored by the *RAMC Training Manual* for 1911, which has entries only for insanity and brain damage. The 1911 manual also makes clear the priorities for military medical officers in their training and practice: 'the interest of the Army require something even more than professional scientific knowledge ... because it is impossible for him to carry out his duties efficiently without a certain general knowledge of military science, especially as regards the administration of the Army in the field'.[35] If Army medical practice was incapable of internal reform, events elsewhere were shortly to challenge the military view of mental medicine.

The new warfare

Technology determined the development of the Great War. From August to November 1914 the conflict was not very much beyond participants' expectation: the Germans made dramatic advances into Belgium and northern France, a defeat for France was narrowly prevented and eventually, despite disastrous Allied casualties on the Marne, some semblance of a counter-attack was launched. Then, in November, the lines froze near Ypres. Stalemate set in. Germany had the powerful tactical advantage of intact supply lines, and struck hard, inflicting high French casualties. So, from November 1914, all through 1915, 1916 and 1917, and on into March 1918, a succession of offensives on either side failed to break the deadlock. By 1917, most armies, the French, Russian and British among them, showed signs of internal discontent, in some cases open mutiny. The British suffered tremendous losses in their summer offensives of 1916 and 1917; the Germans were unable to land their decisive knock-out blow and, with the exception of the Verdun offensive beginning in February 1916, remained on the defensive until March 1918. It was the French Army and the French people who lost most heavily.[36]

The General Staffs, managers of the war, found it difficult to organize their campaigns in the light of the changing conditions of industrial warfare. At the start of the war, leaders believed the Navy and the economy rather than the ground troops would decide who triumphed.[37] Lord Kitchener, the leader of the British military effort at the start of the Great War, alleged (unlike most of the other British generals) that the prudent use of resources, and especially the preservation of fighting force by a planned war of attrition, was the only means to win the war. Charged with raising the New Armies, Kitchener looked back to the American Civil War. Comparing the position of the Confederate States with that of Germany in 1914, he argued that the enemy's defeat required a total exhaustion of their men and supplies.[38] Russia and France, he thought, would exhaust themselves by the end of the third year of war, by which time British troops would be at their peak strength and ready to win the final peace. In the meantime, Britain's policy would be one of preparation rather than offence. However, Kitchener's manner – self-contained, secretive and unfamiliar with challenges to his authority or open debate – left him unable to argue his case in the Cabinet, and in the summer of 1915, the waning of his Cabinet colleagues' confidence led to his loss of power.[39] By this stage, in any case, senior members of the High Command in France, especially Haig and Robertson, were placing greater stress on a more actively offensive strategy. 'In the stage of the wearing out struggle,' Haig wrote at the end of the war, 'losses will necessarily be heavy on both sides, for in it the price of victory is paid.'[40] The Haig–Robertson view was behind the plans for the Somme offensive, but further confusion as to its precise objectives meant that the plan put into action on 1 July 1916 was tragically flawed.

Earlier, at Neuve Chapelle, a relatively brief engagement in March 1915, a template was made for the war as it later developed. In its planning and execution the offensive tested the new methods needed to make strategic advantage, and it contained in embryonic form all the characteristics of offensive, industrialized trench warfare as they later developed.[41]

Neuve Chapelle was organized in part to ease the pressure of the German compaign against Russia on the Eastern Front; Sir John French also hoped to show the French that the British were reliable allies who could break the deadlock of attrition.[42] On the Western Front, the unresolved puzzle was how to convert a defensive capacity of earthworks, rapid-fire weapons and barbed wire into an offensive advantage. The new methods developed for the British by Lieutenant-General Sir Henry Rawlinson and General Haig combined meticulous preparation, concealment of intent and concentration on what the generals hoped would be an overwhelming force of guns, soldiers and shells against the chosen enemy front. Aerial photography and a centrally orchestrated and timetabled barrage assisted them; details of surrounding terrain and mock-up trenches were intended to help the front line soldiers. The bombardment before the troops' advance was a 35-minute 'hurricane' artillery attack using 66 guns. As the war proceeded the size and sophistication of these attacks grew, culminating in the huge shellings at Passchendaele in 1917. At that time the 2nd Army employed 815 heavy guns at Messines, while the 5th Army at '3rd Ypres' used 752 separate pieces of artillery.[43]

The attack at Neuve Chapelle began at 7.30 on 10 March 1915, and shelling lasted until 8.05. Although puny in comparison with later bombardments, this tactic scored a striking, immediate success. The heavy if brief assault tore gaps in the German barbed wire and maintained cover for the first wave of the infantry assault, which captured Neuve Chapelle within 45 minutes, together with the central section of the 8,300 yard-long front. Yet the effort to convert this early advantage failed because all the benefits of preparation and surprise were lost: the lines of communication were unreliable, the artillery could not locate the pockets of resistance that remained along the front, and the troops lacked the necessary speed and accuracy to conclude the assault successfully. In the following two days after the first attack, 11 and 12 March, the British failed to penetrate even half-way across the 4,000-yard front. Instead, the 'battle' deteriorated into a straggle of attacks and counter-attacks, resulting in losses of about 13,000 men for both the British and the German Armies, and with no significant change in the strategic situation over the three days of fighting.[44]

One soldier who participated in the new warfare experiment at Neuve Chapelle was a 42-year-old sergeant from the 1st Seaforth Highlanders.[45] Sergeant C., although he had 15 years' service as a Regular behind him as well as two months in France, had seen little action before March 1915. The time he and his battalion had already spent at the front was employed digging trenches, marching back and forth from the new positions that had to be secured, and making preparations for battle. To this point, shelling was light and casualties were few. Breakfast on the morning of 10 March was at 2.00 am. Sergeant C. then marched with his comrades to the battalion position, each man carrying with him '... great coat and mess tin in his pack with 2 sandbags; unexpended portion days ration & emergency ration in haversack & 250 rounds' and, in addition, each company carrying with it '40 shovels, & 6 picks, 4 full bomb carriers & 30 extra wire cutters ...'[46]

More than two hours after 'the most appalling noise' of the bombardment Sergeant C. moved up to the front line, but the trenches were already blocked with the departing wounded. It took the 1st Seaforths another hour to find their attack position. Finally, well after the advantage of surprise was lost, at about 11.15, Sergeant C. went over the top. Pushing forward through the noise, chaos and hazard of no man's land towards a section of German trenches that would be breached later in the day, a nearby explosion knocked him to the ground. Luckily, his heavy equipment absorbed most of the impact leaving, as he later discovered, metal fragments embedded in his backpack. Shaken by the incident, he nevertheless continued to move forward until German heavy artillery shelling halted all operations later in the day. He carried on with his normal duties until 14 March, and then went off duty, reporting that he felt ill and nervous. A few days later he was on one of C.S. Myers' shell shock wards at Boulogne diagnosed as suffering from 'nervous debility'. Only a month after that, he was back with the 1st Seaforths on active service.[47]

Later in the war the scale of military engagements was magnified many times over; similarly, the psychic trauma of Sergeant C. was replicated, multiplied and intensified as the war dragged on. Piecing together such accounts of battle it becomes apparent that participating in the Great War meant taking part in large-scale battles such as the Somme or Verdun, or their precursors such as Neuve Chapelle, where dramatic attacks were intended to destroy troops, take trenches and create strategic advantage in capturing the ground behind the enemy lines. Equally significant, however, was small-scale attrition such as sniping or bombing raids, where ritualized exchanges maintained trenches and blocked the strategic advantage of capturing the ground behind the enemy lines. From the ordinary soldier's point of view the first was extremely hazardous, costly and often apparently pointless; the second relatively safe, life-preserving and slightly more bearable.[48] Both types of soldiering were intense, unpredictable and dangerous forms of work. To engage in this toil meant making the best of enforced circumstances, and like peacetime labouring, its main constituents were boredom, exhaustion and submission to authority, with the additional fear of mutilation or death.[49]

The battlefields of the Great War became a testing ground for the previous century's social and technological advances as larger, healthier populations fought with more powerful and destructive weapons. While there were technical advances though, the stalemate of the Western Front remained unresolvable. Neuve Chapelle also showed how lack of front line communications for both command and intelligence hampered progress, how support did not get to the right place at the right time, and how artillery and infantry were uncoordinated. The firepower of the artillery also drove troops into the ground. Yet, quickly evolving methods and technical innovations were some help in the new soldiering. Weather records together with gun calibration allowed for variables such as wind, temperature and humidity, and improved gun operating accuracy; gas, explosives, barbed wire, machine guns and concrete emplacements and picture-taking all aided efficiency; as did respirators, automatic weapons, mortars, tanks, aircraft, creeping artillery barrage and manifold increases in manpower.[50]

Great War participants have often described how they experienced the new physical environment of combat that technology helped to forge, and these descriptions are remarkably similar in their response to prolonged battle front exposure. Many soldiers explain the enormous physical force of shell-fire by analogy with seasickness or anaesthetic injection, by reference to a feeling of overwhelming mental and physical exhaustion, or by describing the resultant sense of lost self-identity and individuality. '[The bombardment] raged around our refuge like a typhoon-scoured sea around an island,' wrote the German stormtrooper Ernst Junger. Again, describing subjection to artillery attack as self-annihilation, 'The hail of shells thickened into a throbbing wall of fire. We crouched together, expecting each second the crashing hit that would sweep us up with our concrete blocks and make our position indistinguishable from the desert of craters all around.'[51]

Similarly, P.J. Campbell has described the drawn-out uncertainties of the front line existence, which served only to make such an assault all the worse when it finally came: 'I lost count of the shells and all count of time. There was no past to remember, and no future to think about. Only the present agony of waiting, waiting for the shell that was coming to destroy us. Waiting to die.'[52] Campbell's sense of powerlessness, as if the machinery of war worked its operatives, and the landscape of war dwarfed its occupants, was shared by Paul Dubrille. '[T]o die from a bullet seems to be nothing,' wrote the French Jesuit priest, describing the shell barrage at Verdun, 'parts of our being remain intact; but to be dismembered, torn to pieces, reduced to pulp, this is a fear that flesh cannot support and which is fundamentally the great suffering of the bombardment.'[53] Charles Edmonds, recounting his participation in the Somme campaign of summer 1916, gave equal weight to the struggle for physical and mental survival. The first bound by military rules of duty and discipline, the second by personal rules of morality and self-respect: 'Always the struggle within, fought behind the dark curtains which screen the hidden springs of conduct, was more real than the physical struggle without, and the practical details of life passed by like an illusion,' Edmonds recalled in *A Subaltern's War.*[54]

It was in the large, set-piece battles, Verdun, the Somme, and in the more aggressive zones of routine combat, that casualties multiplied alarmingly, the result of violent surroundings, physical exhaustion, nervous and emotional strain. Like Sergeant C. at Neuve Chapelle, soldiers in battle might be stunned or disoriented in any number of ways. They could lose direction in smoke, flames or debris, be deafened by crashing shells or the noise of gunfire, be distressed by the yells and moans of the wounded. 'Artillery was the great leveller,' according to one front line soldier. 'Nobody could stand more than three hours... The first to be affected were the young ones who'd just come out. They would go to one of the older ones – older in service that is – and maybe even cuddle up to him and start crying.'[55]

Barrage and battle, the hard labour of fighting and surviving, meant a constant physical struggle against exhaustion; feelings of isolation, helplessness and extinction imposed a further psychological strain. None the less, stress and trauma were not only associated with the active phases of the war. Low-level combat shaped trauma just as powerfully. C.E. Montague, explaining how insanitary conditions and exhaustion were psychologically damaging, wrote that when company strength was low it was unusual for men to get off more than an hour at a time over a stretch of eight days. 'Some of the privates were tired the whole of the time; some-times to the point of torment, sometimes much less, but always more or less tired.'[56] Physical fatigue and long bouts of intense combat between periods of calm and boredom: these were the everyday stresses of the war, and even the strongest constitution might eventually be twisted by such conditions and finally snap. Miraculously though, most soldiers survived the mental if not the physical hazards of the new warfare.

Surviving trauma

Not many men broke under the intense psychological pressure of front line warfare because traumatic neurosis was only one of several re-sponses to the stress of industrialized combat. Some soldiers were merely demoralized, others brutalized. More successful adaptation to the cir-cumstances of combat was achieved by holding to the affective frame-work of army life, for example by turning to regimental tradition, to superstition or religion, and metaphorical frameworks within which to assimilate the experience of the war.

Omer Bartov describes the effects of extreme physical hardship, lack of sleep or rest, and unrewarding combat as 'the barbarization of war-fare' in his study of German troops on the Eastern Front during the Second World War. Soldiers lost morale and discipline, and, insensitive to suffering, they became brutal. Moreover, as one doctor reported while describing the effects of five weeks' fighting in the Motorcycle Battalion of the 18th Panzer Division, these soldiers also suffered a rise in nervous disorder and mental instability.[57] The parallels between one conflict and another can never be exact because attitudes, technologies and weapons change, and the social and cultural background to mental disorder also alters constantly; nevertheless, something similar occurred along sections of the Western Front during the Great War. It would be wrong to exaggerate the evidence here, but there is at least one recorded incident that could fit the 'barbarization of warfare' theory. Charles Edmonds, in his account of 3rd Ypres, for instance, recalled being trapped in no man's land with the remnants of his battalion. The assault appeared to be failing and the daylight fading. With a break in the German assault and the arrival of a Lewis gun as well as a reserve platoon, fortunes appeared to reverse when some of the German troops began to surrender. 'At that moment Walker leaped up with a shout and began to shoot in a new direction. Following his aim I saw straight to the front and a hundred yards away a crowd of men running towards us in grey uniforms. Picking up another rifle I joined him in pouring rapid fire into this counter-attack. We saw one at least drop, to Walker's rifle I think, then we noticed that they were running with their hands up. Laughing, we emptied our magazines at them in spite of that...'[58]

The testimony of a temporary RAMC medic, G.N. Kirkwood, provides evidence of another related reaction: the demoralization of soldiers after long-fought, intense combat, which in turn made them more prone to traumatic neurosis.[59] Kirkwood, under orders to pronounce whether the soldiers were fit for combat, on the Somme in July 1916, took the unusual decision to report his men were suffering collective shell shock. Heavily criticized by his senior military commanders, and reporting to the Court of Enquiry that was soon to bar him from front line practice, the medic defended his diagnosis by listing the contributory factors that had led, he believed, to the soldiers' collective collapse. On 1 July, he argued, the battalion lost all its officers and more than half of its men; later rest days were spent at Contray sorting the belongings of deceased comrades. Afterwards they spent their time carrying up rations under heavy and incessant shellfire, digging out the dead in the trenches and carrying them down the line. They lived in an atmosphere of decomposing bodies, were exposed in open trenches to shelling and went without sleep for long periods.[60] Kirkwood's judgement and reasoning seem questionable here as these events and activities were no more severe than those endured by most other soldiers on the Western Front. Nevertheless, the case did indicate, for those few willing to listen, the close alliance between exhaustion, desensitization and trauma on the Western Front.

Most participants in the war even so did manage to keep up the stimulus shield of psychic self-defence and maintain their morale. An important contributory factor in achieving this was a good relationship between soldier and officer. In the British Army before the Great War, labourers, both skilled and unskilled, formed the majority of the lower ranks, while the officers were drawn from the social elite. The relationship between the two was ideally one of mutual respect and paternal authority.[61] During the war paternalism persisted, but the social divisions of rank were broken. The bond between officer and man was usually good and often intense, and comparable to the relationship between husband and wife, or brother and brother. As Charles Carrington noted in *Soldier from the Wars Returning*:

> I was in love with my platoon. The whole of my affection and concern was for the forty Yorkshire miners, collectively and severally, with whom I was so unexpectedly linked. For me the national effort,

Kitchener's Army, the Battalion, were vague concepts while here, concentrated, was an entity in which I could take a sensuous enjoyment. To see their healthy faces, to hear their North Country accents, to feel myself one of them, to cosset them, and even to bully them, gave me the deepest contentment I had yet known . . .[62]

Such qualities of leadership earned the respect and willing cooperation of soldiers from the other ranks, proper conduct and achievement maintained it; the power to encourage and compel men, and thereby help ensure their survival, gave officers their own sense of responsibility and pride. On the one occasion in September 1917 when authority did break down within the British Army, it was the military police and instructor NCOs who were the object of hostility, not the regular regimental officers.[63] The French troops, by contrast, mixed less in the trenches. They divided instead according to social background or even geographical origin, but this still provided social cohesion, which was even more necessary in light of the very heavy losses suffered by the French Army.[64] Losses affected morale, but so did comradeship and belief in the rightness of the cause, and in the case of the French Army, which was in large part drawn from the agrarian class, defence of the land was an ideal to be wholeheartedly espoused by many soldiers.[65] The breakdown of French military authority in May 1917 was not a failure of morale then, but a failure of commanders to treat soldier-citizens with the respect they believed they deserved.[66] In the German Army morale ebbed away as the war dragged on without any decisive success so that following the Somme it was seemingly close to collapse, while the large-scale desertions of August 1917 were near-mutinies. In the German Army too, though non-officers found it difficult to rise higher in the ranks because of their social background and inadequate educational qualifications, NCOs often provided the best leadership for rank-and-file soldiers. Small-group loyalty was also effective, but the loss of a large number of comrades was frequently devastating. By the summer of 1918 then, the loss of the recent offensive and lack of food among the other ranks ignited resentments; political radicals conscripted or entered into the Army in 1917–18 fuelled antipathies still further. As a result, about a million slightly wounded or sick German soldiers abandoned the war between March and July 1918.[67]

The British Army supported its members in a number of ways. It took over responsibility for their day-to-day lives, it reshaped their thought and behaviour, and under the right circumstances, it was able to provide a high level of social, emotional and psychological support. Robert Graves

devotes a passage in *Goodbye to All That* (1929) to the history of the Royal
Welch Fusiliers, describing the Daily Order Book of the 1st Battalion in
the trenches before Sevastopol, the spread of five black ribbons stitched
to the back of the tunic collar, and the struggle to evade spelling standardization and keep the 'c' in Royal Welch Fusiliers,[68] all as if to empha-
size how regimental membership fostered affection and loyalty and
helped soldiers identify with their cause and each other. While Regulars
were still a large contingent of the British war effort during the first year of
the war, they, like Graves, were also strongly attached to the regimental
history and traditions. A smaller administrative, social and fighting unit,
and perhaps more important for conscripts, volunteers and those unused
to military methods and routine, was the battalion. It provided food,
clothing and pay, and answered its members' recreational, religious and
medical needs. Status also varied according to rank and the relative
prestige given to the regular, the volunteer and the conscript. Formal
distinctions changed depending on whether the soldier was a cook, a
Lewis gunner or a signaller, and on how well he did his job. Together with
the platoon, the battalion and the regiment could provide the psychological and emotional support necessary for survival. Formal Army structures, history and group loyalty all fostered group feeling, and promoted,
at least in theory, friendship and emotional support. The Army provided
a framework for affective bonding, but it refused to take preventive
measures against shell shock because this would legitimize the purely
psychological suffering of the troops. Throughout the war, military and
medical officers rejected shell shock because it threatened discipline
among the rank and file. In answer to this threat, the Army promoted
military aggression and masculine virtues, and failure to 'do one's duty'
was therefore seen as a betrayal of the group, as a personal and collective
dishonour. The pleasure and pride that Graves or Carrington felt as
officers made their latent fear and shame all the greater, so that the
potential of affective bonding as psychological support was never fully
realized.[69]

Soldiers also worked out individual survival strategies. Rituals helped
create regularity and stability in the face of uncertainty and confusion.[70]
Mementoes collected in no man's land or from dead soldiers, good luck
charms and routines performed day by day: all of these distanced the
soldier from the arbitrary laws of life and death on the front line. Soldiers
also nursed their raw distress and fear with alcohol: 'I drank three-
quarters of a glass of neat whisky and carried on,' wrote one traumatized
officer. More powerful than this though was the sobering responsibility of
command, as he continues: 'that I was responsible and in charge saved

my reason at the time'.[71] Soldiers also devised metaphors with which to interpret the industrial weaponry of the Great War, making it a super-human fiend or devil; subhuman like the weather or an animal; or domestic and human, which perhaps provided the best chances of survival.[72] Men at war grasped for anything that might help them survive the ordeal of combat. Even the illusion of help mattered, because so much was beyond the combatant's individual control, including the weather and terrain in which he fought, the skill of his medic and the character of his comrades and commanding officer. To give one instance, the minimal, ritualized aggression of the live-and-let-live system was at best unstable and volatile: an eager or naive young officer could insist on more aggressive fighting, the rotation of troops could quickly shift the balance of power, the inevitable result was a flare of aggression on one or both sides.[73]

The discovery of shell shock as an idiom of sickness is to be found not only in soldiers' mental response to the shocks and jolts of the new trench warfare, but also in the disturbed minds of soldiers as they absorbed the censure and support of their comrades and leaders. To understand how this happened it is necessary to turn to the soldiers' rumours, doctors' treatments and Army disciplines of the Western Front.

3
Casualties: On the Western Front

Army medical practice

The front line relationship between war-traumatized soldier and medical officer vexed both parties throughout the war. Many soldiers avoided their medical officer because they knew they would be judged by the requirements of discipline and fighting fitness more than their personal welfare; some found that social background and rank meant their sickness claims were taken more seriously. Many doctors were practically-oriented and empirically-minded, favouring organic, not psychological explanations and treatments for mental disorders; they took less notice of changing medical opinion and research than the strategic requirements of the Army. When patient and doctor met, the medical gaze could soften or harden. These gradations of judgement decisively influenced how the casualty was diagnosed, how quickly his sickness claim was given official validation by the Army bureaucracy, as well as how and where he was treated. So while it is necessary to refer to the Army's changing administrative policy and its administrative re-organization of treatment to explain how shell shock came into being, it is in the confrontation between soldier and doctor serving on the Western Front, and in the relationship of medical officer to commanding officer, soldier to soldier, and soldier to friend and family, that the medical and social discovery of shell shock took place.

There was little agreement between Army authorities and front line soldiers on the nature of 'shell shock' or how to treat it on the Western Front in the early months of the war. The Army flatly rejected any medical diagnosis at first, and took a military, disciplinary view of the condition; soldiers in turn resented the apparent callous disregard of the military authorities.[1] Personal testimony shows that military medics and higher-ranking officers were usually sceptical about the diagnosis of shell shock, and that they turned this disbelief into official policy. The mass of articles and full-length studies on shell shock show too that specialists and professional Army doctors accepted and enforced Army medical policy. There were, therefore, well-defined limits to the medicalization of traumatic neurosis.[2] Front line soldiers for their part often recognized intuitively the psychological injuries of combat, but at the same time they could not help viewing shell shock as a shameful condition, a threat to reputation and peer group status. This shame has meant that very few have spoken about shell shock; what testimony there is indicates that fear of letting down comrades was the greatest anxiety. Many psychological casualties rightly believed too that comrades-in-arms, friends and family saw traumatic neurosis as either cowardice or madness. The guilt was not relieved, perhaps it was even increased, by the knowledge that this was a war-related condition. Consequently some combatants were irrevocably shattered by the war, they suffered guilt and shame in silence, they were either too little or too much aware of their own traumatic neurosis.[3]

The social dynamics of the doctor–patient relationship that often fostered this guilty silence were set in the institutional framework of Army Medical Services. Faced with the harsh conditions of trench warfare the organization of both the hospital network and the methods of military medicine went through a series of alterations between 1914 and 1918. In large part these reforms proved ineffectual, and cure rates were not much improved. While both French and American Army medical services managed to develop a policy of positive expectancy towards traumatic neurosis, which assisted quick, full recovery, the British did not. This reflects a wider failure of the British, a breakdown of military medicine that began with the retreat from Mons, when the RAMC was unable to collect injured soldiers efficiently as the British Army withdrew, and which led thereafter to the abject failure of shell shock treatment. While British soldiers increasingly stayed in France as the war went on and could therefore be treated quickly and efficiently, and while there were extensive reforms in 1916 that made the forward Casualty Clearing Station vital to the whole system on the Western Front, both before and after reforms of 1916, the decisive role remained with the regimental medical officer.[4] He undertook basic health care, acted as the immediate face of military medicine in the front line, and made the first critical diagnosis, and his view of the condition strongly influenced the patient's later fortunes. A soldier just off the battlefield went first to the regimental medical officer at the Regimental Aid Post, then, based on the medical judgement he received there, to an Advanced Dressing Station, a Base Hospital or a transport ship for evacuation to Britain.

In considering how the regimental medical officer exercised his judgement it is important to bear in mind that in both its individual and its communal aspects, medicine in wartime had different objectives from medicine in peacetime. Its purpose was not the well-being and full health of the patient, but the nursing of resources for return to the front line. The relationship between doctor and patient was primarily military then, not medical; consequently, the manpower needs of the war institutionalized scepticism; sickness was tainted with the suspicion of cowardice, dereliction of duty and moral failure. In making medical judgements, the Great War doctor was part of the military system, and his judgements were coloured by this fact.[5] However, some temporary RAMC medics were reluctant to violate the doctor–patient relationship for the needs of the Army.[6] In the opinion of one such temporary doctor, J.H. Dibble, the Army Medical Services had an 'innate suspicion of poor Tommy... alive he is called a malingerer; dead he is accused of being syphilitic'.[7] RAMC hospitals took much the same attitude: 'Army hospitals as one soon finds out to one's sorrow do not exist for the purpose of curing sick men but for indexing them, supplying a name to their disease, ascertaining their religion and "booting them out" elsewhere with as much celerity as possible.'[8]

This approach was hardly unique to the British Army, but a brief survey of the French and German Army Medical Services highlights how the profile of shell shock differed according to medical, administrative and intellectual culture. The French Army's superior size and more extensive engagement in campaigns, for instance, meant the medical system developed with greater speed, and doctors realized as early as 1915 that specialist facilities on the Western Front were essential to effective preventive care.[9] Early on, then, war-related traumatic neurosis was fully medicalized as hysteria; treatment was dispensed through a systematic, centrally coordinated state treatment network.[10] The tenor of treatment was as strict as in the British Army, perhaps more so: in both systems the doctor's aim was to rid the patient of symptoms and return him to active duty, but only the French system institutionalized traumatic hysteria as a form of insolent insubordination.[11] Furthermore, the Société Neurologie believed that the credibility of the profession depended on its ability to rise to the challenge of wartime traumatic hysteria. This meant that French neurologists became involved in a series of policing disputes as they tried to ensure their own control over the examination, diagnosis and treatment of patients.[12] British medics appear to have had no such sense of collective responsibility. Treatment was widely based on positive expectancy, which gave weight to the rapid eradication of symptoms and swift return to action, most notably in Joseph Babinski's 'cure by persuasion' method.[13] Persuasion treatments could routinely include electric therapy, but also hypnotism, or more dramatic displays of mass hypnotic or electric treatment designed to break the patient's symptoms.[14] Clovis Vincent went so far as to use high-intensity electric shocks, again justified by the requirement of a speedy result.[15] If suffering traumatic neurosis was a failure, both moral and mental, the 'refusal' to recover was a graver offence. That some restrictions were placed on medics in late 1916, shifting the balance of power a little towards the military, made a slight difference to the experience of the average French soldier. The point-blank refusal of the French authorities to admit the legitimacy of non-organic war injury meant that they avoided the dilemmas that dogged the British Army throughout the war. With no term like 'shell shock' to imply physical damage, all neurotics were by definition the same as malingerers. Moreover, as there was no organic condition to register or measure, and no discharge from the French Army without admission of full cure, the question of a pension award never arose.[16]

In Germany, too, though medics had thought the war would have a 'cleansing' effect on the national psyche, the rate of traumatic neurosis led, by November 1915, to specialist military centres on the Western Front. The medical and military authorities in Germany established the most 'standardized' and centralized treatment system of all to channel resources as effectively as possible, to recycle the war neurotic who could not fight effectively in the front line into a factory labourer, who might still contribute to the war effort.[17] To this end, field treatment was designed to eliminate symptoms before they were 'fixed'. This made cure in the field all the more urgent because, as one medic argued: 'The neurotic who has crossed the Rhine once, will in almost no case be fit for serving again.'[18] The policy of the German Army was first preventive, then, and keeping potential neurotics near the Western Front was a part of this drive to stop wastage. However, poor medical training and failure to establish an efficient front line hospital system meant this policy was not entirely effective.[19] Just as in Britain, traumatic neurosis was a low-priority condition in times of heavy fighting, so cases would be sent back to clearing stations and war hospitals, many misdiagnosed, and medics even at the end of the war lacked proper training to treat such conditions. Prevention at the front also meant effective leadership and the promotion of high morale; evacuation of 'severe' cases was thus given high priority.[20]

In all the armies, then, mental health and illness were judged according to the military requirements for manpower, as well as by rank and class, which were seen as rough measures of social distinction and dutiful trustworthiness. In the British Army the rigid boundaries of rank became apparent when they were inadvertently violated, and this is illustrated by the experience of a colonial officer, who quickly learned after his arrival on the Western Front how medical science mattered less than officer corps traditions of social privilege, discipline and honour. Leading a hazardous raiding party one of the soldiers under the officer's command broke down: '[He] burst into tears and repeatedly mentioned his wife and children, so there was no alternative to sending him back. As one of the guns was unserviceable there seemed no point in keeping a full gun crew up forward.'[21] Word of this incident quickly spread, to the disapproval of regulars, who felt that the officer should not have stepped in to fill the gunner's role, and that the proper demarcations of rank and discipline had been broken. In an apparently calm exchange between officer and servant (batman) the following morning, the regular soldier tried to put right the colonial officer by arguing there should be a strict demarcation of roles between officer and gunner to maintain full confidence in even a young, inexperienced soldier.[22]

This confrontation between discipline and welfare repeated itself along the Western Front, and in these person-to-person discussions, both official and casual, the true meaning of shell shock was argued out. The working definitions of shell shock that resulted were flawed, variable and tentative, but it is only by examining these exchanges and the institutional framework within which they took place that it is possible to understand the discovery of shell shock and its meaning to those involved in its definition.

Tales from the front line

By 1915 soldiers in the trenches recognized the symptoms and signs of traumatic neurosis more accurately than their professional superiors, and they described it in mixed moods of pity, horror and cynical amusement. For Lance-Sergeant Walton and a number of other soldiers, official recognition of traumatic war neurosis came too late. After a summary court-martial, which dismissed first his plea of nervous breakdown and then the supporting evidence that his desertion near Ypres in early November 1914 was the result of mental confusion and not wilful desertion, he was executed by firing squad on 23 March 1915.[23] The question such executions raise is how organizations and individuals in the front line understood shell shock.

The simplest official definition was physical concussion. However, as early as 1915 front line soldiers such as Gunner Hiram Sturdy, who served with the Royal Artillery Regiment throughout the war, associated the term with mental disorders of all kinds. It might mean poor nerves for instance, since, 'Most of who are here for any length of time are jumpy, and nervous, but the very opposite in action happens, as they can bear a bad situation better than a new man.'[24] In this view any soldier was vulnerable to the mental destruction of war, though by virtue of temperament or experience some were able to resist being affected by 'the sights'. Shell shock was a rather more spectacular version of the fear that every soldier felt then; by repute, closer to insanity or temporary madness, as in the case of one man who after being caught in a bombardment 'gives a scream, jumps off the wall, falls to the ground, foaming at the mouth, jabbering, and starts to tear at himself'. The mood of the men who witness these events was unsurprised, phlegmatic; it was the first case of its sort, but 'we had heard of this kind of case, and when one has been under terrific shellfire, he knows the symptoms all right, as most of us at times have had to fight against this madness caused by pure unadulterated fear.' The belief that shell shock was 'madness caused by fear' was strengthened by the coda to this and similar stories as the soldier – possibly epileptic, rather than hysterical – is restrained, strapped to a stretcher and driven away in an ambulance. 'He never comes back to us.'[25]

As with many other aspects of trench life and warfare, rumours and wild stories surrounded shell shock. Sturdy and his comrades were by no means the only ones who believed the war was driving its participants insane in large numbers. As one VAD nurse from the London Ambulance column reported, 'I noticed another sort of ambulance come into the station, not one of ours. It was completely closed up. I said to one of the men, "What's this ambulance coming in? Haven't we done the train?" He said, "No, Sister, this is from the asylum; it's for the hopeless mental cases." I didn't look. They'd gone off their heads. I didn't want to see them. There was nothing you could do and they were going to a special place. They were terrible.'[26] The imagined horrors of madness made some turn away, but a more common reaction was sorrowful pity, especially where officers were involved, especially because of the stigma attached to mental conditions. This helps explain why the neutral, even noble and certainly organic-sounding term 'shell shock' was so widely used by the spring of 1915. 'I know some people if they have a really bad time do lose their nerve completely (even the strongest nerved in the beginning),' wrote one officer of another in August 1915, 'and it is actually just as much a sacrifice to lose one's nerve in the trenches as to lose an arm, in fact I'm not sure that it's not more so, allied to which when you get back people are in no way inclined to sympathize with you'.[27]

Captain H.W. Kaye, in 1915 a temporary RAMC doctor who was highly critical of what he saw as the antiquated attitudes and practices of the RAMC and the role of the Army in the development of Army medical policy, asked one of his patients to write about his military experiences and the events leading to his traumatic neurosis. This soldier's sickness narrative describes shell shock not as fear-induced madness, but as isolating, wearing distress and doubt, which was only admitted with great reluctance. The soldier's tale begins with a description of the second battle of Ypres in April, May and June 1915, during which his battalion had been destroyed three times, killing and wounding about 30,000 and 'three times it had been my lot as Senior surviving Officer to bring the Battalion out of action practically washed out. After the third time, in June, I knew I was approaching the end of my tether.'[28] Following a brief leave in Britain the officer returned to France to find that the battalion had just completed a successful operation and taken all the trenches on a nearby salient. After a successful attack, there was a harsh counter-attack with heavy, incessant fighting for two days: 'The net result in casualties in those two days and nights was that we lost in killed and wounded 28 officers and over 500 men.'[29]

Two events, Kaye's patient believed, had especially affected him. On 5 June, while sitting in a British reserve trench, a 5.9 inch shell scored a direct hit, killing three of his comrades, severely wounding two others, and singeing his hair, but leaving him 'visibly unhurt'.[30] The officer was now left once again as the senior and had to retain command, which 'saved my position at the time'.[31] He was able to carry on by organizing the disposal of corpses, but with the virtual destruction of his battalion for the fourth time, even this became almost impossible. When two majors finally arrived to take over command the sense of relief was immense, but he then retired into a dugout which was itself struck by a shell and he remained buried for about three or four hours.[32] The breaking point came not long after, during preparations to take the battalion out of the line. The quartermaster, without knowing that only two officers and fewer than 300 men had survived, brought up all the horses 'and there were no officers to ride them. When I saw the horses and realized what had happened, it finished me, I broke down and I do not mind telling you [Dr Kaye] I cried for a week.'[33]

These accounts indicate that during 1914 and 1915, there were varied, often contradictory definitions of shell shock. For many in the lower ranks it was a form of war-induced madness that led to the asylum, for officers it was seen more as a semi-legitimate war injury that might lead, often with genuine reluctance, to a safe haven away from the front line. In the case of Captain Kaye's officer, shell shock was the cumulative effect of emotional and physical exhaustion, triggered by specific traumatic events such as live burial. It is in these circumstances – surrounded by rumour and myth, acute mental distress and the death and mutilation of combat – that soldiers began to discover shell shock for themselves. Speculative imagination played an important role in helping them find the correct postures and gaits, words and images, to express their mental anguish. The idea of shell shock was even a kind of release for the combatants, who described and commented on it in the trenches because it legitimized the discussion of fear. Before the war, hysterical women collapsed and retired to the bedroom there to find a private space away from the pressure and expectation of the male gaze, their collapse matching expectations of femininity and accepted within those limits. Male traumatic neurosis follows a similar pattern.[34] The twisted, paralysed arms and stilted, awkward leg movements of the shell-shocked soldier mentally reproduced and responded to the injuries and broken corpses that they encountered daily. This may explain the similarity of symptoms in the Great War on all sides, but the absence of hysterical paralysis, blindness and mutism in later wars.[35]

Discipline and the medical officer

Events in 1916 helped sharpen definitions of shell shock. The recollections of casualties and doctors show that by this date both groups had a greater wealth of collective experience and folklore to draw on and had become more fully acquainted with the Western Front. Traumatic neurosis quickly became another aspect of life in the combat zone, still an object of ignorant fear, still a source of grim amusement. Writing home on 27 October 1916, and safely away from the Somme where he was injured, 2nd Lieutenant A.H. Crerar described his ward in the No. 1 Red Cross Hospital.[36] 'We get entertainment in the ward,' wrote Crerar, trying to reassure his mother and sisters that he was not too seriously injured and still had his sense of humour, 'from a shell shock case who raves away at his men to dig, dig, and calls his sergeant 6ft of misery.

I don't know how many of his men he's threatened to shoot but I think all of them, I think he did shoot his sergeant.' Returning to the subject a few days later, on 30 October, Crerar describes another incident on the ward: '[A]bout 4 a.m. the old shell case and two new ones start their "turn" and others start their little bits of tuneful moans; sister yells on nurse, nurse yells Webber, Webber yells Rolls, they all sprint into a cubicle where No. 2 was evidently getting up...I promptly hold up our hands, say Kamerad in case he's a case...Oh, its a great life.'[37]

Captain L. Gameson, a doctor who qualified in late 1915 and was on the Western Front by early 1916, gives a more measured account. As a young non-specialist and a temporary RAMC medic, Gameson was particularly frustrated to see the needs of traumatized patients ignored. Late one evening, for instance, he came across a stretcher-bearer in distress: 'The scene is still vivid to me: the deep, German dugout, the usual passage running from end to end, the usual tiers of bunks. The place was dimly lit with a few candles. My patient was sitting up in his cramped bunk, leaning forward gripping hard to an upright with both hands... I quite completely failed to comfort him. Finally I gave him an injection of morphia.'[38] The patient was taken away; the doctor never saw him again. While the initial surprise and the wilder rumours died down by 1916, the difficulties of managing traumatic neurosis, as Gameson's anecdote illustrates, mounted.

The Somme offensive, starting on 1 July 1916, marked a new phase in the fierce conflict on the Western Front, and with it came a sharp rise in shell shock cases, greater public interest and political debate.[39] To the Army, increased attention among the civilian population was an alarming prospect; a blow to morale and discipline because it sanctioned the condition with talk and sympathy and made fighting spirit all the more difficult to preserve.[40] Not much could be done to prevent comment on the Home Front, but on the Western Front military leaders had varied provisions that could help uphold aggression and morale and discourage cowardice or disloyalty. Courts-martial were viewed as a necessary tool in the policing of unmilitary behaviour, and the military doctor was obliged to play his part in this system as fully as the commanding officer.[41] For this reason using shell shock as a defence at courts-martial might have seemed helpful to a temporary RAMC medic, but to military professionals such a plea was a strong argument for prosecution and conviction.[42] The British Army, which executed 307 soldiers during the war, was not the worst offender in this respect: while the German Army executed only 48 men, the French Army put 700 of its combatants to death.[43] Courts-martial were primarily intended, then, to promote the enforcement of obedience. In doing so they dramatized the clash of opinion between the minority of compassionate temporary RAMC doctors who saw shell-shocked soldiers as psychiatric casualties, and the Army authorities, which patrolled the morale of the fighting men and maintained strict discipline along with the majority of medics on the Western Front.[44]

An incident on the Somme in July 1916 highlights this tension between military and civilian medical values. On 9 July Captain H.C. Palmer, acting officer-in-command of the 11th Border Regiment, 97th Infantry Brigade, 32nd Division, received an order from Brigadier General J.B. Jardine to take 200 yards of the enemy's front trench and attack the support line. At the time, the battalion was severely depleted and for the task Captain Palmer found 90 able NCOs and two officers from 250 soldiers.[45] The time for the operation to begin was set at 12.30 am on 10 July. At approximately 9.30 pm on the night of the operation the senior participating officer, 2nd Lieutenant J. Ross, reported that a large number of the men had stated they were unfit for the operation and were refusing to 'go over' later in the night. As the acting officer-in-command, Captain Palmer decided to send for the regimental medical officer, and ordered him to give an opinion on the troop's fitness for the operation. This task fell to Lieutenant G.N. Kirkwood, a temporary RAMC medic who had been in France for about a year. After his examination of the troops, Lieutenant Kirkwood sent a certificate to Brigadier General Jardine stating that, 'In view of the bombing attack to be carried out by the 11th Border Regiment I must hereby testify to their unfitness for such an operation as few, if any, are not suffering from some degree of shell shock.'[46] Jardine received this note and telephoned that the operation should proceed as planned, and these orders were passed on to 2nd Lieutenant Ross. At 1.30 am on 10 July, Ross reported back to Captain Palmer that some of the men had lost their way, others had not arrived in time to begin the operation, and so it had been cancelled.

A court of enquiry was set up, Lieutenant Kirkwood was relieved of his post as regimental medical officer and sent to work behind the lines at a base hospital, though in the opinion of Jardine he was unfit for any further military duty.[47] The many statements made to the court of enquiry show the opposition faced by a lower-ranking medical officer when he gave a diagnosis of shell shock. Kirkwood's job, according to his own statement and the statements of other officers, was not to give independent medical opinion, but to help maintain discipline over the troops by showing his support for the commanding officer. Kirkwood argued that, as noted above, he was right to give a diagnosis of mass shell shock under the circumstances.

Four other opinions are recorded in the existing extracts from the court of enquiry. Two of these were from high-ranking regular Army officers who opposed Kirkwood's decision; the next was from an RAMC officer who held the same view; and finally from Surgeon General Sir A.T. Sloggett, who argued that the Army was blaming Kirkwood to disguise its own failings.[48] Brigadier General Jardine remained unconvinced, arguing that the battalion was under less fire than others in the brigade, with no reported shell shock cases. 'No,' he said, the collapse of the operation 'was caused by failure of the N.C.O.'s to preserve the right spirit – to encourage the men and set a good example in the absence of officers.'[49] Furthermore, 'it is not the M.O. to inform his C.O. that his men are not in a fit state to carry out a military operation'.[50] The men being in the front line should be proof that they are fit for any duty called for.

Sloggett, by contrast, argued that the brigadier had neglected his duties by not being aware of the state of the troops, and that the recommendations for Kirkwood's dismissal should not be acted on, if only because of the chronic shortage of medical staff in France. From his service record, Sloggett argued that Kirkwood had always been conscientious and more interested in the physical and mental welfare of the troops than was proper for a medical officer. The DGMS also pointed out that Kirkwood was ordered to give an opinion, and it was only because his opinion was 'wrong' that he was so vilified. It was also notable, Sloggett continued, that the lieutenant's view was, if anything, supported by the later turn of events, but in any case his judgements were ignored, so he could not be held responsible for the later action of the troops.[51] The Kirkwood incident was never made public, but there was still public and political suspicion that some soldiers might have been unjustly punished or executed. In the autumn of 1917, for instance, a leading shell shock campaigner asked the Under-Secretary for War how it was possible that 'a mere boy overcome by nervousness was executed'. He was reassured that 'I have gone into many of these cases very sympathetically, and I am sure that in every case the utmost consideration is given to all the relevant facts, brought forward, very often by medical officers'.[52]

The War Office accounts of capital court-martial cases show a very different story. On 8 October, for example, Private Harry Farr, of the 1st Battalion West Yorkshire Regiment, was executed despite five months in a military hospital at Boulogne and a further two weeks in a dressing station, also suffering traumatic neurosis, during the Somme campaign.[53] Farr's offence was to refuse to enter the line either voluntarily or under escort. By his own account he could no longer cope with the noise of gunfire. Similarly, and very unusually because he was an officer, 2nd Lieutenant Eric Poole, of the 11th Battalion West Yorkshire Regiment, was executed for desertion on 21 November 1916.[54] In both cases witnesses made statements testifying that the accused were suffering mental confusion, effectively an admission of guilt. In both cases the courts-martial lasted a matter of minutes and the verdict was little more than a foregone conclusion.[55]

The Army authorities on the Western Front continued to prosecute, convict and execute war-traumatized neurotics until the Armistice in November 1918. On 24 January 1918 a private in the Royal Iniskilling Fusiliers was executed; on 10 September another private, a BEF volunteer since 1915 with previous convictions for desertion and self-mutilation; on 1 September a third private, this time from the Machine Gun Corps. In each case, the soldier had served for several years on the Western Front; in the second and third case, both men had poor military service records for desertion or self-mutilation and the circumstances surrounding the case give the suspicion of mental instability. In no instance was medical evidence allowed.[56] In September 1918 Captain Gameson, acting as a medical witness, defended Gunner 'X', and made a detailed examination only to be told that the court-martial had already taken place and the capital charge of cowardice found proven. Unable to submit his report on the mental condition of the patient, Gameson could only attach it to the report on the trial proceedings before the papers were sent off to a higher authority. Gameson believed the capital charge was dropped after his intervention.[57] Later, 'a curious order came from the Corps. It flagrantly limited the scope of Medical Officers in cases seemingly patterned on that of Gunner "X". It was, in effect, a censure on those who it might concern. I flatter myself that it concerned me.'[58]

Officers were very rarely court-martialled, but were more vulnerable to traumatic neurosis than members of the other ranks. The admission figures in *The Hydra*, the magazine for the Craiglockhart Special Hospital for Officers, show the greatest stress was on lower-ranking officers: on 4 August 1917, for example, the new arrivals included four majors, five captains, six lieutenants and eighteen 2nd lieutenants, one of whom was Siegfried Sassoon. One soldier noted that many men, including officers, 'simply broke', becoming 'more or less gibbering idiots'. Two officers to his knowledge had committed suicide, while older men found the psychological strain difficult because 'they hadn't been hit and they hadn't been there for long really, and they just couldn't stand it'.[59] The story of one officer documents the gradual onset of shell shock as well as the management techniques of military and medical authorities. After heavy fighting during the spring and summer of 1917, the soldier was wounded twice within a very short period. Exactly what kind of trauma he suffered is unclear, but what does emerge is the collapse of his self-confidence, the sense of guilt he felt, and the ease with which he was able, as an officer, to leave the front without any overt social stigma and without any loss of his pension rights: 'we got heavily trench mortared and I got slightly wounded again... And this being hit by a shell the second time, it shattered me so much, and I'm ashamed to say this, but I went to the adjutant and said: "look here, I don't know what to do. I have no real control over myself any longer, if I get into a sticky position again, I'm afraid I shall simply panic and run away".'[60] The officer got a transfer, thereafter helping run the Lewis machine gun school.

The diary of another high-ranking officer traces his mental decline between February and October 1917, at which time he too left the front line, in this case to return to Britain.[61] Guilt and concealment are the dominant themes of this account: 'It didn't affect me so far as the outsider was concerned. I did the work...the only thing is that I began to feel... "I wonder how much longer I can go on",' he wrote, on Saturday 14 April 1917.[62] He records too the names of dead and wounded comrades, the marches and halts, the feelings of insecurity and fear, and the continual, draining insomnia. Heavy and continuous shellfire and the dispiriting effects of intense fighting are both prominent themes in the May entries. On 2 and 3 May, for instance: 'The whole show seems to have failed & God knows how many were lost. I began to think this sort of thing cannot go on. The pressure is very great on both sides. Are losing enormous quantities of men + something is bound to break soon. Even though one feels we are winning there is not much pleasure in killing the Boche in the awful numbers we are now.'[63] The entries get shorter and more anxious over the following weeks. The greatest struggle of all was not to let his comrades see the anguish.

Anxiety, guilt and fear also meant that the officer's mental condition was aggravated and accelerated for lack of any treatment. To cope with this throughout the summer and into the autumn of 1917 he increasingly kept away from the front, but his distress and sleep loss worsened. On 29 June, for example: 'I am much more nervy than I ought to be.'[64] The entry for 14–15 September 1917 describes the officer's decision to leave the front. 'In the end I went to my Battery commander and said "look, don't send me on any more [such demanding missions]...because I may let you down"...I think they thought I'd had enough.'[65] We can infer from this and other accounts that an important distinction between the experience of officers and members of the other ranks arose from the informal ways psychological casualties were dealt with in the field. Shell shock was seen widely as a matter of guilt and shame, among both individual soldiers and the Army authorities, yet some soldiers were punished while others with very similar conditions were dealt with sympathetically and rewarded for their bravery.

War's end

Given the guilty, silent distress of soldiers and the disciplinary approach of the British Army, it is not surprising that despite the growth of medical knowledge and military experience the quality of care and treatment for psychological casualties improved only marginally in France between the Declaration of War and the Armistice. In March 1918, two medics left their work in Britain to spend about twelve months each on the mental wards of the Western Front. Both their accounts show that what advances there were depended largely on the initiative of individual doctors, not on changes in Army medical policy or informal attitudes. Dr Hills was one of these medics: a professional neurologist who became the first psychological specialist attached to the 4th Army, dealing with all types of mental cases.[66] Dr Chambers was the second doctor: an asylum practitioner by training, who took charge of the major hospital for 'mental cases' in the Boulogne and Calais areas, situated at Wimeraux.[67] The two represent very different approaches to the practice of psychological medicine: Dr Hills the 'progressive', and Dr Chambers the asylum-trained, traditional nerve specialist. One of the few points where the two agreed was in their dislike of Army medical policy towards shell shock.

Dr Harold Hills arrived in France in early 1918 sympathetic to mental casualties, but as a temporary RAMC medic he had no knowledge of practices and attitudes within the British Army in France. His education began immediately on arrival as he discussed his new post with another neurologist before going on to the 4th Army Headquarters. 'I read "Private..., Number..., was on...charged and found guilty before a Field General Court Martial with Desertion. He was found guilty and sentenced to death. The sentence has been carried out."'[68] The new doctor's colleague explained that the private had been sent for a psychological examination and based on the medical view that there was no mental disorder, he was executed. Medical testimony, Hills realized, was sometimes taken seriously; more importantly he saw that he would have to do similar work and that his expertise affected the life or death of other soldiers.

At the 4th Army Headquarters, Hills found many of the soldiers suspicious and unfriendly; he saw this not as personal malice, but disquiet at the first appointment of a mental specialist. Several soldiers were quick to give Hills their own view on the subject. 'In the mess someone said, "we like you but we don't like your circus. We think they ought to be shut up, better still shot." I said "Some are going to be shot, if that satisfies you." '[69] Like Gameson, Kaye and Kirkwood before him, an important part of Hills' duties became the medical defence of shell shock cases in court-martial proceedings, which meant submitting full and accurate medical reports on all cases referred to him. Since he had no experience as a medical witness, Dr Hills often found it difficult to reason with soldiers within what seemed a capricious and vindictive justice system. In the doctor's view, it was not the arguments that he put forward that were important, but the sense of doubt that the presence of the medical witness gave to the court-martial proceedings. 'I found it hard to get across to the board the idea that a grown man could have the mind of a child and, childlike, could not hold out.'[70] Hills was reduced even to deception at times after he discovered one of the most effective forms of defence was to blind the court with medical science. 'I began to learn something of the ways of Courts-Martial. If I called a man a Paranoic or a Schizophrenic I was not questioned; anyone with such a horribly named diseases ought to be in hospital.'[71] The better he learned military protocol the easier it was for Hills to gain credibility and respect from the 4th Army staff. Within a few months, the doctor was able to make an effective case for the medical, not military, treatment of psychological casualties on trial, a feat which many other doctors had found impossible earlier in the war. However, as the recollections of other doctors working in France at the same time show, Hills was an exception within the shell shock treatment system.

W.D. Chambers was a professional asylum doctor and an assistant senior physician before he went from Dumfries to Wimeraux to take charge of the mental wards of the Boulogne area from March 1918 to January 1919.[72] His training and medical opinion were those of a nerve specialist in the age of psychiatric Darwinism, while his article on 'Mental Wards with the B.E.F.' was published in the *Journal of Mental Science*, for many years edited by Sir George Savage.[73] Wimeraux was one of the largest and busiest mental hospitals in France, and it followed Army medical policy by never segregating or sorting soldiers by disorder. In diagnosing the numbers and types of cases on the wards during his stay, Chambers reported 153 soldiers as Feeble Minded, 136 as Confusional Insanity and 92 as Melancholy; smaller numbers suffered Moral Imbecility, Mania and Stupor.[74] These classifications show Chambers' asylum training and the inadequacy of Army admission policy, but also that, as the medic himself admitted, cases of traumatic neurosis would very likely go unnoticed.[75] Similarly the pressure of numbers meant the treatment that could be made available was almost valueless.[76] Even the location of the hospital made effective care a hazard. 'The first considerable concussion put these out, leaving the ward full of unreliable patients of various tendencies perilously free scope for their activities.'[77] Beyond the black humour, there were strict limits on the provision of Army medical services towards the end of the war. Chambers believed the Army 'mental' wards were near disintegration at Wimeraux because of the resignation of Lieutenant-Colonel C.S. Myers, the leading consultant psychiatrist in France, in December 1917. W.A. Turner, a senior Army neurologist who had opposed many of the reforms Myers wanted to introduce, was the replacement, and thereafter the mental wards 'compared unfavourably with that provision for surgical and medical cases'.[78]

With the discovery of shell shock by soldiers in France came discussion and controversy among the civilian population in Britain. Part II examines the repercussions that followed the appearance of mass shell shock, and the very different ways in which it was treated, experienced and understood by soldier-patients.

Part II
Wartime

4
Enlistment: Army Policy, Politics and the Press

The enlistment of shell shock

Throughout the Great War, newspaper journalists, politicians and medics made public pronouncements claiming that the conflict was witness to new and revolutionary accomplishments in modern medical science which amounted to a triumph of state control and organization on behalf of the ordinary man. On 12 August 1916, for instance, *The Times* stated that 'the public have an utterly inadequate idea of the debt they owe to modern surgery at a time like this. Day by day the surgeons are giving the nation new men for old. They are doing more than would have been credible 20 years ago to rob war of its ultimate horror.'[1] Here, as elsewhere, medicine was depicted as a progressive force for healing, well-being and healthfulness, doctors were compassionate and wise, nurses were ministering angels in white, hospitals were havens of calm and sanity.[2] As one aspect of military medicine in the Great War the care of shell shock casualties was supposedly another instance of scientific progress, and it too was enlisted for the purposes of Home Front morale. The bodies of men were used in a similar manner: either displayed as evidence that physically injured men could be visibly healed, or else discreetly kept at a distance so as not to offend casual observers.

However, while shell shock doctors could easily serve the same purpose as those who performed restorative facial surgery or prosthetics, shell shock casualties differed from other injured men because they were less easy to assimilate or to confine. While a physically injured man might be distressing to look at, his condition was nevertheless understandable. Shell shock casualties, meanwhile, despite their condition's apparently self-explanatory name and its public 'celebrity', were never so easy to comprehend. They sometimes offered outward visible signs of the war in a stutter or a shuffling walk, but the damage of war was mostly unseen, at first located in the brain, and later relocated to the psyche. Without bandages, scars or missing limbs, the shell shock casualty could not lay claim properly to a wound; without the prestige of a wound, he was under suspicion. In private his manhood could be doubted, in public his patriotism might be questioned. Military pronouncements on the Western Front made this distinction a guide to the formation of policy, while on the Home Front there were no open accusations, but still an emphasis on the marked difference between an imaginary, mental condition and an empirical, physical disorder. Moreover for a shell-shocked soldier to claim he was suffering some form of sickness was equally damning. In the case of a mental condition, this still carried the taint of heredity and degeneracy, and this lent the interest of newspapers, politicians and public in shell shock a hint of morbid curiosity. Because of this mismatch between curiously invisible symptoms and high-profile public campaigns to rehabilitate the condition so that no aspect of the war was entirely incomprehensible or alien, civilian feelings towards shell-shocked soldiers were mixed.

These seemingly contradictory views are evident in volume VII of *The Times History of the War* (1916), a populist, patriotic series, which plays on the mingling of curiosity and concern aroused by shell shock, 'so remarkable and so interesting as to merit a careful description'.[3] Sympathetic to the empirical approach held in such high regard by the Army Medical Services, this account stresses 'nervous life-history', 'physical bankruptcy' and 'those circumstances which, generally, favour the onset of ill-health' as contributing causes. Despite these attempts to domesticate the condition, there is nevertheless something mysterious in it. F.W. Mott, the neurologist who first defined shell shock as concussion-like physical trauma, gives a description that makes the sickness into an eerie mental void: '[T]he soldier's face was a blank. He might not remember his name; he might have no idea who he is, or how he came to be in the position in which he found himself. Near relations who visited him often found that he had no idea regarding their identity, and viewed their coming with the same stony indifference with which he regarded the whole world around him.'[4] Lacking the visible signs of wounding, the definitive characteristic of the shell shock casualty here is that he is empty of emotion or memory. He is also a puzzle. Neither he nor his condition seems to have a past that can be traced: the shell shock casualty here stands in for what is unspeakable or unknowable about the war for those who had not experienced it. As a symbol of the public's innocence and ignorance, and as an embodiment of incomprehensible, existential damage to the human spirit, the shell shock casualty, like the war itself, commanded respect, but special pity and fear too.[5]

To understand how shell shock achieved its complex, ambiguous reputation it is necessary to describe the various parties who took an interest in it, the conflicting values they brought to bear in understanding it and the contradictory demands they placed on it.

Army medical policy

Officially, shell shock was unnamed and invisible – effectively it did not exist – until the Army authorities recognized it was a potential threat to military manpower in early 1915. Those cases that existed before the term 'shell shock' was recognized were treated as concussion, head or brain injuries, as were many after that time.[6] If one section of military opinion expanded its definition when shell shock acquired a name and became visible, another section doggedly argued for the brain damage thesis throughout the war. Consequently, the suffering of many soldiers was prolonged by inappropriate treatment; still worse, others were wrongly certified and most probably lost to the asylum. Once named, the shell shock epidemic quickly multiplied. The first specialist hospital in Britain, Maghull, opened near Liverpool in November 1914. By January 1915 Maghull was full and two further hospitals – the Royal Victoria Hospital Netley, near Aldershot, and the 4th London General, Denmark Hill – opened neurological sections.[7] Meanwhile in France, late 1914 saw the compilation of a report listing the number and type of 'neurological' cases in the first four months of the war. On 12 January 1915, the Director General of Medical Services sent this account to fifty officers-in-charge of Field Medical Units.[8] Appointed consultant neurologist to the War Office on 30 January 1915, one of these officers was Lieutenant-Colonel William Aldren Turner, who reported that among the cases at Netley were instances of functional paraplegia, amnesia, deaf-muteness, motor agitation, depression and confusion.[9] Yet beneath this apparently efficient and coordinated (if limited) response, the RAMC was struggling to maintain and extend its professional influence. As one newspaper reporter hinted on 13 October 1914, on the grounds that they were not accustomed to Army discipline and life, the military authorities were reluctant from the very beginning to accept assistance from voluntary organizations such as the Red Cross.[10] If the RAMC had been more willing to accept the assistance of outsiders, *The Times* correspondent argued, the disastrous failure to cope with the large numbers of casualties in the beginning of the war could have been avoided. This reluctance to use non-military doctors, which persisted throughout the war, was also a part of the Army's attempt to keep control over the definition and treatment of shell shock.

A year later, in December 1915, the Army Medical Service was still battling to meet the demands of the war effort and failing to keep the support of the civilian medical profession. In an internal RAMC memorandum a number of possible reforms came under discussion to help increase the efficiency of the organization. Three of the authors were highly placed members of the civilian medical profession in London who had been arguing for reform of the RAMC on Advisory Boards and Committees since the Boer War. The fourth author was another civilian doctor who had 'recently returned from France'. Poor relations between regular RAMC doctors and military authorities with temporary RAMC medics were the doctors' greatest worry. Without making any accusations of outright incompetence, the authors state their disquiet at widespread inefficiencies.[11] The failure of the RAMC, it was argued, was often self-imposed: temporary Army medics had been effectively intimidated into silence, senior staff of Army Medical Services were oblivious to the dissatisfaction of lower-ranking regulars, temporary RAMC doctors and patients. The professional Army medics, argued the authors, failed to see that a change in the quantitative requirements of the Army required new practices to cope with the scale and complexity of the new warfare and to incorporate the New Armies.[12] Overstaffing at the hospitals set up early in the war, shortage of staff at the more recently established centres and underuse of specialist skills were the result.

The treatment of shell shock cases provides an important example of the Army's failure. Over a year after the outbreak of hostilities the majority of soldiers still returned to Britain with no medical notes at all, or only very brief and inadequate comments on their case history, even in acute cases where some treatment would have been given.[13] The treatment of shell shock is also singled out as an especially noteworthy example of the way the Army authorities imposed clinical judgements. Though there were two (unspecified) opinions as to the best method of organization and treatment of the numerous cases of nerve shock and exhaustion with serious temporary mental disturbances, the authors argued, the civilian profession had never been asked to discuss the subject. 'The question is a very important one. Whichever method is adopted the Government is responsible to the Public and in a lesser degree the whole of the Medical Profession is responsible. Surely the Profession might be consulted and led rather than driven to assist in the administration.'[14] Furthermore, the effect of RAMC military discipline on the medical profession would eventually become self-defeating. Both medical profession and public opinion would turn against them: 'More officers are being called for, but there are many complaints from those already in the service that they are not being given appropriate work. There is also a feeling that the present method of thinly veiled compulsion is threatening grave dislocation of civil practices with injustice to those who go...'[15]

Thinly veiled compulsion and disregard for the finer points of medical science had been the order of the day in both front line and home front Army medical practice from August 1914, for example, in the Army's cursory investigation of the mental health of enlisting men. In the rush to arms at the start of the war such considerations must have seemed irrelevant to authorities and men alike, but even in the revised Army medical examination of 1917, doctors spared only a few cursory moments to consider the potential recruit's 'mental condition'.[16] Although often quickly rendered unfit for military service, and thereafter becoming an expensive liability to the state, the recruitment of mentally unstable and inadequate men continued all through the war.[17] Similarly, under Army medical policy, psychiatric casualties were a low priority, so the quality of care they received was often poor. Shortages of staff and facilities were commonplace, while the higher-ranking authorities wanted to avoid any policy that might appear to sanction traumatic neurosis, to avoid making it an acceptable alternative to fighting.[18] In this light the makeshift conditions that C.S. Myers noted at Boulogne in early 1915, where shell-shocked soldiers were kept on the top floor of a semi-converted hotel, were not only the result of the need to improvise under adverse conditions.[19]

In spite of the initial concern raised by reports on shell shock in late 1914 and early 1915, the Army's attitude varied between apathy at the higher levels and some hostility among medics and soldiers in the batteries and battalions. Innovations and improvements were rare; consequently, mild cases stayed in unsuitable non-specialist hospitals and wards, either at Boulogne or in the UK.[20] On return to the UK, other soldiers received incomplete treatments, went back to the front and soon broke down again.[21] Improvements in France came after cases increased fivefold on the Somme in the second half of 1916; in an attempt to maximize the number of cases returned to active service in the minimum recovery period, non-officer ranks were now to be treated in France, not in Britain.[22] Such changes did improve standards of shell shock care in France, but there were limits to the Army's willingness to adapt, as is illustrated by the expulsion of the leading reformist RAMC specialist in France, C.S. Myers, in December 1917. For Myers, the Army would not go far enough; for the Army, Myers overstepped his authority.

Field doctors working at battery or battalion level observed the constant revisions in policy and regulation with some incredulity. Leonard Gameson, for instance, the temporary RAMC captain who served on the Somme in 1916 and at Arras during the remainder of the war, notes in his memoirs (written from a diary and letters some five years after the Armistice) his own growing disillusion at developments. As an inexperienced doctor who qualified in late 1915 and went to France in early 1916, he particularly noticed that the classification of shell shock seemed a highly contentious issue that had financial implications for both soldiers and the state. One particular rule caught his attention. From the second half of 1916 until the end of the war, cases were diagnosed as 'Wound' or 'Shock', or a variant of this.[23] As a doctor treating shell shock casualties in the field, Gameson was concerned by the use of these categories because they were such imprecise terms which might easily be amended to suit immediate needs, for example to reduce the appearance of large numbers of cases by changing them from the 'Shock' to the 'Wound' category.[24] Alternatively, they could be amended to limit state financial liability. As Gameson argues, the distinction between a 'Shock' and a 'Wound' case was a 'question of the employers liabilities: PENSIONS, that is to say... in the sphere of damaged men Authority was curiously inhibited. In every other conceivable sphere money appeared to be poured out freely and even squandered.'[25] This system was further refined in 1917 when the term 'Shell Shock' was banished from official terminology and in its place suspected mental cases were to be designated as 'Not Yet Diagnosed (Nervous)'. This temporary label was to be given to 'officers and other ranks who, without any visible wound, became non-effective from the physical conditions claimed or presumed to have originated from the effect of British or enemy weapons in action'.[26]

Shell shock casualties were increasingly marginalized in France after the departure of Myers. Under the NYD(N) system, reports were made on each soldier's character and the genesis of his complaint, and it was on the basis of this rather than the medical report that 'sick' or 'wounded' men were divided. Summing up his thoughts on the shell shock treatment system, Gameson succinctly describes the policy of the Army medical authorities: 'Discourage the diagnosis therefore. The fewer there were of such cases the better, the easier, the cheaper. It was, as I've said, a sound move to prevent the abuse of a diagnosis, but we seemed to be getting dangerously near the abuse of preventing a diagnosis. I felt there was a gap somewhere, that something was missing.'[27]

Army medical policy on nervous disorders in the examination of recruits, attitudes to temporary doctors and specialists, and questions of diagnosis and training, thus amounted to little more than a series of improvised reactions and revisions. Captain Gameson's view was that the only coherent theme running through Army policies was 'The fine traditions of "to hell with the nerves"...' which, he argued, persisted in large measure to the end of the war.[28] 'To hell with the nerves' was always a part of the military view of traumatic neurosis, but once the condition was named and recognized, it could not so easily be ignored. The Army's instinct and training meant discipline was the first and most forceful response, and one that might have proved adequate in earlier wars. In the Great War though, shell shock cases could be court-martialled and shot, or sentenced to hard labour or sent to the asylum, but they could not be fully contained. There would always be those doctors unwilling to militarize the condition and more concerned to treat it medically. Potentially, then, the appearance of mental casualties on the Western Front was a public relations disaster for the Army, but first to its relief and later to its chagrin, on the Home Front shell shock became a rallying call for both patriot and dissenter.

Press and political campaigns

In France, regimental medical officers and senior RAMC administrators limited and refined the official definition of traumatic neurosis until it suited their purposes; in Britain journalists and politicians did the same, making the condition a special emblem of heroism and sacrifice, as well as a focus for discontent. There was intermittent discussion on shell shock in the press and in Parliament well beyond the Armistice, while public appeals had a limited impact on the War Office and Ministry of Pensions. In 1915, the initial concern was wrongful certification, and throughout the war there was public apprehension that war heroes were locked in asylums against their will and to the shame of the nation. Related to this was the question of treatment in France where, it was suspected, soldiers were being court-martialled and executed as cowards. Towards 1918 there was also renewed public discussion on the most effective forms of treatment and convalescence. Throughout, traumatic neurosis was considered a real and disturbing condition, a subject of press speculation and of various related fund-raising campaigns which provided a way to express support for the war effort and show solidarity with the suffering of the troops in the front line.

Lord Knutsford, Chairman of the London Hospital and one of the earliest and most consistent advocates of the rights of mental casualties, helped fix their Home Front image at the start of the war. On 4 November 1914, before any serious medical investigation had begun, he made an appeal for funds to set up a specialist treatment centre, noting that 'There are a number of our gallant soldiers for whom at present no proper provision is obtained, but is sorely needed. They are men suffering from severe mental and nervous shock due to exposure, excessive strain and tension. They can be cured if only they can receive the proper attention. If not cured they will drift back into the world as miserable wrecks for the rest of their lives.'[29] The national response to Lord Knutsford's appeal was both swift and generous. The notion that war could produce mental as well as physical casualties was soon accepted and caught the public's imagination because it seemed a manageable problem that could be dealt with quickly and easily. Yet almost immediately squabbles began over the most effective forms of treatment. The Chairman of the Queen Square Hospital for Nervous Diseases argued that funds should go towards the extension of existing provision rather than a separate hospital.[30] Lord Knutsford, though he was no expert, argued adamantly that a neurasthenic-type cure should be used which took full advantage of the possibilities for 'absolute quiet and isolation in separate rooms'.[31] The appeal had raised £7,700 by the start of 1915, and the home for officers opened at Palace Green. Within six months of August 1914 too, the rough boundaries of opinion were laid: public supporters and private campaigners were mobilized; disagreement between military and medical interests was evident.

Queen Alexandra's visit to Palace Green in January 1915 shows how quickly shell shock took on a promotional public role in the war effort; wider interest in the medical profession was stirring around the same time.[32] That same month Sir John Collie in a speech on his specialist area, malingering, gave his first public speech on officer cases of traumatic neurasthenia returning to the UK.[33] By the start of February, Queen Square Hospital, in response to criticism that the old pre-war methods of treatment were ineffective, set up specialist treatment wards.[34] Palace Green remained the centre of attention, though, and throughout the war it was one of the best-known centres of its kind. This reflects the greater interest in higher-ranking soldiers: all appeals and funds for the extension of facilities and opening new homes were in the name of officers; the first admission that a psychiatric casualty had been wrongfully executed, later in the war, was also linked to the case of an officer.[35]

The public discussion of two subjects related to shell shock in 1915 – on its medical status and on the question of certification – shows how officers were privileged. Surgeon General Macpherson argued that shell shock had been widely misunderstood, with the result that 'misguided public opinion had raised the psychoneuroses to the dignity of a new war disease, before which doctors seemed nigh hopeless'. Similarly '[t]his view became rapidly widespread among the soldiers in France. Officers, men and even in some instances medical officers, imbibed the new doctrine. It wrought untold evil among the patients.'[36] The Army was particularly concerned that shell shock had become a media- and rumour-driven epidemic, and alarmed by the prospect of what they saw as the prospect of an outbreak of fear and low morale spread by rumour and ignorance. For this reason, they tended not to comment in public on the subject. At the same time, the War Office, and later the Ministry of Pensions, were keenly aware of the financial liabilities involved if shell shock were to acquire the status of a legitimate disorder. While these wider policy issues were not necessarily clear to ordinary soldiers or civilians, the military approach did arouse suspicion and resentment. Moreover, despite all the bluster and fuss of the Army, their policy towards shell shock seems to have remained ineffective. Finally, the military instinct to insulate soldiers and civilians against the condition failed because it held too strong a grip on the public imagination and it proved impossible to separate the fate of officers and the other ranks.

In addition to the public attention at the very beginning of the war, shell shock remained in the public realm in 1915 because of the question of certification. On 20 April the Assistant Home Secretary, Cecil Harmsworth, introduced a Bill into the House of Commons which became the Mental Treatment Act 1915.[37] Under the existing legislation, the Lunacy Act of 1890, soldiers could not receive treatment in nursing homes without being certified as insane and then sent to an asylum or hospital. All agreed that certification was an unnecessary stigma and that sending soldiers to asylums was inappropriate and ineffective. Both the 'temporary nature' of shell shock, as Harmsworth argued, and the battalions of cases succumbing to it, led to the decision that soldiers should be treated for six months before being certified. Consequently, it became impossible to detain psychological casualties for treatment against their will. The matter received further public attention when, on 22 May 1915, the Under-Secretary for War, Mr

Tennant, answered the first of many questions in the House of Commons on the arrangements for the treatment of cases in France and Britain. Indicating that there was unease about the treatment of the complaint as insanity, he stated that 'at large hospital centres in France specialists in nervous diseases, not alienists, saw all cases of nerve strain and determined to which clearing hospital they are to be sent'.[38]

At the same time as these assurances were being given, the argument that shell shock was based on little more than misguided public opinion was also vigorously promoted. The medical correspondent of *The Times* was convinced that what passed for a genuine disease of war was a failure of willpower and a loss of self-control. A suitable cure for this temporary lapse was thus a positive atmosphere, and, in a phrase that echoed all through the war, 'the larger psycho-therapy of cheerfulness and encouragement'.[39] What continued to worry journalists and politicians most was the mistreatment of cases, of which there were a significant number. Later, in July, Lord Knutsford himself addressed the issue of alienists when the question was again raised in the House of Lords. 'It was true,' he said, 'that those doctors who were mainly concerned in treating lunatics were called alienists, but they bitterly resented the agitation that had been got up against them and the representation that because they were alienists every man who went to them was necessarily mad.'[40] After the war, these assurances proved hollow; asylum methods and 'alienist' doctors were used in the treatment of traumatic neurosis throughout the war.[41]

By early 1916 in Britain, as on the Western Front, there was widespread acceptance of shell shock. Its novelty spent, public attention shifted to other, more urgent aspects of the war. In spite of this declining interest, psychological casualties were returning to the UK in increasing numbers. The fund-raising efforts of Lord Knutsford for officers' hospitals continued, but the steady growth of research into shell shock already showed that Knutsford's 'common-sense' treatment might be inadequate. The developing medical literature was shifting away from hereditary and organic views of the complaint towards a psychological aetiology, while influential public commentators such as Sir John Collie continued to maintain that 'wrong perspective' and 'insufficient willpower' were the causes of wartime mental disorders.[42] The best cure, in Sir John's opinion, remained to keep busy, stay cheerful and return to active service as quickly as possible.[43] The widespread view that shell shock was a form of nerve exhaustion, little different from pre-war complaints, is illustrated too by the increasing use in official and medical circles of the term 'neurasthenia'.[44]

In 1917 many of the issues which affected shell shock cases attracted new public attention and public discussion. Increasing concern is indicated by the growth of private funds for setting up officer treatment centres; as Sir John Collie reported, in late 1916 and early 1917 there had been 'a wholehearted and generous response' to appeal funds. An offer was even made by a generous member of the House of Lords to set up a scholarship for research into the complaint.[45] *The Times*, on 1 February 1917, also noted that in the newly opened centre there would be no changes in the neurasthenia-type cures introduced at the first Special Hospital early in 1915. Treatments at the new Golders Green Hospital would instead attempt to protect soldiers from what was considered a harmful environment. In February 1917 came new evidence that soldiers were being treated in asylums, although this was not in the public domain. The issue arose because of a meeting of the Executive Council of the County Councils Association, who were concerned about the continued policy of sending soldiers to county asylums for classification and treatment.[46] This, it was said, caused great expense and overcrowding, while no effective form of treatment or training for staff was available at the local level. Despite the deputations sent to the Pensions Minister and the Board of Control, who administered the asylum network, the argument that the government should take full responsibility for shell shock provision was ignored.

Meanwhile, Sir John Collie was assuming the role formerly held by Lord Knutsford as leading public educator on the rights and duties of shell-shocked soldiers.[47] These two important figures on the British scene both took the 'common-sense' approach that appealed to public and authorities alike. Where they differed was in their views of the best interests of casualties; while Knutsford remained relatively independent in his concern for the welfare of shell-shocked soldiers, Collie was the public voice of the government on the subject. Like the Army authorities in France, Sir John was acutely aware of the financial burden of long-term or in-depth treatment, including those mentally unfit when they enlisted, and he pared his definition of shell shock accordingly. Consequently, while Collie's public attitude bore little resemblance to medical knowledge his views were nevertheless widely publicized and influential.[48] He explained his approach in a speech in 1917 on 'The Management of Neurasthenia and Allied Disorders in the Army', given at the Royal Institute of Public Health. The subject was of such interest that the talk was reprinted in two journals and reported in the national press. 'Most, if not all cases of neurasthenia arising in the Army were,' he said, 'directly or indirectly, the result of actual concussions – shell shock

– or the conditions prevailing in modern warfare.'[49] Just as his understanding of the origins of the complaint lagged behind medical knowledge, so did Sir John's thoughts on treatment. The cure regime, he argued, should help the soldier regain self-confidence and a positive frame of mind through outdoor work and recreation. Some therapeutic treatments such as massage and electricity might also be incorporated.

Psychiatric casualties also attracted attention in 1917 because of several administrative changes, the most important of which was the increase in numbers of public and privately funded treatment centres.[50] New homes were opened by the state, as were privately funded officers' hospitals run by the Red Cross and other voluntary agencies. One example of this growth of public involvement was the 'Country Host' scheme, a state-funded convalescence programme started by the Ministry of Pensions in August 1917, which discharged shell shock cases to volunteer private households in rural areas for up to three months' recuperation. In full accord with Sir John Collie's view, it was believed that light agricultural labour and a quiet environment were all that was required for recovery.[51] This may be the source of one shell shock image – the disillusioned soldier going to the countryside to 'forget' about the war.[52] The public response was typically mixed: within a few days there was keen public interest and support and the programme was widely used, but some expressed reservations. Was it possible, doubters asked, that 'hosts' might be sent unhinged or dangerous men?[53]

During the latter part of the year, political and public disquiet over Army and Ministry of Pensions treatment methods made traumatic neurosis into a newly controversial public issue. Differences of opinion also emerged among those who felt that the 'rest and quiet' cure was inadequate, and that the 'Country Host' scheme was a pretext for the Army to discharge poorly treated soldiers prematurely. Instead of making veterans dependent on the charity of volunteers, it was argued, full treatment should have been given by specialists before soldiers left the Army. Thousands of soldiers remained curable but retained functional symptoms such as paralysis or deafness, because their conditions were not properly diagnosed. One doctor described the situation for the readers of *The Times* in October 1917: ' "There are many thousands of *discharged* soldiers in our midst suffering from 'shell-shock', neurasthenia, and other equally distressing though purely functional and *curable* disorders"... This statement, coming from one who speaks from a position as Medical Referee for Pensions etc., speaks with authority, constitutes to my mind a very serious indictment against the Department responsible for the treatment of our soldiers, why are they not cured?'[54]

The increasing tensions between the Army and public over shell shock also emerged in the issue of exemptions. The military view was that they should have the final say, despite any medical opinion as to the fitness for service of soldiers who had been treated for shell shock. Sir John Collie's view was that under the 1917 Military Service (Review of Exemptions) Act the Special Medical Board which dealt with all shell shock pensions and medical certificates, had the right to give absolute exemptions to cases as this was necessary to ensure full recovery.[55] The Army view prevailed, and another policy introduced in 1917 also passed with little comment. This was the regulation that excluded soldiers whose mental condition was said to be the result of pre-war factors from the right to a pension. Given that Special Medical Board doctors often used a broad definition of the term 'pre-war', the ruling denied many ex-servicemen any kind of compensation.[56]

The ambivalent view of both Army and government towards shell shock is apparent too in the issues of courts-martial and exemptions from service. The question of wrongful trial and punishment of mental casualties was first raised in 1915, and journalistic interest as well as political concern prompted five questions in the Commons between October 1917 and March 1918. On 19 February 1918, for instance, in reply to a question from Mr Snowden, the Labour MP for Blackburn, the Under-Secretary for War, Mr Macpherson, stated that 'in the case of trials of soldiers for desertion in the field every care was taken that the men should be medically examined with the view to ascertaining whether they had been suffering from shell shock...' To which the Labour MP for Mid-Lanarkshire, Mr Whitehouse, responded, 'Then why have they been shot?'[57] To criticize the Army, no matter on what grounds, was disloyal and unpatriotic, yet after several months of persistent questioning the final clash of the war on courts-martial in the House of Commons resulted in an admission from Under-Secretary Macpherson: in one instance an officer had been wrongfully executed. On 14 March 1918 Macpherson stated: 'It was said in this particular case grave doubt existed as to whether the officer was not suffering from shell-shock, and therefore irresponsible for his action. Undoubtedly the idea that shell-shock meant "cold feet" was an exploded idea. (Hear, Hear.) One knows of scores of gallant young fellows who after shell-shock retained only a part of their bodily strength and mental vigour.'[58] On the question of exemptions from military service, however, there was no change in the decision that cases not discharged should be given only a short rest cure and then returned quickly to active service.[59]

The final phase of public discussion on shell shock before the Armistice came in the early months of 1918. It was during the last year of the war that Ministry of Pensions facilities grew to accommodate the increasing numbers of psychiatric casualties returning from the front, and professional neurologists were first employed on shell shock pensions tribunals.[60] The continuing discussion over treatment policy went a step further when the Ministry of Pensions decided specialist medical advice was largely unnecessary for cases in the UK. This affected the care of soldiers in various ways. In March 1918, during a speech at Worcester, the Minister of Pensions, Mr John Hodge, argued that the existing location of one of the most famous shell shock hospitals at Golders Green was too near to areas where air raids were feared, and that patients would be better off in the country's peace and quiet. As doctors pointed out at the time, however, there was no real evidence that such raids would adversely affect shell shock cases as they were more used to such occurrences than the civilian population. The change in policy that this statement represented was, rather, a pretext to reduce the 'special' status of psychiatric casualties; as the minister argued, the best form of therapy was to have 'neurasthenic cases mixed up with other cases, so that the cheery chap might shed some of the sunshine of his presence over those suffering from neurasthenia'.[61]

Specialists quickly pointed out that the effects of integration were highly destructive to the patient's chances of recovery. One such physician was G. Elliot Smith, co-author of *Shell-Shock and its Lessons* (1917), who argued that the minister was backing out of an agreement made only three months earlier to save psychological casualties from the 'morbid curiosity' of other patients. It was preferable that casualties should instead be aided by those with similar experiences instead of being subjected to 'misplaced joviality'.[62] Shell-shocked soldiers were rarely able to express their opinions in public, but on this occasion some of the patients at Golders Green did make a statement. In a letter to *The Times* on 28 March 1918, they explained why they too disagreed with the Ministry of Pensions, arguing: 'Our past experiences in general hospitals have taught us to appreciate being separated from other cases, especially from the so-called "cheery man"', and 'all patients are agreed that after the experience of other hospitals and the company of the so-called "cheery chap" they prefer to risk the air raid results before that of going to another hospital'.[63] By 14 May, two months after his original speech at Worcester, Hodge made it finally clear that Golders Green would close.[64] Despite the objection, made by doctors, patients and campaigners, that specialist doctors and specialist facilities were in

London and that doctors would refuse to travel out to treat former patients, the closure went ahead.[65]

This incident shows how the Ministry of Pensions functioned towards the end of the war, and how it continued to work into the 1920s. The appointments made by the Ministry provide additional evidence of their thinking; in 1918 Sir John Collie, one of the leading advocates of the 'cheery chap' school of shell shock treatment, was appointed Director of the Ministry of Pensions Medical Services Section. Under his direction, and with guidance from the Ministry of Pensions, shell shock facilities were 'upgraded'. By November 1918, Under-Secretary of War Macpherson could announce there were 15 institutions treating shell shock and that none was segregated. These were not new hospitals however, but the same centres that had been treating cases since 1915. In addition, case note samples, including cases from these hospitals, indicate that centres such as the Springfield, Upper Tooting, the First Southern General, Birmingham, and Seale Hayne, Newton Abbot had limited specialist facilities or expertise.[66] The Ministry of Pensions intended to pursue the 'cheery chap' treatment regime despite all objections and disagreements. The approach was symptomatic of a similar 'common-sense' view of shell shock which prevailed throughout the war in Britain aided by the public perception of the complaint as neurasthenic-type nerve exhaustion.

Disputed definitions in wartime

As the institution most directly involved with psychiatric casualties throughout the war, the Army did everything in its power to enlist shell shock into the war effort by defining it according to strictly pragmatic criteria. Disciplinary issues were, therefore, of greatest urgency in France; in Britain, shell shock took on a broader role. Having caught the public's imagination, the notion of 'shell shock' was beyond the control of military or state authorities. As the official line that shell shock was an entirely illusory collective loss of confidence that spread through gossip and misinformation went unheard, controlling public perception of the condition became a question of 'damage limitation'. Initially a potential threat to morale on both the Western Front and the Home Front then, shell shock was later used to help promote the war effort and enhance the idea that the state was engaged in a dedicated campaign to assist the well-being and health of its soldiers. Preserving manpower and financial resources was an additional task that neither generals nor politicians could afford to ignore.

Ultimately, the Army believed, these procedures were justified by the requirements of the war effort.

In France, the most important consequence of the military approach was the requirement on the part of the Army not to lend credibility to the idea of a legitimate mental disorder of war. Restricting and guiding the related language and terminology helped achieve this, for example through field orders, which used strictly pragmatic definitions of sickness and stressed the requirements that discipline took priority over medical opinion. Consequently, in many minds, especially on the Western Front, shell shock remained a rumour, a phantom in no man's land, whose existence was unconfirmed or denied outright. This served the Army well, especially early in the war, when shell shock was dismissed as a confidence trick based on the credulity, ignorance and low morale of soldiers, who were both its advocates and its victims. On the Home Front, the Army could not completely ignore the journalists, politicians and soldiers who discussed shell shock, so here too it became necessary to limit the condition's definition and rework its meanings, especially by promoting a limited, empirically defined view of the disorder in educational talks and semi-official public appeals. With the exception of some showcase officer centres such as Golders Green, however, standards of treatment and facilities for soldiers were consistently lower than for physical casualties; forms of shell shock that did not fit the military definition were only begrudgingly treated.

The Army's 'damage limitation' policy was somewhat hampered by its inability to control the public and political sympathy and interest that shell shock aroused, especially in the investigation into such unsavoury aspects as misdiagnosis and mistreatment, but by promoting the cure of officers in 'special' hospitals, it nevertheless became possible to incorporate the condition into public notions of 'honourable' suffering. The example of shell-shocked men helped to make the sacrifices that the war demanded imaginable, as well as to show how well men could cope with its trials: hence the stress on 'cheerful' cures. At the same time, the newspapers and war histories of the day paraded the more lurid view of shell shock before the public too. This only added to the uncanny view of wartime mental disorders seen on the Western Front and in Britain. On balance, the public interest in shell shock, and its presentation as an example of successful wartime medical practice, benefited patients by making possible fuller medical care and legislative protection. It gave only a vague hint, however, of the realities of wartime medicine for the vast majority of psychiatric casualties who did not receive the privileges of officers at Golders Green. The next chapter begins a consideration of the circumstances faced by the majority of patients by outlining the development of the British treatment network, defining the peculiarities of its medical outlook, and examining the theory and practice of more specialist doctors.

5
Treatment: On the Home Front

The British treatment network

From its first appearance in the autumn of 1914, when cases of lost speech and limb paralysis began to arrive in Britain, doctors, generals and politicians disputed the likely origins and best treatments of shell shock; they also set about establishing a makeshift treatment network to allow the evacuation of casualties across the Channel. In the first few months of the war this system delivered men haphazardly, wherever beds were free, to asylums, specialist hospitals and general wards. As the number of cases began to rise steadily, it became obvious that a specialist state hospital was necessary, and 'D' Block at Netley was quickly converted into a reception and clearing centre.[1] Having established this first base towards the end of 1914, a special investigation into the needs of patients was made, and in December the Moss Side State Institute at Maghull was taken over by the War Office. However, the continued sharp rise in the number of cases meant that even with Maghull all the available places quickly filled. Many patients were, as a result, still going into the neurological sections of general hospitals in early 1915, but the more seriously disturbed went to specialist hospitals such as the National Hospital for Paralysed and Epileptic, Queen Square, London, which opened a specialist ward in February 1915.[2]

In the first half of 1915, the shell shock treatment network began to expand quickly. The 4th London Territorial General Hospital was the next addition; the Middlesex County Asylum was also taken over and renamed the Springfield War Hospital.[3] The Middlesex was one of a group of asylums converted in 1915 into medical centres for all types of war casualties, including mental cases. The Warncliffe War Hospital, at Wadsley, near Sheffield, for example, was the South Yorkshire Asylum until the West Riding Asylum Board transferred patients into surrounding institutions and in early 1915 offered 1,500 beds to the War Office.[4] With this expansion, hospitals began to specialize. The Royal Victoria at Netley took some acute cases; Napesbury took the certifiably insane. In England, other chronic and acute cases also went to Springfield, Maghull and Queen Square; in Scotland they went to the Royal Victoria, Edinburgh; in Ireland to the King George V, Dublin.[5]

By 1916 several of the converted asylums had become significant shell shock treatment centres, including: the Northumberland (Newcastle upon Tyne), the Warncliffe (Sheffield), the Lord Derby (Warrington), the 1st Birmingham (Rubery), the 2nd Birmingham (Hollymore), the Norfolk, the Welsh Metropolitan (Cardiff), the Grayling (Chichester), the Beaufort (Bristol), the County of London (Epsom), as well as the Napesbury (St Albans) and the Springfield (Middlesex), and later the Northants Asylum (Berrywood).[6] Large enough to achieve some stability in the latter part of the war, this treatment system constantly diversified and readjusted itself according to military requirements and to a lesser extent political will. The events of the war also affected treatment: pressure of numbers during the Somme campaign in the summer and early autumn of 1916 reduced the length of hospital stays; the start of unrestrained submarine warfare shortly thereafter, which constricted the movement of transport ships across the Channel, meant that from late 1916 many more cases were treated in France. By this time, in any case, the experience of seeing so many soldiers pensioned off from the Army because they were apparently incurable had led the authorities to recognize the value of 'forward treatment'.[7] This meant rapid diagnosis followed by placement in a hospital near the front line, and if this first-tier hospital failed, a further back-up level was available away from the front. The important treatment centres in France included Havre, Boulogne, Rouen and Etaples. The other ranks were returned to Britain only as a final resort. Officers had largely separate treatment centres throughout the war, first at the Special Hospital for Officers, at Palace Green, which was opened early in 1915.[8] Later officer hospitals included the Lennel Convalescent Home at Coldstream, and from October 1916, a much larger Special Hospital for Officers at Craiglockhart, near Edinburgh.[9]

Cultures of treatment: Britain, France and Germany

This outline of the treatment network gives a framework within which to analyse how doctors tried to understand and cure shell shock, but having established where the war-traumatized neurotic might have been treated, it is much more difficult to ascertain what form his treatment took. This is not just a question of printed sources, there is no shortage of articles and monographs on the subject, nor is it a problem of insufficient or inadequate medical records or first-hand testimony, although these are less readily available. Rather, it is the near-impossibility of recreating clearly the encounter between medic and patient that frustrates the historian's ambition to know what attitudes and expectations were brought to the consulting room, and how they shaped a peculiarly malleable form of hysteria such as shell shock. One way to compensate for this limitation is to compare the treatment systems of Britain, France and Germany, first to discover the institutional and medical specifics of each system, second to understand what assumptions lay behind treatment, and by this means infer the unspoken views that British medics brought to the consulting room. What follows is a study of medical culture then, which considers both the theory and practice of treatment, as far as it can be understood from the extant sources and from the specialist medic's perspective.

The enduring tradition of empiricism guided British medical thought and practice both before and during the Great War. British psychiatrists, for instance, preferred not to adhere to strict schools of thought, but to take a generalist, 'objective' approach to mental conditions: to consider causes a question of genetics, toxicology and biochemistry.[10] F.W. Mott took this approach to shell shock when he catalogued and analysed the first cases in late 1914 and early 1915; the medical notes in general hospitals throughout the war both in Britain and in France indicate that by training and temperament other British doctors did the same. Mott's major published work is *War Neurosis and Shell Shock* (1919); however, it was through a series of wartime articles on mental hygiene, the physical impact of shell explosions on the brain, neurasthenia as a disorder of fear and the effects of inheritance on mental disposition that he disseminated his empiricist view.[11] In 1916, E.E. Southard, then director of a 'Psychopathic Hospital' in Boston, reviewed a lecture by Mott, who at that time was a temporary RAMC doctor at the 4th London General Hospital.[12] Summing up Mott's view, Southard says, the effects of high explosives fell into three categories: instant fatalities from violence or burial, sometimes without physical visible injury; non-fatal wounds and injuries of the body, including the central nervous system; and injuries of the central nervous system without visible damage.[13] Accordingly, when Mott came to advise a group of non-specialist doctors in treatment techniques he suggested a benign form of 'positive expectation' and the use of baths. 'Be cheerful and look cheerful is the note which should be sounded to these functional cases. Sympathy should not be misplaced although it should be shown to all these poor fellows who have a fixed idea of never recovering...I do not find hypnosis or psychoanalysis necessary or even desirable...' Mott went on to praise what he saw as the ideal treatment conditions at the Maudsley Hospital, with its 'light, airy wards, and day rooms for meals and recreations, plenty of single rooms for the isolation of cases that are troubled by noises or require separate attention; and especially valuable are the baths, so that every soldier can get a warm spray bath every day. The warm baths, and especially the continuous warm baths, of which there are eight, are especially valuable.'[14] This was perhaps a continuation of the earliest hydrotherapeutic techniques used for the treatment of mental patients, but it may also have been a less severe variation on the 'active therapy' technique adopted at the University Psychiatric Clinic in Frankfurt.[15] Here Rafael Weichbrodt cured his patients by continuous immersion in hot baths; on one, admittedly exceptional, occasion, this process lasted for 40 hours.

The contrast between Mott and Weichbrodt's use of baths is one instance of how each society reshapes and renames like treatment and symptom in its own image. There are other cultural variants, for instance in the differences in criteria and accuracy in recorded rates of traumatic neurosis in each country; the French, for instance, recorded much higher rates than the British, reaching 50 or 60 per cent of all cases in some neurological centres.[16] In a similar manner, while British medics spoke of shell shock during the first part of the war, and only reluctantly admitted its psychological sources, French doctors immediately labelled psychiatric casualties as hysterics. The varied institutions and objectives of the national medical professions offer another instance of cultural disparity: while the British medics responded to shell shock with improvization, with doctors from asylum work, academic and civilian life contributing to the war effort according to the dictates of conscience, the French neurologists were coordinated by a centralized Association which created a coherent and unified reaction for reasons of patriotic duty and collective professional advancement.[17] On both sides of the Channel there were medics who explicitly connected the situation of soldiers to that of the insured factory worker: both would prolong their treatment and hospitalization because it was a comfortable alternative to the harsh environment of the factory floor or the worse hardships of the trenches.[18] Hence in France the extensive use of Vincent's electric shock and 'persuasion' method, known as *torpillage*, and Babinski's isolation and persuasion technique, known as *méthode brusque*. Both these techniques contributed to what Mark Roudebush calls the 'war of nerves': an antagonistic, combative view of war hysteria on the part of the French medical profession, and unsurprisingly a similar resistance and antagonism on the part of soldiers under treatment. French neurologists would not discharge uncured patients from service, but at the same time, they were not able to cure all the patients they encountered. Some patients found themselves trapped inside the system: symptoms cured, they went to the front; suffering relapse, they then went to another hospital to be cured again.[19]

In Germany too the associations between the mental anguish of war, hysteria and patriotism were compelling in a way that was absent in Britain.[20] Before 1916, soldiers were often unsuccessfully treated as victims of 'traumatic neurosis'. The failure of these treatments led to the reconception of mental casualties as 'war hysterics' and to the increased use of 'active therapy', which included Fritz Kaufmann's extended and painful application of electric shocks in a technique he called *Überumpelungsmethode* (surprise attack method).[21] As in France, the objective of 'active therapy' was to save pension funds and return the soldier as an able worker to the front, or to become a labourer in a factory.[22] Again, although preserving manpower and money were British priorities too, medics nevertheless took a different approach. Lewis Yealland most notably used methods that resembled those of Babinski or Kaufmann, but as we shall see, such techniques were not as extensively or systematically applied, nor were former shell shock cases seen as potential factory workers because, it was believed, the noise and activity of the shop floor might provoke relapse. If he was lucky, long-term treatment or a pension was the likely fate of the British shell shock casualty, not a job in a munitions factory. One other aspect of the German approach to medicine during the war was its extensive use of both scientific and persuasive 'magical' therapies.[23] As Paul Lerner notes, French medics rejected hypnosis because of its anti-scientific associations, and British medics were reluctant to embrace any psychological explanation for shell shock. However, in Germany hypnotic techniques were used, and known usually as Nonne's method, after Max Nonne, who worked at Eppendorf Hospital, Army Reserve Hospital Station III in Hamburg, where, by his own account, he treated around 1,600 patients successfully.[24] Suggestion through display and mystification were the rationale for these techniques: in Nonne's case by encouraging the expectation of cure, and in Kaufmann's by provoking a 'counter-trauma'.

French and German medics were, then, much more willing to central-
ize, patriotize and psychologize the treatment of shell shock than their
British counterparts, whose treatment system by contrast was relatively
dispersed, un-ideological, and empirical in its outlook. There was less
pressure on doctors to cure soldiers before discharge and less reason why
the medical profession should assert its authority over shell shock cases.
Unlike the 'hot' French or German 'war of nerves', then, the British
hostilities were, if not cold, at least 'cool'. Suggestion, coercion and
active therapy were all present in Britain, but the 'physicalist' view
tempered them. Because the vast majority of doctors treating psychological casualties were non-specialist RAMC medics or civilians in uni-
form, when confronted with limb paralysis or hysterical blindness they
fell back on their empiricist training or the views of like-minded asylum
doctors or nerve specialists to help understand the aetiology of mental
disorders. Furthermore, the opinions of doctors like Mott, Wolfsohn or
Southard coloured the outlook of many British medics because this was
the tradition in which they trained and because the 'physicalist' approach fitted military expectation and needs. The military doctor's
objectives were to dampen the perceived threat to morale and to treat
the patient just enough to return him to duty, but this requirement was
complicated by the fact that the pressure to send soldiers back to the
front did not affect all doctors and all patients equally. To understand
how doctors approached their shell shock patients it is necessary, then,
to re-examine the most widely used model of shell shock treatment,
which makes a sharp distinction between disciplinary and analytic
methods.

Queen Square: disciplinary practice

Throughout the war, debates and case studies on shell shock clogged the
medical journals, and it is based on this evidence that historians have
built their understanding of shell shock treatment.[25] One influential
model, put forward by Eric Leed in 1979, divides treatment into two
categories: disciplinary and analytic. This distinction first appears in
No Man's Land (1979) as Leed is discussing the 'reacculturation' of
soldiers to the war. 'In the acute treatment of war neurosis one can
identify two very different therapeutic scenes, two different techniques
of domination, rooted in two different conceptual frameworks and
visions of human nature,' says Leed. 'The moral view of neurosis that
fashioned disciplinary treatment contrasts sharply with the "analytic"
view, which is best represented by, but by no means identical with,

psychoanalysis.'[26] In Britain Leed identifies the disciplinary method closely with the 'quick cure' or 'Queen Square method'. This entailed the use by doctors of high pressure 'persuasion' techniques principally, according to Leed, 'derived from animal training', such as painful electric shocks, shouted commands or isolation. The 'Queen Square' method is a variation on the procedures employed by Kaufmann and Babinski then, but what cannot be ascertained from the published literature on shell shock is how widespread or effective was the use of such techniques at Queen Square or elsewhere. By considering the treatment regime at the hospital itself it should be possible to establish this, to gain an insight into the everyday work of specialist medics and to ascertain how they understood and treated shell shock.

The leading exponent of 'disciplinary' therapy in Britain was Dr L.R. Yealland, a young Canadian medic who worked as a specialist at Queen Square during the war and in 1918 published *Hysterical Disorders of Warfare*. In *No Man's Land*, and in almost all the subsequent studies on the subject, one particular example of Yealland's method is quoted: the case of a 24-year-old private, a highly decorated soldier who had been unable to speak for nine months.[27] For Showalter and other of Leed's supporters, the details of this case are evidence that medics effectively tortured their patients into submission, and especially that electrical faradization was 'at the most punitive end of the treatment spectrum'.[28] In Showalter's view, for instance, 'Yealland was probably the most extreme advocate of disciplinary treatment among the English doctors'.[29] This is a fair judgement, but it leaves open the wider question of what other kinds of treatment medics used at Queen Square, and whether Yealland was in any way representative of national therapeutic practices. On examination, Yealland appears to have been isolated not only within the treatment regime of Queen Square, but on the national stage.

The National Hospital for Paralysed and Epileptic, Queen Square, London, opened in 1860, had a long-established reputation as a leading centre for the treatment of psychological and neurological disorders.[30] In February 1915 the then President of the National, Lord Beauchamp, announced the opening, in conjunction with the War Office, of a specialist ward for psychological casualties; the medical case notes and records show that Queen Square continued to treat war-related cases until 1924.[31] The bulk of these patients were admitted from late 1915 and through 1916. Following the Armistice a smaller group passed through the wards, men who had suffered severe psychological damage. Soldiers admitted to the National during the war were not the all-too-common cases of nerve exhaustion, memory loss or limb paralysis, they had frequently been through the non-specialist war hospital treatment network without any improvement, and were sent to the specialist centre as a last resort. The records, preserved at the Institute of Neurology Library also in Queen Square, give a detailed account of shell shock treatment unlike any in the existing histories of the complaint.

The extant medical notes and records from the National appear, however, to be incomplete, lacking especially Dr Yealland's separate medical treatment file. Despite this gap, they do give a clear picture of the numbers and types of war cases dealt with, and of the treatments and aetiologies used by various medics. None of the doctors at Queen Square, all psychological specialists, dealt exclusively with the variously classified war cases. Nevertheless, among the extensive surviving case notes for patients in all categories are the records of 200 soldiers whose nervous and mental complaints related to active war service. These come in the form of complete sets of records for each doctor and for each year from 1915 onwards. Thus, Dr Russell had one volume for 1916 and one for 1917, while Dr Collier had three volumes, for 1916, 1917 and 1919. In this way, the notes of nine medics are preserved for the period 1915–24 in 14 volumes, although not all doctors had cases recorded for treatment in every year.

Over the nine-year period from 1914, civilian and military neurasthenics amounted to 651 patients – 381 women and 270 men – with a sharp decrease in the male cases following the closure of the specialist shell shock ward in 1918. Two hundred military cases passed through the National between 1915 and 1924; a minority in all diagnostic categories, their numbers were also relatively small within the hospital as a whole. Five cases of mutism, eight cases of hysterical mutism, 37 cases of shell shock (1915–18); 13 cases of hysterical monoplegia (1916); 20 cases of traumatic neurasthenia, and 117 cases of neurasthenia (1915–24).[32] The National dealt with more cases than the shell shock wards of general hospitals, but by any standard 200 is only a small fraction of the nation's cases. By comparison, Maghull treated 3,638 patients between November 1914 and June 1919. In their article of June 1917, Adrian and Yealland indicate themselves that their treatment techniques were not widespread, noting that the cure 'had been applied to upwards of 250 cases which have included all the most common types of hysterical disorder...'[33] The influence of the Queen Square method seems, therefore, to have rested more on Yealland's published work than on the number of cases he treated.

Considering the Queen Square notes generally and surveying the varieties of treatment, one finds what were clearly common practices and conventions in examination and the production of case sheets. These tend to make the medical case notes themselves rather difficult to discern; nevertheless, they do give a picture of the variety of medical practice within Queen Square. The Queen Square notes show that about a third of war-related cases were treated with some form of faradization (non-punitive electric shock therapy), but what exactly that meant depended on the doctor's clinical outlook rather than his technological resources. The following examination of case notes shows how widely the relationship between doctor and patient varied, and how a variety of approaches were used at Queen Square.

'Shell shock' was the diagnostic term used to describe 37 of the cases treated at Queen Square; it was used in the case of patients principally but not exclusively suffering physical shock rather than from recognizably psychological symptoms. Dr Taylor, a close associate of Yealland's, dealt with one such case, a 25-year-old private, between 29 March and 27 May 1916. The patient had been ill since September 1915 and had improved, but complained of pains in the head, amnesia and 'dreams'.[34] Faradism, bromide and massage were his treatment throughout the next two months, and although not fully cured, his symptoms slowly improved. Dr Tooth used similar methods, but placed little emphasis on the use of electricity, as in the instance of a private treated in the autumn of 1916. Aged 34, J.A. stayed at Queen Square between 5 October 1916 and 13 January 1917, two and a half months in total, and was eventually discharged fully cured. He had joined up in April 1915 and went to the Dardanelles in October 1915, Egypt in January 1916 and France in May 1916. Dr Tooth describes his patient as a '[w]ell built man of 34. Lies quietly in bed with a rather vacant expression. Coarse tremor of both hands. His extremities are very clammy. He speaks in a halting fashion and gives a fairly connected account of his illness.' The only recorded treatment is 'massage'.[35]

Wherever possible Dr Tooth identified a particular incident that caused the symptoms. The case of a 27-year-old in the North Fusiliers, for example: a man who had joined the Army in September 1914, gone to France in September 1915, was then transferred to Armentieres diagnosed with shell shock and treated from 19 May to 12 July 1916. Reportedly quite well when he arrived near Albert in March 1916, 'on Thursday 27th April, a shell burst 100 yards in front of the trench he was in. He was buried for two hours and when dug out remained unconscious for two hours more ... he jumps in his sleep, but is not troubled with dreams ... Massage and bromide t[reatment].'[36] Dr Tooth gave effective assistance to many soldier patients, a 21-year-old private, for example. Admitted to No. 12 General Hospital at Rouen, then to No. 1 Stationary Hospital Rouen in April 1916, and finally arriving at Queen Square on 11 May, he received treatment for 'shell shock'.

> Progress. Has improved by slow degrees. Speech returned but some extreme difficulty owing to great stammering and stuttering. His facial muscles all tremble more or less when he attempts to speak. The stammer is now almost away (he had no stammer previous to shock). Pains in head much less severe. Feet had improved greatly but are still numb to some extent and he has not attempted to stand... Feels less apprehensive and is much brighter. Sleeps very well now but has occasional nightmare.[37]

He was finally discharged as fully recovered on 10 August 1916.

Dr Tooth provides a strong counter-example to the view that techniques of domination were the basis of war neurosis treatment. All his case notes reveal a medic who was considerate and efficient, not just in the treatment of war cases, but with all his patients. The attentions of such a medic did not guarantee that the wider treatment regime of the hospital was not disciplinary, but it did moderate the influence of some of the more radical doctors, such as Yealland or Taylor.

'Neurasthenia' and 'traumatic neurasthenia', apart from 'shell shock', made up the largest diagnostic categories at Queen Square. These two groups of cases also provided the greatest challenge, as doctors were often unable to find fully effective treatments. One married man, aged 37, was treated for neurasthenia between 22 December 1915 and 26 March 1916 with some improvement. This case highlights too the inadequacy of the Army medical system, which was unable to identify or treat him correctly, and by contrast the efficiency of Queen Square:

> When on a long march he fell exhausted, his comrades having to carry him along. Cramp-like pains soon developed in the legs and arms and he was soon forced to give up...He was at hospitals... Convalescent camps and so forth but did not improve. He was sent back twice to join the ranks but on each occasion had to return to a hospital. He soon began shaking all over and was sent to England.[38]

The detail and attention given to these and many other case notes at Queen Square are unusual. In comparison to most other British hospitals, these records give greater attention to the patient's history, his symptoms, and his daily treatment regime. The quality of medical notes cannot prove the efficiency of the treatment regime, but do give an indication of how much time each doctor might allot to individual patients. By contrast, the doctor who wrote the medical notes for a regular sergeant major, for example, who was admitted to the Lincoln 4th General Hospital 18 July 1915, gives no space to the patient's history, noting only that he had been in France from the beginning of the war, and that he had reported in on 13 July with pain in the head, eyes and over the heart. The patient was, his medic wrote, suffering from 'disturbed sleep & nasty dreams – nervous system shattered by long hours at work & not enough sleep & rest'.[39] The prescribed cure was bromide, light duty and bed rest.

It might be argued that these variations in the aetiology and treatment of war-traumatized neurotics are immaterial to the fundamental point of Leed's argument: that the 'therapeutic scenes' of treatment were based within coherent visions of human nature, conceptual frameworks and consequent techniques of domination. This argument holds up when considering certain forms of treatment, yet within a more detailed examination of clinical practices the clarity of the distinction between analytic and disciplinary therapy is lost. Even within the Queen Square records, many of the case notes demonstrate the difficulty in adhering to the disciplinary/analytic dichotomy. To give two generic examples when this dichotomy does not hold: cases clearly thought to be the result of physical injury, or subject to a concussion/wound form of shell shock, and cases where electric shock is applied in a non-punitive form.

Given its empiricist traditions, it is not surprising that concussion and neurological conditions accounted for a high proportion of the cases at Queen Square. However, there were also other, less clear-cut instances where patients seemed to be on the borderline between concussion and neurosis. There were also instances where a doctor at the front gave one diagnosis, a base hospital medic another, and the Queen Square specialist an opinion that again was entirely different. This confusion or ambiguity is illustrated by the case notes of a 26-year-old private, who came down the line labelled N.Y.D. (N) [Not Yet Diagnosed (Nervous)]. 'He was very excitable and noisy on arrival but quickly improved. He has evidence of severe shock usually associated with shell concussion, most marked symptoms knee jerks, unequal pupils, and a spasmodic "Tic" of knee with frequent jerking of the head to the right. He is not insane. Speech and general behaviour normal.'[40] 'Dementia' was the diagnosis at the 10th General Hospital. Travelling on to the mental ward at Queen Square on 17 April 1918, where he remained until 11 June 1918, 'nervous exhaustion' was the diagnosis for his headaches, trembling and giddiness.

As in the following instance of a soldier who was admitted on 6 January 1916, and discharged on 15 March with no improvement, with Dr Yealland acting as House Physician, Dr Tooth noted headaches, weakness, backache and difficulty passing water as the principal symptoms. 'Patient is conscientious; answers questions very intelligently. Has no delusions or hallucinations and is well oriented. There are no speech defects... hyperanaesthesia of ankles & feet + analgesia below knees both legs... High frequency... three times a week + bromide & massage + [hospital] discharge & furlough [followed by] L[ight] D[uty].'[41] Looked at from the perspective of the medical notes, without the accompanying commentaries that have made Yealland's method seem so repulsive, in particular types of cases it clearly proved very successful. 'High frequency', 'faradism' and 'isolation' were similarly applied to a 28-year-old private who had suffered 'functional monoplegia' – involuntary movements of the left arm. Ill from 1915, he spent his two months at Queen Square between 26 May and 15 July 1916; his health was fully restored when he left hospital.[42] Under well-defined circumstances then, faradism was an effective therapeutic tool.

A few of the Queen Square notes and records do clearly fit into Yealland's own description of his method. A lance-corporal diagnosed with 'neurosis and functional aphonia' entered the hospital on 11 April 1916 and left the following day. R. had been with the Gordon Highlanders since mid-August 1914, and subsequently at Mons, Aisne, La Basee, First Battle of Ypres, Kemmel, Hill 60, Hooge and the International Trenches. Like most of the soldiers treated at the National, R. received ineffective treatment at several medical centres before final referral. 'States that his voice has been leaving him for six months, but the 2nd March finished it... cured by faradism.'[43] Passed from one unqualified doctor to another and treated ineffectively throughout, this soldier's quick cure must surely have brought him some peace of mind, though its long-term efficacy is doubtful. He was not made well by the method Yealland describes, but he might have proclaimed, together with 'Case A1 – Mutism', 'Doctor, doctor, I am champion.'[44]

Another case illustrates how Queen Square was, in many respects, one of the best wartime hospitals. It shows too how faradization did not necessarily entail a protracted interrogation session. Admitted to the National on 18 October 1917 and discharged on 5 January 1918, Private W. of the Rifle Brigade was 19 years old. He had been ill for a total of seven months before admission, and his symptoms were '(1) Mutism,

(2) General restlessness and trembling. (3) Both hands useless with athetiosis... Treatment: Voice treated by Faradism, returned at first with a stammer. Re-educated to talk within five minutes. Hands were faradized, power returned. Legs next treated by Faradism, re-educated to walk.'[45] According to the hospital records, Queen Square received all its cases of 'hysterical' or 'functional' monoplegia during 1916. Dr Taylor dealt with many similar cases between 1916 and 1918; two of the soldiers were relieved of symptoms within the same day, the remaining nine stayed at the hospital for a matter of days or weeks. It should be noted too that faradization was usually used within a wider therapeutic regime that also included sedatives, baths and massage. Another case that could fall into the category of punitive treatment was a 36-year-old volunteer. Admitted on 29 March 1916 suffering loss of power and feeling in the right leg from the knee down, he also had a painful right hip. 'Treatment: Strong faradism was applied to his right leg for about an hour, feeling returned quickly and power came back to a considerable extent. He walks fairly well ... without crutches and without holding on to anything.'[46]

Faradism worked best in this kind of case. Where the psychological disorder was more complicated, doctors had less success. In these instances treatment involved long stays on the specialist wards, as in the case of one 19-year-old officer who suffered severe memory loss and was treated daily with massage, sodium bromide, 'liquid Strych.' and pints of milk. Admitted on 2 September 1916 and diagnosed with 'Neurasthenia (Shell Shock)', after 14 weeks of this regime he had improved and was transferred to the Officers' Home of Recovery at Golders Green.[47] In this case the boundary between a pre-war case of neurasthenia and a wartime case of 'shell shock' as physical concussion is uncertain. The notes on family history show an interest in hereditary and organic explanations, while the milk diet prescription harks back to the older cures for neurasthenia that would readily come to mind in a hospital like the National.

The density and brevity of the case notes make it difficult to go beyond the commonplace statement that clinical practice and opinion at the National, as in any institution, depended on the temperament and approach of the individual medic. What we can say for certain, however, is that Queen Square employed skilled specialists whose methods were empirical and pragmatic, and that a variety of resourceful techniques were tried in the treatment of war-related cases. Furthermore, the Queen Square approach had many of the 'common-sense' attitudes used by less skilled medics within the General War Hospital network. For Yealland, as for other medics, heredity and physical injury were the first point of diagnostic reference, and only then were other explanations and treatments tried.[48] Standard methods included a milk diet, bromide and massage, which together with rest was a sufficient cure for some patients, though in other instances, sick soldiers remained at the hospital for several months before recovery. In this hospital as elsewhere the role of willpower was severely limited by heredity, physical concussion and neurological damage, all of which rendered persuasion techniques useless. Yealland's role in all this remains ambiguous. If his techniques were regrettable, they also seem to have been remarkably effective. Where other medics pronounced the patient incurable, Yealland persisted, a significant achievement given the large numbers of British patients who remained uncured after the war.

Maghull: analytic practice

As well as the pre-war treatment regimes used and modified at Queen Square and elsewhere, a second approach to traumatic neurosis was attempted. Analytic therapy during the Great War centred on the work and experience of a loosely associated group of specialist and academic doctors known as the 'School of Integral Psychology'; this group included W.H.R. Rivers, William Brown, C.S. Myers and William McDougall.[49] The two groups were not mutually exclusive, however. Dr Farquhar Buzzard, for instance, treated wartime mental disorders at the National within a 'disciplinary' regime, but also worked after the war at the more 'analytically' oriented Cassel Hospital. Like the Queen Square medics, but unlike the majority of medics who dealt with shell shock, the Maghull doctors were also members of the professional and academic elite who turned to applied psychology as their contribution to the war effort. Myers and McDougall, for instance, were two of Rivers' brightest students at Cambridge before the war, and in 1898 all three went on an anthropological expedition to the Torres Straits.[50] With the onset of the war, Myers expressed a common sentiment among his contemporaries that these former academic pursuits had lost all meaning. Now the urgent priority was practical treatment.[51]

Rivers and his associates were a part of a larger band of psychoanalytically minded doctors spread thinly over the treatment network of Britain and France, sometimes coming together and sharing knowledge in a large specialist centre, at other times working in relative isolation at or near the front. The centre where almost all of the analytic medics went, sometimes briefly, was Maghull, run by R.G. Rows throughout the war.[52] The hospital's distinguished staff included at one time or another a long list of specialists: Henry Yellowlees, J.T. McCurdy, T.A. Ross, R.G. Gordon, C.S. Myers, W. McDougall, A.B. Howlitt, Rivers, L.F. Reeve, William Brown, C.G. Seligman and Ernest Mapother.[53] In the summer of 1915 Rivers worked there with, among others, T.H. Pear.[54] Other doctors at the hospital during that summer included the Freudian Ernest Jones, Bernard Hart and G.E. Smith. When Myers left France at the end of 1917 to work as inspector and coordinator of UK treatment on the Western Front, he chose to go to Maghull to work with Rows.

Maghull provided its doctors with a thought-provoking intellectual environment and the challenge of an urgent, difficult job, and although it proved hard to transfer the hospital's methods elsewhere, several doctors built on the theories they had developed at Maghull in articles or books that dealt with their work.[55] In *Instinct and the Unconscious* (1920), for example, Rivers states that his theories evolved continually as a result of his work at Maghull with Dr Rows, at Craiglockhart with Dr W.H. Bryce, and at an air force base working with pilots. His 1920 study was, he wrote, 'to put into a biological setting the system of psychotherapy which came to be generally adopted in Great Britain in the treatment of the psycho-neuroses of war'.[56] Perhaps the most widely read of the studies that came out of the war, though, was the populist and progressive *Shell Shock and its Lessons* (1917), by G. Elliot Smith and T.H. Pear.[57] In 'D' Block Netley too, at the 4th London General Hospital, the urgent needs of psychological casualties deeply impressed many of the doctors. 'D' Block, run by Dr C. Stanford Read, was a second centre for analytically inclined shell shock doctors, and a central hospital in Britain's treatment network. It included among its staff Hugh Crichton Miller and William McDougall.[58] In *An Outline of Abnormal Psychology* (1926) William McDougall wrote how 'it was my duty to select and care for, from among this immense and steady flowing stream [of mental casualties of war], all cases that were capable of being managed in open wards. In this way there came under my care a series of cases of functional disorders which, in respect of variety and severity, was probably unique.'[59]

However, 'D' Block could not rival Maghull. The 11,000 men who passed through 'D' Block stayed there no more than a few days. C. Stanford Read describes the hospital as a reception centre, where cases were cleared and then sent into the War Hospital network for supposedly substantive treatment.[60] Rivers was in a better position than McDougall at 'D' Block because Craiglockhart was an officers' treatment centre and not just a clearing hospital. However, while Craiglockhart dealt with 1,560 officers between October 1916 and February 1919, Maghull processed 3,638 men between 1914 and mid-1919.[61]

Rivers, McDougall and others used their wartime clinical experience to help treat psychological casualties, and then after the war to develop new theories. Rivers is representative of the revised psychoanalytic approach, which viewed repression, mental conflicts and the content of the unconscious as the genesis of war neuroses. The source of these mental disorders was, he said, not the emotional battlefield of childhood sexuality, but the physical battlefield of the Western Front. The repression of fear and the desire for self-preservation were sufficient explanation for 'almost every case'.[62] Conditions and practices in the hospitals did not always match the theory of analytic treatment, however. Hypnosis and dream analysis were used, but bringing to consciousness unresolved mental conflicts could be a long, complicated process. Even if the military authorities at Maghull tolerated such practices, they were not always useful under wartime conditions.

There were some signs of analytic methods gaining in authority and use towards the end of the war. A series of short courses in analytic techniques began at Maghull in late 1917, when for three months 50 RAMC officers received training in the latest 'abreactive' techniques.[63] The Ministry of Pensions also argued that new methods could be justified only if they reduced the cost of supporting war neurotic ex-servicemen.[64] Rivers' article on 'Freud's Theory of the Unconscious', published in the summer of 1917, may also have marked a significant change in the mood of the profession.[65] The influence of analytic therapy was limited for several reasons, though. The doctors trained at Maghull were few in number and all the evidence points to hostility or indifference towards the hospitals' methods within the treatment network as a whole.[66] The complex restructuring of theories that resulted from academic medical encounters with traumatic neurosis was a slow process that bore fruit in the postwar studies of doctors like McDougall and Rivers. During the war moreover, although new forms of 'talking cure' were indeed developed, they were used within few hospitals and only among a handful of specialists. At Maghull, and to a lesser extent at Netley and Craiglockhart, such methods were certainly practised, but beyond this there is little evidence that advanced desexualized analytic techniques made a contribution to the treatment of psychological casualties. The impact of Rivers' article on the medical community is beyond question. Yet this was only one instance of a wider proliferation of interest in the complaint signalled by an increasing number of articles by specialists in psychological medicine. With the establishment of the Ministry of Pensions in the latter part of 1916, there was renewed discussion on the social and military implications of shell shock. Rivers' article stimulated the interest of one section of the medical community, the publication of Adrian and Yealland's articles in the same year prompted interest in entirely different forms of treatment.[67]

The following two chapters examine the wider shell shock treatment network within Britain. This is not, though, an attempt to review the many and varied schools of medical thought related to shell shock, however; rather, it is an exploration of the formation of shell shock as a disease shaped by varied pressures. Medical debates in journals and the medical practice of specialists are a part of this disease formation, but so too are institutional regimes, non-specialist practice, patient perception, military requirements and political opinion. Thus if, as Eric Leed maintains, doctors sometimes deliberately played on soldiers' guilt and feelings of shame, this was only a reflection of how they saw their own condition. 'Sometimes I had an uncomfortable notion that none of us respected one another,' wrote Siegfried Sassoon, 'it was as if there were a tacit understanding that we were all failures, and this made me want to reassure myself that I wasn't the same as the others.'[68] Shell shock treatment was not just the play of external disciplinary forces against the individual then, but also the interplay of internal and external forces that produced, eventually, a compromise agreement. By the terms of this agreement the individual could tolerate his shame, while society could tolerate his shell shock.

6
Patients: The Other Ranks

The other ranks and the Army Medical Service

The disciplinary and analytic models of shell shock treatment at Queen Square and Maghull give some indication of how soldiers encountered military medicine and hospitals during the Great War. In this and the following chapter, by exploring both soldiers' and doctors' perspectives on treatment in practice, a more detailed picture emerges of how institutions and individuals were involved in making shell shock; of how the condition emerged in the interaction between doctor and patient, in the implementation of institutional rules and treatment techniques, in the antagonistic friction between doctor, patient and military authority. One instance of the way traumatic neurosis was marked by social interaction is in its definition and treatment according to rank. Within the Army, and therefore within the Army Medical Service, rank decisively influenced the opportunities and rights of the individual soldier. In combat rank shaped life-chances, in social encounter rank defined peer group reaction and self-perception, and in sickness too, rank fashioned attitude and expectation, which then guided the formation and presentation of symptoms as well as sanctioning the type and extent of treatment. The collective, popular memory of shell shock treatment is also influenced by rank. United by upbringing, education and social status, officers have been better able to describe their experiences of combat, and these accounts are more widely known in both the medical literature and memoirs of the Great War. Most shell shock casualties were not officers though, but members of the other ranks.

The physical conditions and administrative framework of treatment are also important to understand fully shell shock's social context, because they too influenced, however subtly, soldiers' self-perception.

Writing of the British Army Medical Services for the treatment of injured and disabled soldiers in 1917, Sir Alfred Keogh, Director, stressed that all soldiers were treated within a system that was stretched almost to breaking point. The facilities and treatments in the Military and Auxiliary Hospitals of England, Ireland and Scotland were limited, he observed, by the need to maintain the armies in the field:

> Questions of accommodation, equipment and staff soon become embarrassing. The necessity for not disturbing civil conditions and for maintaining, as far as may be in peacetime, the great philanthropic institutions and educational establishments, at once limits the possibilities of providing sufficient hospitals and appropriate staffs for a sufficiently long period for all cases of injured and disease...[1]

For both social and economic reasons therefore, hospitalization was minimized.

Nevertheless, a range of treatment was available in British hospitals. For instance, Dr E. Bramwell at the Royal Edinburgh Infirmary was one of many medics who in cases of 'neurasthenia' combined the traditional rest cure regime with non-punitive faradization, employed to persuade the patient that his condition was mental, not organic, and therefore curable.[2] Elsewhere, some doctors used intimidating behaviour and equipment to 'convince' patients that they were not beyond cure, but many of their colleagues rejected such procedures as unethical. Numerous physicians also used hydrotherapy, to relax; harmless drugs, to give the impression of medicine in action; perhaps most common of all, bromides to reduce restlessness or nervous irritability. Yet as the war progressed, and cases of hysterical conversion gave way to nervous exhaustion and chronic fatigue, new treatments were widely adopted, including suggestion and persuasion as practised, for instance, by J.A. Hadfield at the Ashurst Hospital, Oxford.[3] Authority and expectation were essential in these later treatments, which included both waking suggestion and hypnotic suggestion, but as happened very often in cases of all ranks, even where such techniques were judiciously applied, the incidence of postwar neurosis shows that they alleviated symptoms without eradicating the underlying cause. Unusually, Hadfield also recommended collective [group] hypnosis because it saved time, adding that respect for the patient, expressed through 'reassurance, elucidation, demonstration, re-education', was essential to effect a proper cure.[4] These conditions were, though, often entirely absent.

Hadfield's preferred treatment regime was more likely, but not guaranteed, where some form of analytic psychology was practised, such as at Maghull, or at the Central RAF Hospital in Hampstead. According to Nicholl and Young, at Maghull 'psycho-analysis' was concerned with the deeper mechanisms that lay behind neurotic symptoms.[5] This type of labour-intensive therapy emphasized that neurosis resulted from failure of the individual to adapt to changed circumstances and that symptoms were often an expression of this failure. The outward signs – a stammer, an immovably clenched fist – tended to dictate the use of psycho-analytic techniques where other methods had failed; functional palsies were one such category and anxiety neurosis a second. The inward signs – dreams, and especially battle dreams – provided material for analysis, but talking cures or hypnosis were also sometimes a part of treatment. W.H.R. Rivers' eloquent, moving account of the talking cure, used to treat officers with repressed memories of the war, is a good example of the psycho-analytic approach.[6] Nicholl and Young claim the method could cure quickly; in wartime it could seem impracticably drawn out, and as a technique it was confined mostly to Maghull and Craiglockhart. The privileged medics in these centres – by means of professional prestige and social position – were able and wanted to resist the pressures of military administrators.

The best-known shell shock hospitals, including Springfield and Queen Square (London), Maghull (near Liverpool) and Craiglockhart (near Edinburgh), were in the top tier of a tripartite treatment system in Britain.[7] These centres, with at least some staff and facilities, were above average, either because they were larger centres for the treatment of more serious cases or because of their exceptional standard of care. In such institutions the patient:staff ratio was favourable and the specialists in psychological medicine, the authors of medical texts, like Yealland and Rivers, more employable. These hospitals varied in size from the relatively large, like Craiglockhart, to the smaller voluntary recovery centres, usually reserved for officers, like the Lennel (Scotland), Osborne Palace (Isle of Wight) and Lord Knutsford's Special Hospital for Officers (Golders Green, London). Level two had 23 General War Hospitals' neurological sections, each with very limited specialist personnel and resources. Most important of these were the central reception hospitals in Britain that took cases directly from France, especially 'D' Block, Netley (London). At the lowest level, for quality of treatment and facilities, there were the 80 or so non-specialist wards throughout Britain in the General War Hospitals, such as the First Southern General (Birmingham).[8] While specialist institutions immediately recognized the damaging effects of mixing psychological casualties with other types of patients such as the physically injured and non-war mental cases, and psychiatric casualties too felt awkward in this situation, many men were nevertheless dispersed in small groups or individually across the country, receiving treatment on general wards.[9] The medics who worked at this level, if they were specialists at all, often had a background in medical insurance fraud, for instance Llewellyn J. Llewellyn at Bath, the co-author of *Malingering, or the Simulation of Disease* (1917).

Maghull: a mental hospital at war

Conditions at Maghull illustrate the common circumstances of many of the hospitals in all three tiers of the treatment system, and provide an insight into the everyday conditions and treatments at one of the more prestigious and successful shell shock hospitals in Britain. Situated at Maghull on the northern border of Liverpool, some 4 miles north of Ormskirk, the Moss Side Hospital began its life as a medical centre in the late 1870s.[10] At the outbreak of the war, the Board of Control (the late Lunacy Commission) had just taken over the premises. The hospital was quickly converted to the treatment of soldiers, renamed the military Red Cross Hospital, and accepted 20 patients, soldiers among the initial wave of psychological casualties returning from France at the start of the war, in late 1914. By January 1915 there were 83 patients. Maghull quickly established itself as one of the foremost centres for the treatment of war-related mental disorder, remaining open until the summer of 1919 to treat cases and train doctors for service on Ministry of Pensions assessment boards.[11] In addition to treating 1 in 50 of all wartime cases, after the Armistice it took another 500 men.[12] T.H. Pear, one of Maghull's leading physicians, noted in his memoir that the reasons for establishing the hospital were pragmatic. 'Firing squad therapy', as Pear describes it, had little success among the volunteer army in France. It was feared that some psychiatric casualties who were court-martialled or sentenced to death, whether officers or members of the other ranks, would be well connected, which might lead to embarrassing questions in the House of Commons. Worst of all, if MPs began asking questions in public, information might become available on the ignorance of psycho-pathology among alienists or members of the Board of Control. Such knowledge, Pear believed, would have damaged the medical profession, undermined military authority among the civilian population and horrified the parents of a boy who had broken down in the trenches after a fortnight's incessant bombing.[13] Maghull, then, was the Army's reluctant answer to accusations of negligence.

Every type of case was treated at Maghull. Many were the products of the emotional and psychological effects of front line service, others had head injuries, and some were epileptics or mental defectives. In the 16-month period between November 1914 and March 1916, 748 patients were admitted to the hospital. Of these 385 were discharged as fit for service, and 219 were retained, 107 were classed as chronic lunatics, 18 were transferred for physical conditions, 18 were classified as epileptics, seven deserted and four died.[14] Between April 1916 and July 1919 the proportion of serious cases increased, and new methods of treatment that drew on Freud and Janet were developed.[15] In 1917, the decision was taken to begin admission of soldiers with limb paralyses such as hemiplegia and monoplegia. By conventional military standards Maghull failed miserably, as less than 50 per cent of patients were returned to active service. By civilian standards, however, Maghull was in many ways a model shell shock hospital where soldiers received specialist care from leading experts. It was also probably the most humane of the British centres for the other ranks with its emphasis on re-education, persuasion and careful attention to the individual. The idea of the 'therapeutic acts of kindness' towards the lower ranks, for example, is almost unimaginable anywhere else in the military medical treatment system.[16]

In common with other military hospitals, Maghull was constantly beset with practical troubles. Inconvenient renovation and rebuilding work, for instance, continued through much of the war; wards were filled to capacity, though the number of places had expanded from 300 to 500 by the Armistice; conditions were always overcrowded and uncomfortable. Adequate food supply was a constant problem too. By the end of 1915, contractors were able to obtain only poor quality fish, which was barely edible. In the following year rationing reduced outside supplies even further, so that each week patients were allowed two sausages, a pickle as a treat and brawn when this was not available. In 1917, staff and patients alike were reduced to a diet mainly of bread, turnips and rice, while all the available land was used to grow vegetables, which were sold to raise funds.

Material limitations were matched by administrative restrictions. As admissions grew in number and severity and resources declined, the everyday running of the wards became increasingly difficult: concussed and traumatized patients disliked sharing rooms with mental defectives who had never been fit for military service; nursing orderly staff detested working with patients whose 'character and habits', they said, made it impossible to maintain surgical or medical standards.[17] Unlike most military hospitals, the medical regime at Maghull made running the hospital more difficult because the military authorities were suspicious of its activities. Furthermore, like Bryce at Craiglockhart, Colonel Rows as the head of Maghull had to find ways to circumvent military restrictions. On one occasion when some senior soldiers came to Maghull believing all the patients were 'scrimshankers', 'malingerers' or 'hysterics', Pear reports, Rows devised his own way of convincing the 'top brass' that the hospital made an active contribution to the war effort: 'After giving them a good meal, he saw that they got the full treatment: a leisurely tour of mental defectives, schizophrenics and maniacs (I daresay he showed them the padded cell, hardly ever used). And at the end, a very fierce higher-up breathed a prayer "I hope to God my boy doesn't go this way!"'[18] If confusion, shortage and patient discontent were in the top tier of the system, the limitations in less specialized institutions must surely have been all the greater. A detailed examination of medical records from a variety of shell shock treatment centres reveals the policy and practice of treatment in the lower tiers of the treatment system.

Non-specialist treatment

The following survey of non-specialist shell shock treatment is based on personal medical notes collected during and immediately after the Great War by the Medical Research Council and the British Museum, and used as the basis of the statistical studies of injuries and treatments for British troops published after the war, especially *The History of the Great War*, Volume 7. *Medical Services, Casualties and Medical Statistics*, published in 1931.[19] A selection of these has been preserved at the Public Record Office in the form of standard medical case sheets, chosen to illustrate the diversity of disease, injuries and treatments received in the Great War. The collection has two boxes labelled 'Shell Shock, Neurosis, Neurasthenia' and 'Mental Illness', respectively, containing a total of 746 complete and semi-complete cases illustrating psychological cases from the war.[20] Close inspection shows that these labels do not correspond to the box contents as both boxes contain cases of all types. Notes representing the upper tier of the shell shock treatment system are present, notably from Maghull, Netley and Springfield, but the vast majority of the case notes were written in 78 lower-tier hospitals. The selection process used by the Public Record Officer to gather this sample remains uncertain, but it is heavily skewed towards the early part of the war and mainly refers to cases that originated in 1915.

For the purposes of this investigation, the sample is divided into three groups ('slight', 'borderline' and 'acute') in accordance with the diagnostic terminology and variety of symptoms described in each set of case notes. From each group, a smaller set of examples was selected searching for individual case notes that were complete or complete enough to give a clear picture of the case, and to establish the variety of symptoms and treatments described in the notes. In practice, this selection process excluded all the medical notes that had inadequate information on case history, symptoms and treatment. The imprecise contents of the larger groups of sketchy medical notes requires cautious interpretation. To give one instance, sometimes brief medical notes may indicate nothing more than a busy, efficient doctor, but may show something of a medic's or an institution's working style. After eliminating those sets of medical case notes that lacked detailed information, then, there were 57 sets that provided fuller information. The size and content of this smaller group of medical notes also calls for some caution in drawing conclusions. These notes cannot claim to be a representative sample, but they can give an insight into the background history and symptoms of some of the psychological casualties of the early part of the war, into the terminology and treatments used by medics in less specialized and non-specialist hospitals, and into some varieties of shell-shocked soldiers' hospital experience.

'Slight' cases

This set of medical notes included details of 29 soldiers with relatively mild symptoms: physical exhaustion, chronic fatigue, giddiness, irritability, various aches and pains, sometimes diagnosed as organic. Length of hospital stay was not a criterion for inclusion in this group, as some serious cases were discharged within a few days. Twelve were aged under 30, twelve between 31 and 40, and five aged between 41 and 50. Sixteen of the soldiers were regulars and the remaining thirteen were volunteers. This reflects the equal distribution of regular and volunteer cases within the sample as a whole where the information is recorded. Within the 57 cases, 29 were regulars, 25 were volunteers and the remaining three unrecorded.

The first striking feature of these medical notes is that often patients were treated haphazardly, with little coordination between medics or hospitals. This was the fate of Corporal S.L., of the 1st South Staffs, a

regular with 13 years' service and aged 31 at the time of his hospitalization on 3 July 1915, who had been in France since October 1914.[21] S.L.'s
condition had been noted as early as December 1914 and he had been
treated with varied remedies in several hospitals, but was not returned to
an unspecified Birmingham medical centre (probably Rubery or Hollymore) until 3 July 1915. On arrival he looked well, despite rheumatism
and a finger wound, and on 19 July he was recommended for a convalescent home. By 12 September, however, he had not recovered, and his
back and right leg were being treated with massage and strong faradism.
On 16 September the medical notes state: 'Pt. seems in a stationary
condition – I think he would be better if occupied...'[22] S.L.'s medical
notes, unusually, recommend faradism, and as a result three days later
his condition was much improved. Despite this success, the administration of this case shows the treatment network was chaotic and consequently its physicians sometimes confused. The medical notes give no
obvious diagnosis, for instance: symptoms, it appears, were puzzling;
treatment was hesitant; and no obvious or decisive therapeutic decisions
are recorded.

Some soldiers at specialist centres were treated with greater care and
coordination. Private H.R. of the 3rd Rifle Brigade, aged 32 and with 14
years' service, was admitted to the Maghull on 4 January 1915 and his
medical notes show careful attention to detail. The form of medical
examination and diagnosis resembles that recorded at Queen Square,
as in the following entry:

> Patient is quiet and well mannered and says he has served 3 years
> with the colours and 11 in the reserve. States that he was in good
> health when he went to France. Was under shell fire in the trenches
> at the battle of Aisne. Was sent back to Rouen with blistered feet and
> when recovered was attached as escort to an ammunition train.
> While on one journey he is said to have threatened his comrades
> with a bayonet (at least he says this is what he was charged with
> before the officers). Stoutly denies that he did it, although he admits
> that he can recall nothing of his doings after he got on the train that
> day, until the following morning...[23]

The remainder of this record is an extended checklist of all the possible
signs of mental disorder, all of which were absent, but the War Diaries of
the 3rd Rifle Brigade show how the doctor accounted for the case. Its
probable origin lay in the tension of waiting in the trenches noted by
other soldiers, in the futile fighting on H.R.'s stretch of the line, and in

the 36 consecutive days spent in the trenches during October and November 1914.[24] The later fate of H.R. goes unrecorded, but as in some other Maghull cases, he was discharged uncured because his condition could not be further improved. Even in a well-known specialist centre then, early in the war, expertise was still developing and the success of treatments was far from certain.

'Shell shock' cases sometimes turned out to be partly or wholly epileptics or mental defectives, and again this caused confusion as doctors had varied interpretations of the same case. Private E.M. of the 2nd Battalion of the Royal Sussex Regiment was 35 with only three months' service when he was admitted to Maghull in mid-February 1915. His medics could not locate the source of his condition, though 'fits' in childhood were noted. The relevant Battalion War Diary entries suggest Private E.M. was in heavy fighting; for instance, on 29 January 1915: 'A determined attack was made upon the KEEP and trenches each side of it this morning... The enemy at once massed behind the Brickstacks for a second attempt but were so accurately shelled by our guns that apparently the attempt was abandoned. The enemy continued to shell until 12.30 pm.'[25] The medical notes are confused and disjointed. Initial reports and statements in France as well as on the returning hospital ship in February focused on the diagnosed insanity of the patient's brother and father; at Maghull, where E.M. was admitted on 15 January 1915 (and discharged on 31 March), he reported his childhood fits, which returned on 27 January 1915. The doctor wrote: 'He appears to have been markedly impressed and somewhat upset by the death of some friends in his own company. Self-control and judgement at present appear to be normal. From the mental examination of the patient one has come to the conclusion that he shows marked instability without definite evidence of any mental aberration.'[26] Unusually, these notes reveal the contrasting responses of professional Army medics and specialists to the same case. Without generalizing too far from one example, there is clearly a difference in approach and emphasis: non-specialists searched for signs of insanity and tell-tale childhood incidents; doctors at Maghull looked into the soldier's experiences in France. It remains unclear whether these doctors were examining different aspects of the same case, or whether they had entirely unrelated views on the symptoms.

'Borderline' cases

This set of medical notes included 12 soldiers unlikely to be treated in a specialist centre, but given specialist care within the General War

Hospital network. Their symptoms included short- as well as long-term memory loss, loss of speech and hearing, disorientation and confusion, together with the signs of mental disorder commonly associated with 'slight' cases. Ten were under the age of 31, and the other two aged 52 and 53 respectively. Seven were volunteers and five were regulars; volunteers had between six months' and two years' service, regulars between six and 33 years' service. Length of hospital stay varied between four days and nine months.

Neurasthenia was often the diagnosis for soldiers suffering some form of war-related mental disorder, though within this category there were wide variations in the symptoms that doctors would describe as neurasthenic. Private C.D. of the 1st Rifle Brigade, aged 27 with eight years' service, was given this diagnosis when admitted to the 3rd Northern General Hospital on 28 January 1915. From October to mid-December the 1st Battalion of the Rifle Brigade was engaged in skirmishes, continual sniper fire and bombardments, with some more serious offensive operations by the German troops. Private C.D. was at Ploegsteert Wood on 19 December 1914 and the War Diary indicates the chaos of the failed British offensive on that day.[27] C.D. was also present during the preparations and build-up to the offensive, and in the following month's operations.[28] The effects of trench life and bombardment put the private in hospital for over two months, where his treatment was one commonly prescribed in the General Hospitals: mild sedation and plenty of rest. 'He left trenches 17-1-15,' state the medical notes:

> He attributes cause to tension caused by waiting, and to shell fire. He was in trenches over two months. He felt restless, weak and irritable, and lost a great deal of hair from his head. On examination knee jerks are very brisk. He has marked tremor of fingers, now gone. Pulse normal. Considerable improvement under small doses of bromide.[29]

On 6 April he was given furlough. On the basis of these and similar case notes 'Neurasthenia' seems to have been a default diagnosis, given in the absence of any other obvious or revealing symptoms, and it is one of many instances where medics found the diagnosis and treatment of psychiatric casualties troublesome.

Two cases illustrate some of the difficulties doctors faced. Private F.G., a volunteer aged 31 who had served only three months in the field when admitted to the York Military Hospital on 12 July 1915 with pains in the stomach, was clearly an awkward patient. His doctor noted that 'Three months ago he was laid up with gastritis and states that three years ago he vomited blood. He is a bootmaker by trade and has worked a great deal with things pressed against his stomach.' The notes are sparse here, with the next entry on 19 July stating only that 'He complains of pain a good deal in the abdomen'. By 26 July, however, a clearer medical opinion seems to have formed when the patient was described as 'highly neurotic'. On 3 August he had become a disciplinary problem too: 'Patient this morning refused to have electrical treatment and has been put on fluid which is strictly measured.'[30] It is difficult not to conclude that the medics reprimanded F.G. for his refusal to accept electrical treatment by changing his diet, and that this was a routine response when patients were uncooperative. Patients who refused to accept treatment were one group who troubled doctors; patients who were unable to communicate effectively were another. Private J.C., aged 53 with 36 years' service in Britain, was at the front for only one week before being hospitalized and diagnosed with 'melancholia' on 24 March 1915. 'He is a very difficult person to get anything like a coherent account of his illness, complaint or history – he won't answer questions, but simply bursts out crying and sobbing when spoken to. Says he is not ill and nothing is the matter with him. Memory bad: will not say why he is crying.' Depression, weeping fits, deficiency of intellect and dementia were all noted in his condition: '. . . is in a kind of dream during the day. He does not look you in the face when spoken to, but turns his head deliberately to the left or right away from you.' The following day his condition appeared much the same: 'Above observations confirmed. Pt. very difficult to get anything out of. No signs of organic disease. Past and family histories – nil given.'[31] Whether this was dementia, mental deficiency or traumatic neurosis remains unclear. The doctors at Maghull found it hard to diagnose Private J.C., as would doctors in any other part of the treatment network.

'Acute' cases

This group included 16 sets of case notes describing varied mental disorders, among them symptoms included recurrent dreams and nightmares, hallucinations and insomnia, as well as paralysis, hysterical gait, tics or stereotypical movements, fits, mental regression, somnambulism and severe depression. Thirteen were under 30, and three aged between 31 and 40. Eight were regulars, five were volunteers and in three cases details were not recorded. Volunteers had active service records between seven weeks and 18 months, regulars had served between four and twelve years. Despite the severity of the symptoms, length of treatment varied dramatically between nine days and 14 months.

Psychological casualties were from time to time also diagnosed with associated physical injuries, as in the case of Private F.F., a 27-year-old regular with five years' service in the 2nd Lancs. Fusiliers when he was involved in a gas attack on 2 May 1915. Admitted to the Northumberland War Hospital he was diagnosed as suffering 'neurasthenia and effects of poison gas' and appears to have been treated for the second but not the first of these complaints. 'On admission the patient was in a highly neurotic condition, all physical signs of bronchitis which he had been treated for at Havre had disappeared – no abnormal physical signs except a shaky condition of hands. Treatments – ordinary diet.' By 13 July this 'treatment' seemed to be working, but by late August the patient's condition had deteriorated again. '29 Aug. Patients' condition is very unsatisfactory; he lose [*sic*] weight steadily, 3lbs during last 5 weeks. 22-9-15. Has made a slow recovery.'[32] The staff at the Northumberland seem to have been unable to give further assistance or treatment, so F.F. was discharged, still 'very neurotic and shaky', and placed in a convalescent home for rest and recuperation. His chances of full recovery were slim.

In other cases too, medics seem to have been powerless. As with Rifleman W.B. of the 7th Rifle Brigade, aged 20, who spent 14 months in hospital following his return from France in May 1915, apparently curing himself, as the attention of doctors during the year or so he spent in the Dublin V.A.D. Auxiliary Hospital had little effect. According to his medical notes entry for August 1916 W.B. was

> Sent home from Flanders May 1915, suffering from Shock (Shell) with symptoms of loss of memory, almost total, complete loss of speech, partial loss of sight and hearing. Tremor, sweating, sleeplessness, probable hallucinations of sight. Slow improvement till Oct 1915, when suddenly he received speech and for 72 hours he remembered about his time in Flanders, forgetting meanwhile all he knew of the Dublin University V.A.D. Hospital ... where he was being cared for.[33]

In February 1916, W.B. was transferred, but despite constant treatment he seemed little improved.

Among the cases in this group W.B. was one of the most difficult patients to treat because the origins of his condition were almost entirely obscure. For another soldier, Sergeant D., the difficulties of effectively coping with the front line were all too clear, and were made worse by worries over a complicated domestic crisis, as a note attached to the medical file, written by a comrade, reports:

When I returned to billets last evening about 8.20 pm he was calling for someone by the name of Jack, thinking he was the man sleeping next to him that he was calling for I told him he was out, but found he meant his brother-in-law and he thought I was him and asked me to put something cold on his forehead as he was dying and his head was bursting. I did so and he seemed more settled for the time being. Then he told me that they (but mentioned no names) were saying that he starved his wife to death and that could not be true, as he had always given her plenty of money and that she had £850 of her own. He started crying and caught hold of me so that I could not leave him, crying all the time about his wife and child...[34]

What we can reasonably infer from this testimony is the expression of Sergeant D.'s unconscious, but devastating feelings of guilt about deserting his family. Although this is a particularly poignant and un-usually well-documented instance of the mixed effects of war environ-ment and domestic anxiety, it would nevertheless seem plausible that such feelings about one's family were common. They were another of the mental burdens soldiers had to carry and medics had to unpack. After a short stay at a non-specialist centre in Britain, the sergeant was returned to the front line.

Several conclusions spring from this selective discussion of 57 case notes. Doctors were occasionally reluctant to treat cases that they saw as entirely psychological, although they showed every concern for those who had been buried or suffered trauma as a result of gas attacks. There are many cases attributed to pre-war origin, which reflects Army recruit-ment policy as well as the empirical training and predilection of the British medical profession. The overwhelming impression is that doctors were barely able to cope with the various mental cases that they encoun-tered. Often they responded intelligently and with some concern for the fate of the men placed in their care. However, attention and treatment were just as often minimal, and collective military interests were invari-ably more important than the fate of the individual. These medical notes relate mainly to 1915, and at this stage of the war many of the complaints were less severe than the fatigue and anxiety cases of 1916 and 1917, but this cannot fully account for the brief periods (often weeks or even days) that patients were hospitalized. Military doctors returned men to duty when they could do no more for them, and the limits of medical knowledge together with wartime conditions meant that often they could give little or no help. Treatment was also patchy and uncoordinated so that, for instance, on some occasions soldiers with similar complaints were kept in hospital for a matter of days, on others for months on end.

Considering the whole sample of 746 case notes, the majority of soldiers were not treated in specialist centres, but mainly on the specialist wards of the large General War Hospitals. Alternatively they were treated in the non-specialist wards of small medical centres which were spread throughout Britain. Of the 81 hospitals represented among the 746 sets of case notes, 62 had five or fewer psychological casualties, indicating that soldiers were just as likely to be spread throughout the country in small numbers as placed in concentrated communities for specialist treatment. Distinctive policies also emerged in separate hospitals. For example at the 1st Southern General Hospital at Stafford Road, Handsworth (Birmingham), the length of hospital stay was noticeably shorter than for other centres; also cases were usually sent direct to duty rather than to furlough. At Lincoln the RAMC major used bromide as the sole form of treatment. At the Warncliffe War Hospital, Sheffield, cases without exception were recommended for ten days' furlough or, if well enough, sent directly to duty. At Maghull, Dr Rows made it a policy always to recommend patients for one month's furlough. At the King George Hospital, Dublin soldiers were given either light duty or furlough, and in a high proportion of cases soldiers were invalided directly out of military service. After hospital, patients could be sent to an active service assignment, a convalescent home, a specialist shell shock ward or a longer-stay medical centre. Furlough was given when the soldier was fit or almost fit, and could last between a few days and one month. Light duty could be temporary or permanent; in the former case it was a prelude to a return to active duty. Hospital discharge cases include all those where there is no other indication of the patient's future; service discharge cases were considered useless for any further Army activities.

The experience of shell shock cure for the other ranks varied according to when the patient was hospitalized, in what type of hospital he was treated and how his medic was qualified. All medical centres within the three-tier system had difficulties with providing the necessary specialist care; lack of facilities or training or basic resources worsened the situation. Although these common themes hold true within the PRO sample and gain some corroboration from the Queen Square notes, they must be treated cautiously. Medical case sheets are always a partial source of evidence, while this collection was also preselected by an unknown method and heavily skewed to the early part of the war. Nevertheless, they reveal the sequence of logical steps medics used to create for themselves and their colleagues a convincing chain of cause and effect that could account for the symptoms of shell shock. More discretely, they demonstrate how patients might form and maintain their understanding of shell shock in opposition to both military and medical opinion.

Writing shell shock

As this last statement implies, though it is not overtly registered in their medical notes, shell-shocked patients from the non-officer ranks were often quick to give opinions on their condition, their time spent in hospital wards, and their treatments, and often they were critical. In passing comment they displayed the same satirical humour recorded by front line combatants in trench magazines like *The Wipers Times.* Rather than attacking the generals though, hospital journal writers retrained their sights on Army doctors, nurses and fellow patients, giving lower-ranking soldiers a forum for both light-hearted banter and serious comment. Gossip and argument, reflection on front line experience, satirical fantasies, jokes and poems were the most common forms. Army authorities in Britain, because they seemed to know little of the fighting in France, and as a result were seen as not sufficiently expert to help wounded soldiers, were one of the regular targets. However, since the sale of hospital journals served two purposes – to raise hospital funds and to keep relatives informed – if any soldier were likely to offend seriously either hospital or relatives, he would probably never get into print. For practical reasons then, criticism had strict limits. In spite of this, and since articles and contributors were always presumably in short supply, editors seem to have mostly printed what patients handed them, and a variety of opinion and critical comment found a small but knowledgeable audience.

Soldiers in British hospitals continued to joke about shell shock, just as they had done in the trenches. For lower-ranking soldiers this was the pretext for Chaplinesque slapstick cartoons: a bell rings, a martial casualty jumps out of bed and runs off into the night; a soldier in a bed sheet wakes the ward shell shock case, frightening him half to death. These sketches had titles like '"The Entertainment Bureau." Night Effects arranged for the Amusement of a patient suffering from Nervous Breakdown' or 'Shell-Shock – Who'd be a Night Nurse?'. Shell shock was an easy target for hospital humour, but there was a nervous edge to this laughter. Moreover, when shell shock stopped being funny in itself, it could still act as a sounding board for other issues.[35] One regular contributor to the *Springfield War Hospital Gazette* here comments on a rumour that 'the Crown Prince is now in retirement after suffering from Shell Shock'.

> Shell Shock! What! The Crown Prince!
> 'Ang it man, yer mocking,
> I ain't never met the bloke
> An' doant want to bust yer joke,
> That there kind's PAST shocking.[36]

What this (and similar pieces) suggest is that the main cause for regret among lower-ranking casualties was not shame or stigma, but guilt at being unable to continue active service and participation in the defeat of enemy forces. This made petty bureaucracy and medical ignorance all the more frustrating. Incomprehensible War Office forms or pointless administrative procedures, the delays and unfair treatment of Medical Boards, all of these were accordingly a part of the soldiers' gripe.[37]

'K.W.S.' wrote a long, critical article, for instance, on the Army medical view of shell shock, for the May 1917 issue of the *Springfield War Hospital Gazette*. The author frames his thoughts as a dream, thereby granting himself a licence to fantasize, and in it – presumably as in real life – he is a shell-shocked soldier interviewed by a specialist medic in a British hospital. 'In Shell Shock Land' takes its cue from *Alice in Wonderland* by inventing a world of nonsense and absurdity. Obscure jokes and a jerky style mar the article, but beneath these faults is a strong sense of injustice, a belief that the military doctor had no real interest in treating his patient. K.W.S. describes first the doctor's office, filled with the privileges of his position, tins of 'Gold Flake 50' tobacco and 'Ideal Milk'. He continues:

> Books, books, books. Of all shapes and sizes, evidently the belongings of the Great One (who, by the way, was closely viewing me by looking into a mirror behind him). One huge red book was entitled '*Charlie Chaplinism and Shock. Connections*'. Others respectively, '*Moons and Loos*' (whatever might that mean), '*Will and Can*', and there were many with long names. I was completely forgetting the Presence near me whilst wondering whether '*Will and Can*' was related to '*Jack and Jill*' . . .[38]

Book learning, medical theory and common-sense exhortations to exercise willpower are, then, the familiar, inadequate currency of the medical profession whose vanity is boosted by ignorance of combat and military non-combat decorations, which 'seemed to say I'm small but I mean a lot'. Following these descriptive passages and reported speech, K.W.S. gives the doctor a long, condescending speech that may be read as a reflection of how such medics made real patients feel:

'So so,' he drawled out, 'I'm going to cure *you*, but really there's nothing wrong with you – really you know... Pull yourself together! In *your* case (this most deliberately) it's simply imagination – pure imagination... Now, directly you can forget about the "Front", etc. you will get the cheque. We don't want to keep you. Think of it – a new suit and... Well, you must put it all aside. Your brain has been playing tricks you see...'[39]

Interestingly, there were no objections to this belittling portrait of an Army doctor, or to his dismissal of those injured in the war. Soldier-patients, including shell-shocked soldiers, no doubt took some pleasure in showing themselves as long-suffering Tommies, yet in this case all the evidence justifies their complaints. If patients criticized doctors for their treatment of the other ranks in General Hospitals like Craigleith, Springfield and the 3rd London, it was for good reason.

Perhaps the most forthright instance of this type of writing comes from a 'Gunner McPhail', who placed 'Just Shell Shock' in the *Springfield War Hospital Gazette* in September 1916. In the context of the magazine, which also contained homilies by chaplains and morale-boosting exhortations from officers, the author pithily summarizes the situation of psychological casualties.

Of course you've heard of shell shock,
But I don't suppose you think,
What a wreck it leaves a chap
After being in the pink...
Or suppose you loose your speech sir,
Perhaps you're deaf and dumb as well,
But you don't get no gold stripe to show,
Although you've fought and fell.[40]

Here there is a special pleading on behalf of lower-ranking shell-shocked soldiers that contests the apparent medical ignorance of the public, the low prestige of the condition compared to the heroic status as the physically wounded, and the bureaucratic obstruction of the Army and Ministry of Pensions. McPhail illustrates too the psychological casualty's sense that war-related mental disorder was misunderstood and mistreated, the power of the condition to command the attention and support of its audience, and the self-indulgence of soldiers who played for sympathy in asking members of 'the public' to imagine themselves as the psychological casualties of war. The boundaries and conventions of such an address are described too. There is no hint of disillusion or critical comment in these lines, only a dramatized appeal for greater understanding. Despite his critical comments then, McPhail takes it for granted that his peers would be sympathetic to his pleas, understanding of his views and willing to take his opinions seriously.

Like the majority of participants in the Great War, shell-shocked soldiers made a sharp distinction between those who had seen action and the non-combatants who ran the Army bureaucracy and often treated cases in Britain. Thus, doctors who viewed shell shock with derision were themselves considered ignorant or worse. While some soldiers were so seriously ill that they could not take any part in hospital life or pass any comment on it, many psychological casualties were very aware of their situation and surroundings and the way they were treated. On the basis of their testimony these patients did not passively receive treatment, but rather engaged in a contest to establish their right to be ill and to be properly treated: they therefore on occasions refused to accept certain forms of therapy and blocked the daily running of hospitals. There is no evidence of a generalized disillusionment with the war, or indeed of alienation from the community of the other ranks. At the Casualty Clearing Station and in the General Hospital ward soldiers maintained a pro-war and anti-German attitude, though they were sometimes repelled by the actuality of warfare and the way they were treated by the Army. Although shell-shocked soldiers were aware that their disease was questionable to many doctors, derided among the other ranks and suspected as a form of malingering, they knew too that many of their peers in the Army considered the psychological damage of war genuinely disabling. Evidence of this support can be found in both pieces written for hospital journals and the comments of front line soldiers.

Having established the types of treatment, the structure of the hospital network and the view of the majority of patients towards their own condition, it becomes possible to examine the smaller group of shell shock cases whose experience is, misleadingly, often considered typical: the officers.

7
Patients: The Officer Ranks

The officers and the Army Medical Services

Officers and other ranks experienced the same awful trench conditions and bombardments, felt the same fear of mutilation or dismemberment, and suffered the same distress or numbness as comrades and friends were injured and killed. However, the Army Medical Services believed that having led by example, worked closely with the soldiers under their command and been pressured to take trenches and win attacks, shell-shocked officers in the field and in British treatment centres should receive certain traditional privileges. Although traumatic neurosis was a threat to discipline and a violation of the established code of military behaviour in the ranks, hysterical officers were in various ways accommodated. They were shielded more than exposed to the taint of dishonour, cowardice and insanity; treated more than disciplined; viewed with sympathy more than suspicion. Consequently, diagnostic expectation and examination was unlike that of the other ranks, as was the view of their condition according to both regimental medical officers in the field and doctors in Britain. Moreover, officers' education, social position and military function gave them a different vocabulary in which to express their feelings and thoughts. Despite the patronage of the Army though, war-traumatized officers still had an ambiguous public image. In the eyes of the press, in politics and in Army treatment, it was officers who suffered shell shock and who were heroes willing to sacrifice their sanity for the war effort, yet at the same time they, like the other ranks, were subject to an habitual, if muted, prejudice against mental disorders and to gratuitous curiosity. Privately, officers felt far from heroic. From the moment of diagnosis or early doubts in the field about 'nerves', they were disturbed and shamed by their condition.

The facilities for treating shell-shocked officers sometimes overlapped with those for the other ranks (at Maghull, for example, separate quarters were provided for 40 officers in 1917) but in the main, the officer treatment network was separate and often privately funded. Consequently, less evidence on its working has survived, the sources that do remain are even more fragmented than for the other ranks, and so any conclusions are necessarily tentative.[1] What can be described with some certainty is the usual pattern of treatment and recovery for officers who returned to Britain. One of Lord Knutsford's centres – or some very similar small hospital – was usually the main location for treatment, while later in the war larger, more professional and state-funded treatment facilities were made available at Craiglockhart as well as Maghull. After treatment, officers routinely went for a further stay at a convalescent centre such as the Lennel or Osborne Palace on the Isle of Wight. The following account explores the experience of officer rank patients using medical case notes, officers' letters and administrative records from the Craiglockhart Special Hospital for Officers and the Lennel Auxiliary Convalescent Home.[2]

Craiglockhart: an officers' hospital at war

Craiglockhart was the largest and most important of the centres for the treatment of shell-shocked officers during the war. The events of 1917 draw most attention, but the broader workings of the hospital are also of interest because this Special Hospital was important in many officers' experience of traumatic neurosis, and because it provides a contrast against which to measure the ministrations of other centres such as Maghull. The immediate origins of the decision to open a large shell shock hospital exclusively for the treatment of officers in October 1916 date back to the summer offensive on the Somme. The official figures show that shell shock reached its height during the second half of 1916. The highest six-monthly figure to June 1916 was 3,951; but this rises sharply to 16,138 cases between June and December.[3]

In 1916, Craiglockhart was able to do little more than begin operations as a working medical centre, but from its inception the hospital had opponents, including the local director of Army Medical Services, who favoured a strict military management regime, and stated that he 'never had and never would recognize the existence of such a thing as shell shock'.[4] Events came to a head three months after the hospital opened when the first commandant was dismissed for mistreating patients, the hospital abandoned its first, strictly military model of treatment, appointed a new commandant, and established a modified medical regime.[5] Eventually, in 1917, a stable, properly medical treatment system was established. At the tail end of the previous year, the hospital had acquired W.H.R. Rivers as its best-known senior physician. By the summer of 1917, under the leadership of Commandant Bryce, relations between staff and patients were much improved and the therapeutic regime more eclectic.[6]

The Craiglockhart Admission and Discharge Registers give a vivid insight into the running of the hospital and the lives of the men who were treated there.[7] The Registers cover a period of two years and three months, during which time 1,560 patients were treated. Both the partial Lennel records and the full Craiglockhart Registers indicate that officers below the rank of captain formed by far the largest group of admissions, around three-quarters of all cases.[8] The records provide five classes of information that help explain how the hospital was run and how individuals experienced traumatic neurosis: monthly admission rates, age of officers on admission during each month, length of Army service, length of active service (not synonymous with active combat duty) and length of treatment at the hospital.

Monthly admission rates, based on the daily admission figures, give an indication of the overall number of cases. Apart from the exceptionally high number of 111 for September 1917 and the low of 41 for June 1918, admissions remained between 50 and 100 throughout the time the hospital was open. Sharp rises and dips in admissions reflect the number of vacancies left after each medical board review, while a large influx of cases or a relatively quiet month had a lesser impact on the number of beds available. The age profile of officers admitted each month shows that in the earlier phase of the hospital's life the majority were in their late teens and early twenties, while at the end of the war most men were in their late twenties and early thirties. With the exception of four of the 23 months, shell-shocked officers admitted to Craiglockhart were aged between 25 and 30, and this can be taken as a reflection of age structure in the British Army as a whole. If Army training, discipline and combat experience were decisive features in the onset of the condition, based on the assumption that longer-serving regulars would be least vulnerable to war neurosis, length of Army service ought to remain lower for shell shock casualties than for other groups. In the event, the length of service varies dramatically between two and five years, including many men who enlisted well before August 1914. There is no clear evidence in the Craiglockhart records, therefore, to link length of Army service and shell shock rates. However, length of active service was important as one of several elements, especially prolonged exposure in an active front line sector, which coalesced to produce the symptoms of neurotic trauma. Toward the end of the war, smaller groups of officers with long service stayed for brief periods of treatment. The efficacy of drawn-out treatment remains highly debatable though, because convention rather than clinical judgement fixed the length of hospital stay and gives no real guide to the severity of the treatment or the outcome of the condition. Like every medical centre, Craiglockhart tried to contain the tension between the need to treat cases effectively and the pressure to take as many new cases as possible. Patients lost out in this equation because, wherever the number of cases increased, the figure for length of treatment went down. Thus when fighting was at its most intense in France and more disturbed cases needed treatment, the time available to each patient was reduced.

The doctors at Craiglockhart took a variety of approaches, but just as important as their individual preferences was the therapeutic atmosphere within the whole medical centre. The second director, Commandant Bryce, for example, saw 're-education' as a social and occupational activity. Men recovered their muscular skills and coordination with gymnastics exercises; musical and theatrical entertainment encouraged them to be active and sociable, and it was excellent for memory training.[9] As the admission and discharge registers show, though there was continual pressure on the hospital to take new cases, there was nothing like a standard treatment period. Patients re-established their confidence at their own pace through work, games and hobbies. Other centres used the same approach. 'In a hospital for men work will naturally begin with light duties in ward and kitchen. The next step will depend on local possibilities – for example, at Maghull the men next passed to the farm where work could be graded in any way desired.'[10] Where the other ranks did farm work or carpentry, officers at Lennel and Craiglockhart were allowed therapeutic hobbies, and it is at this point that the officer's hospital experience begins to resemble an extended retreat at a country house. Photography, for example, was thought to be an ideal activity. It was relatively simple and untaxing, and at the same time it engaged the officer's interest and occupied his time in a variety of tasks from choosing subjects, to taking snapshots, developing and printing pictures. Bryce gives another instance: 'At Craiglockhart we had a model-yacht club. Each member had to make his own boat from a block of wood, cut the sails, rig her, and then sail her. Many other occupations can be devised on similar lines.'[11] While for the other ranks 'outdoor activities' meant growing and harvesting vegetables for the hospital table, for the officers it meant football or golf, and on rainy days billiards.

The doctor's therapeutic approach was not easy to reconcile with the Army's requirement for the swift return of officers to the front line, and this conflict of interest led to another crisis in the autumn of 1917. At that time, a little more than a year after the dismissal of the first commandant, a high-ranking RAMC officer visited the hospital. According to the 'in house' account, Commandant Bryce

> decided that authority should see the hospital as it was. It would serve no purpose to apply all the rigour of army discipline in such a hospital. Result: the great man could not see his face in the frying pans, Sam Browne belts were conspicuous by their absence. There may even have been officers going about in slippers. As for the staff, they busied themselves with their patients, instead of waiting about. Dr Bryce was notified by the authorities that he should give over, and all the staff gave in their resignations as a demonstration of their loyalty.[12]

As at Maghull, where a group of specialized medics with significant social standing were gathered, it became possible to moderate the demands of the Army. Moreover, that the Army authorities should reluctantly accede to purely medical considerations indicates that the successful treatment of officers was a high priority. Craiglockhart could thus maintain relatively low admission rates, about 150 soldiers at any one time, but because officers sometimes stayed for extended periods, the hospital treated 714 cases in 1917 and 708 in 1918. When there was greater pressure to take more soldiers, they spent shorter periods at Craiglockhart, and longer periods at less medically oriented convalescent homes, such as Palace Green or the Lennel.

Officers' treatment

Examining the wide range of evidence on the experience of the other ranks, it is quickly apparent that medical treatment varied drastically in British hospitals. The evidence on the treatment of officers is much more limited and relates especially to the work done at Craiglockhart and the Lennel convalescent hospital. Only a handful of medical notes are extant from the former hospital, but further confirmation on the nature of cases and the workings of medics is available from other sources. The Craiglockhart register lists cases individually according to date of admission. By tracing the regiment of each individual and the history of the case before admission, it is possible to identify the war environment from which the soldier-patients emerged in France, and the general circumstances under which some of the patients were first diagnosed.[13]

The second major source on the treatment of officers comes in the form of 111 sets of medical case notes preserved from the Lennel Convalescent Home at the National Archives of Scotland.[14] The Lennel regime, designed as a final stage between recovery and return to duty, was organized much like that of a reception or treatment centre. In the Lennel notes there appears to have been effective communication between hospitals on both original causes and earlier treatments: thus medics could give a detailed case history from the reports of previous records and add a description of the patient's medical condition at the time of admission. Sometimes case sheets were not even copied out, but sent on from Palace Green or Craiglockhart and added to the Lennel records. The notes, therefore, give a broad outline of each case, but evidence on treatment was infrequent and lacking in detail. Depending on which doctor took the case, the notes placed special emphasis on family background, on the origin of symptoms in the field or on the extent and type of symptoms. There was no standardized form of note taking, although there were observable common practices and conventions of language and medical perception within the regime. A set of medical case notes at the Lennel was not the working tool (added to daily, constantly reinterpreted and revised) found in a large General War Hospital. Rather, patients were often near to full recovery or to discharge, and in this context their medical reports became a highly ritualized part of the bureaucracy of the medical centre.

In addition to the set of medical case notes, the Lennel archive contains an incomplete Admission and Discharge Register dating from 1916–17, although the notes cover 1915–18. Of the 59 in the register, 11 were lieutenants and 34 were 2nd lieutenants, making 45 junior officers in all. A further nine held the rank of captain, while the remaining held the rank of major; 27 of the soldiers were volunteers, 11 were regulars and in 21 instances there was no record.[15]

As the cases at the convalescent home were at roughly the same stage of recovery, and the form of the Lennel notes so distinctive, the 111 sets of case notes in this sample can best be examined under three headings to illustrate the variations in the officers' experience of shell shock and show changing medical practice and perception at Lennel between 1915 and 1918. The three categories are: sickness attribution, symptom variation, and medical perception.

Sickness attribution

The psychological impact of the war environment and participation in combat on officers was largely defined, in the eyes of Lennel medics, by rank-related activities. Throughout, the Lennel and Craiglockhart records stress the psychological cost of leadership for more senior officers, and of trench ecology and prolonged active duty, especially in the winter of 1916–17 (though not specific incidents or family traits, as in the case of the other ranks) for more junior officers. Equally, they place little emphasis on hereditary explanations. Some case notes demonstrate officers' strong adherence to traditional military principles and codes of conduct, which in turn influenced doctor's diagnosis and patient's self-image. The case of Major E.P. illustrates these points especially well. Aged 34, he had been in France since the beginning of the war and gained a commission after only three months: 'In all the fighting for two and a half years, with only 28 days' leave. Was buried three times; much shaken; has been getting very tired, sleeping badly, losing power of concentration, etc. Dreams so vivid that he was in doubt as to what orders were real and what only dream products. Sent home 13/4/17. To Craiglockhart ... 10/5/17 Condition much improved ... Is simply overstrain of campaign.'[16] The major was obviously determined to remain on active service. He did so until he was unable to function effectively and this extended exposure to the front as well as the responsibilities of rank led to what medics saw as an excessive mental and physical burden.

That subalterns were noticeably more vulnerable than other officers because they acted as leaders in the field and were both responsible to higher-ranking officers as well as working closely with men under their own immediate command is borne out by several cases. Lieutenant E.S., for example, aged 20 with seven months' experience in the field during the winter of 1916–17, was admitted to the Lennel in mid-August 1917, having previously stayed four months at Craiglockhart. He had joined the ranks in September 1914 and underwent the usual training in full health. E.S. received his commission in the Royal Marines in June 1915 and in September 1916 went to France. Particular emphasis is laid in these notes on the remorseless combat environment at the front, and the patient's acute symptoms. As in a number of other instances at the Lennel, the recommendation to send Lieutenant E.S. down the line came from a fellow officer rather than the regimental medical officer.

On 10th Feb. was badly shaken when he was under heavy barrage fire for a whole night with little shelter. Was sent down the line to No. 3 British General Hos. and was there for a fortnight...On the 15th April again went into the line before Arras. On 18th he was in a heavy bombardment without cover and felt very shaky. He was sent down by another officer for being unfit for any duty.[17]

On his admission to the Lennel in August 1917 the examining doctor noted severe headaches brought on by exertion and resulting in restlessness, excessive reaction to sudden noises, tremors, inability to concentrate and a partial loss of memory.

The least likely explanation for a case like this at the Lennel, in its medics' eyes, was heredity. Within the Lennel sample, doctors identified one case out of 111 with a possible pre-war origin. In the other rank case notes, the possibility of an hereditary explanation was routinely discussed, while pre-war and temperamental origins were often suggested. The use of an hereditary diagnosis for cases in the other ranks was, in other words, a matter of conventional medical interpretation. As the war continued, promotions eroded the social profile of the officer class. This raises the question of whether temperamental explanations were absent in officers' medical notes because no pre-war causes were present in officer cases; or rather, because doctors treating officers preferred not to raise the issue for reasons of social etiquette. The source material prevents any definitive answer to this question; however, it does seem reasonable to argue in this instance that medical perception at the Lennel was altered by social convention. The single reported instance of a pre-war condition is also noticeably different from those described in the other ranks: 'After being wounded, while in hospital, he developed a hesitation in his speech. He was in hospital at La Treport three and a half weeks and then evacuated to Endsleigh Palace Hospital from whence he was transferred to this Hospital.' J.N.'s symptoms are described in neutral, if not partial language. 'Defective Nervous stability with *over-reaction* to quick noises. (no history of loss of confidence under shell fire). *Physical Fatigue.* Insomnia. No Dreams. Headaches in morning. *Emotionalism.* Loss of *Appetite.* Failure of Nutrition. Slight hesitation of speech. Fatigue – Early.'[18] In this instance, mention of the pre-war condition serves to underline the patient's credibility.

Thus on the evidence of the Lennel case notes there were wide variations in the doctors' ascription of sickness among officers. Symptoms were not solely the consequence of large-scale bombardment or long-term active warfare then, but of particular strains. Formal factors such as

Army medical policy shaped symptoms, informal practices and attitudes within the Army and the officer ranks helped define both the attributes and the attribution of hysterical sickness.

Symptom variation

Surprisingly, given the intense and prolonged combat in which they were involved, the Lennel notes show that compared to the other ranks, symptoms were often only vaguely defined in officer cases. A close examination of case notes gives clues as to why this was so. Admitted to Craiglockhart on 6 June 1917, Captain S.F. had joined the Army at the beginning of the war and served in France for the previous 15 months. The War Diary records that throughout May the battalion had been involved in intense combat, with soldiers removed from the field as psychological casualties on two notable occasions:

> 20 [OR wounded] + 2 shell shock + 1 officer shell shock 23rd–24th . . . The conditions in the trenches were very bad. A very large number of unburied dead were scattered in and near the trenches, while a large number were lightly buried in the parapet or in the trenches them- selves . . . movement during the day was reduced to a minimum and most of the work was carried on during the night. During the day the enemy artillery and snipers were very active, and accurate.[19]

The captain was diagnosed as suffering from shell shock, but under these circumstances it is unclear exactly what this might mean: concussion and traumatic neurosis are both possibilities under these circumstances. This vagueness was perhaps a matter of mutual convenience for both patient and doctor, as it allowed a veil to be drawn over the more disturbing implications of mental breakdown. In the event it allowed the captain to spend a total of 123 days in the hospital following the events of May 1917.

In the rare instances at the Lennel where a soldier had symptoms that were both chronic and acute, they were hardly ever 'functional' condi- tions such as paralysis or tics. The case notes of Major P.I., aged 27, best represent the conditions which seriously disturbed patients tended to suffer at the Lennel. The major was a regular who had spent the whole of the war in France. He had been involved in extended periods of active service, including 2nd Ypres in 1915, and although nervous symptoms had been noted at that time, no action was taken until his performance in the field began to deteriorate toward the end of 1916. After a month in Britain on leave and training P.I. returned to France in January 1917 and remained in the trenches until mid-April when he was caught up in the Battle of Arras and at the front for another two and a half months without relief. His medical notes, written on admission to the Lennel in July 1917, describe the effects of this long stretch on active service:

> Two and a half months without the Batty being relieved. During the last 5 weeks of this time, he says he was no use at all. He heard of his brother's death on April 14/17 and this considerably upset him. Toward the end of the Arras Battle, he felt very languid, and had no keenness, no energy, had lost his power and found it very difficult to concentrate and was also very irritable. He applied for one month's leave and was given ten days leave on June 19/17.[20]

Apart from severe physical exhaustion, the medical notes describe loss of concentration and lapses of memory, depression and emotional instability, as well as 'loss of nervous stability under fire'. According to his case notes, Major P.I. was also notably fearful in his anticipation of coming stress. This can be interpreted simply as an indication that he hoped to avoid the nervous tension of the front line, but also implies that he was afraid of breaking down in front of fellow officers or members of the other ranks. In either case, late diagnosis and extended periods of recovery stemmed in part from this refusal of officers to admit their nervous, emotional or other psychological difficulties, as they found it too difficult to identify in themselves the cumulative and gradual effects of nervous disorder. Similarly, Major W.P.'s records show a close relationship between doctor and patient, and a strong connection made between the environment of war and the attitude of the officer:

> On June 4th in Ypres Salient he was subjected to heavy shelling and while rescuing two of his telephonists was himself buried in a dugout. He lost consciousness and when he came round found himself in hospital. His head ached terribly but as he felt fit otherwise he refused to remain any longer in the Dressing Station and went back to his unit. He had a good sleep and remained with his battery, until he went out to rest about the middle of July.[21]

Medical history was given great weight in the identification and appraisal of symptoms by shell shock doctors: particularly the extent and severity of exposure to active warfare, and the stage of illness at which the patient was diagnosed, treated and returned to service. At the same time, in their treatment of officer patients, medics adjusted infor-

mation according to social position and rank. It therefore remains difficult to distinguish actual and assumed differences in the types of psychological disorder found in officers.

Medical perception

While the sources and symptoms of war-related trauma can be measured
with relative objectivity, medical perception is obliquely recorded in
officers' case notes. Descriptions of aetiology and symptoms, as well as
the general approach of medics to officer patients, differ from those of
the other ranks in several ways. First, doctors had more time and specialist knowledge to give to each individual case; second, communication between hospitals, especially in continuous case notes, was much
more efficient; and third, treatment was better by virtue of rank and
status. Even case notes differed according to seniority of rank. In non-
officer patients the quality of case sheets ranged from a scribbled record
on name and rank or scanty notes of symptoms and date of discharge, to
extensive battlefield histories and character or eyewitness reports. While
the most professional and informative notes were from Queen Square,
the Lennel notes were of a high standard too, and the use of common
phrases and methods for the description of symptoms indicates close
cooperation between the medics in this relatively small centre. Finally,
written at leisure and with thought, these dossiers reveal the permuta-
tions of treatment for officers in France and Britain and the delicate
negotiations between medic and officer-patient as the two worked out a
mutually agreeable definition of shell shock.

The absence of severe and long-term 'functional' symptoms in officer
psychological casualty cases was striking in the Lennel notes, just as
such symptoms were a notable part of other rank medical histories.
There is only one instance of naming and describing serious hysterical
symptoms at the convalescent hospital. Lieutenant P.H. was aged 23
when admitted to the Lennel in September 1917 after seven weeks in
the field, between September and October 1916:

> On Oct 21, during an infantry attack his company suffered very
> severe losses, he carried on until the evening – following this, there
> occurred a period of clouding of consciousness (Hysterical) and he
> recalls no further experiences until he returned to consciousness in
> No. 1 Red Cross Hospital, Etaples: he was then transferred to the
> Hospital in Birmingham (3 weeks) and then here after 3 months at
> Latchmere. Boarded ... Sept 13/17. 2 months in the country. 10.12.17.
> Lt ... has just heard that a brother is 'missing' in France: this has

somewhat upset him + thrown him back. Weight on arrival 8 stn 4lbs . . . Restless movements of face and hands . . . [22]

On admission, the lieutenant was suffering from severe amnesia. His only memories were from his schooldays in England and fighting incidents around Thiepval before he lost consciousness. His symptoms included severe paraplegia 'with weakness of trunk', stammering speech, insomnia and vivid dreams of fighting, as well as 'emotionality'. Though this case indicates that functional symptoms were present irrespective of rank, they were unusual among the Lennel notes. On this evidence, then, physicians lay emphasis on the nervous disorders; 'functional' disorders were justified forms of exhaustion produced by responsibility and toil at the front.

A number of cases at the Lennel would have been dealt with differently were they not officers. For example, only in officer notes were there references to 'clouding of consciousness'. This vague description was associated with memory loss, confusion and disorientation, sometimes with depression and nightmares; this and similar blanket phrases disguised associations with lunacy, hysteria or mental deficiency. The tendency towards elision is seen in the medical records of Lieutenant H.C., a 19-year-old volunteer who spent nine months at Gallipoli and a further six months at the Front in France. The lieutenant arrived in Britain in mid-September 1916 after a head injury sustained falling from a car, and only later was mental disorder noted:

He was sent in a motor for a rest 23-9-16 when he fell out of the car . . . and when picked up asked what had happened . . . complained of cold and was dazed, could not answer questions and replied very slowly . . . He was overworked but did not realise this for some time. Cloudy of Consciousness. Disorientation on time and place towards persons. Depression – at times agitated.[23]

Another notable feature of the Lennel notes is, on the one hand, the way medics discharged or considered discharging officers prematurely, apparently at their own request, back to duty, and then saw them later suffer chronic or acute relapse; and on the other hand, the periods of many months officers spent recovering. Lieutenant W.T., who had volunteered in August 1914 and was in France until wounded in May 1915, wanted to return to duty most of all for reasons of professional ambition. He joined the Royal Flying Corps in July 1916 and went to France as a pilot between December 1916 and April 1917 when he suffered concussion during a landing accident, and returned to Britain. Once there, he received treatment at a London hospital for officers between April and July 1917. His symptoms were various: severe and continual headaches, depression, weight loss and vertigo. The officer then went on to the Lennel for an extended stay in September, and during that month suffered two blackouts. 'Nov. 5th. His attacks of giddiness are much less frequent and can master them almost immediately. He has been working hard and regularly... He is anxious... as he has promise of an assistant adjutancy, if the board will recommend him for duty. In my opinion he is quite fit for light duty...' This apparent recovery preceded a relapse. '22.XI. Bad head – 23 much worse – went round to see D. at his original hospt. 53 Cadogan Sq – arrived all but unconscious... Roused occasionally managed to give his address about 2–3 hours after admission. Gradually improved – fully conscious.'[24] After four months of treatment and rest, the cure ought to have worked, both the officer and the Medical Board doctors agreed on it, but Lieutenant W.T. went back prematurely and was still very ill. On this evidence, then, medics could be swayed by the traditional military values and virtues that officers often held dear and, as a consequence, their patients were sometimes misdiagnosed or mistreated.

Considering the Lennel records as a whole, the absence of diagnosed functional symptoms and references to pre-war and hereditary or organic explanations are perhaps the most significant characteristics of the notes. 'Neurasthenia' was a diagnostic label used for patients of all ranks, although the term could well have been applied more accurately in its pre-war sense to officer rank cases. Medics believed officers' war-related mental conditions were distinct from those among other ranks. The nature of the actual differences remains debatable because doctors treating officers used different criteria for the assessment of health and illness. Thus early diagnosis, the use of blanket phrases in the descriptions of symptoms, and extended periods of treatment and convalescence compared to the other ranks might partly account for the apparently distinctive nature of officer rank symptoms. However, they cannot fully explain the characteristic ascription of disorders to officers and non-officers. The attribution of symptoms appears to have been substantially genuine, but this is not quite the same as a social distribution *per se*. In civilian society before the war a similar division had existed and was undoubtedly present in medical wartime observation. However, unless military rank and its attendant differences in military function can be categorized as class, the observation has only a limited significance. There would have to be many exceptions, such as soldiers promoted from the ranks or those of more humble social origins because of the extraordinary shortages caused by the war. The more convincing argument remains that doctors reported a distribution of symptoms that related to the distribution of military functions between ranks.

Writing shell shock

The development of the two systems of treatment resulted partly from social considerations, and partly from the progressive revision of the officer shell shock treatment network, which also illustrates the more general shift away from the voluntary service work of the first 18 months of the war towards a state collectivist approach in the latter part. In late 1914 and into 1915 – the early, heady days, when enthusiasm and patriotism for the just cause was at its peak – a number of appeals went out for various war-related causes, including 'men suffering from a very severe mental and nervous shock, due to exposure, excessive strain, and tension'.[25] This description comes from Lord Knutsford's appeal notice in *The Times* in early November 1914 at a moment when there was little practical distinction between the treatment of officers and the other ranks. As soon as the War Office became involved however, early in 1915, they reserved the first hospital to result from the appeal – and subsequently another four – for officers. In January 1915, Knutsford described the centre to *The Times* audience that had willingly contributed to its establishment:

> The house is quiet, 'detached,' overlooking Kensington Palace, with a small garden of its own. The War Office has asked us to restrict the hospital to Officers, as they are providing a similar hospital for the men . . . the hospital is to be called 'The Special Hospital for Officers,' as we are anxious not unnecessarily to emphasise to its inmates that they are suffering from shock, or nervous breakdown . . . [26]

Following the public success of this first Special Hospital, in cooperation with the War Office and the Red Cross, Lord Knutsford developed a network of officer treatment homes. These were not the only centres of their kind, but they were important examples of the sort of regime in use to treat commissioned soldiers. The preservation and promotion of willpower and a positive frame of mind was often the basis of treatment in such hospitals. As a report on Palace Green emphasized in May 1915, the medical centre was 'home like, large and comfortable, and above all cheerful'.[27] Faradization for functional symptoms, massage and restricted diets were all available at Palace Green. However, five months after the opening, rest, quiet, light distractions such as gardening were the most highly prized components of the cure. Psychological therapies, by contrast, were suspect.[28] Over the following two years, Knutsford was closely involved in the fund-raising campaign and the setting up of more hospitals, each of the five homes treating between 50 and 100 patients a year.[29]

That the public profile of shell-shocked officers was very different from the soldiers' view of themselves is evident from the archives of the Lennel and Craiglockhart, and from *The Hydra. The Magazine of the Craiglockhart War Hospital*, which ran from April 1917 to June 1918. In its early editions, *The Hydra* was a straightforward 'in-house' hospital magazine with information on clubs and activities to orient new arrivals and keep resident patients up to date. Like all hospital journals, there is plenty of gossip, veiled allusion to clandestine romance and the progress of the war. Doctors and Army bureaucracy were not the subject of critical comments, perhaps because as officers the contributors were themselves engaged in the Army hierarchy – giving orders as often as they received them. The Craiglockhart patients' magazine describes the Special Hospital and its patients both obliquely and openly in the hospital reports, in articles and stories, and in that most popular of all forms, the poem. On occasions patients could be quite candid in the way they reported their condition and the responses it evoked.

The author of one poem, *To be Stared At*, for example, which appeared in the June 1918 edition of *The Hydra*, shows an especially keen sensitivity to the social stigma of shell shock and a related sense of guilt and lost self-respect. Setting the scene for what will follow the author first locates himself not among his fellow soldiers, but in the main thoroughfare of Edinburgh:

> Now if I walk in Princess Street,
> Or smile at friends I chance to meet
> Or, perhaps a joke with laughter greet,
> I'm stared at.

In the following two stanzas the author describes the blue armband that identifies him as a Craiglockhart inmate, and which inescapably describes who he is, and how going out for a drink of 'Adam's wine' in the town centre is itself an unnerving experience because it drew the attention of the local community. In stanza 4 he confesses unease at being associated with Craiglockhart and the shame that through the hospital has attached itself to him:

> Craiglockhart mem'ries will be sad,
> Your name will never make us glad;
> The self-respect we ever had
> We've lost – all people think us mad.

The final stanza stresses this mildly self-dramatizing theme in the lines 'If "Someone" knew who wrote this verse,/My simple life would be much worse'. There is more than a touch of self-pity in these lines too, which may account for the reference to the disapproval of ' "Someone" ' (a relative perhaps, or a doctor), but like Gunner McPhail in his poem *Just Shell Shock*, this soldier is also concerned with what he sees as the unfair prejudice against his condition: 'And on my tomb would be this curse,/"To be stared at." '[30] Neither writer's audience would have disagreed with the sentiment they expressed. In this case, however, the author is evidently more worried for his reputation, confessing a sense of failure, of having let others down – comrades, friends or family – but also himself. To make matters worse, by this account the local Edinburgh community too was wary of Craiglockhart patients. From the poem one senses that, whatever the public willingness to provide funds for 'special hospitals', shell shock sufferers were the object of a malign curiosity that was part of a wider, customary prejudice against mental disorder.

In the summer of 1917, Wilfred Owen became the editor of *The Hydra*. Unlike the author of 'To be Stared At', Owen was able to inject some humour into the magazine. In the 15 September issue, for instance, the editor published 'Extract from ye Chronicles of Wilfred de Salope, Knight'.

> The Castle that is called Craiglockhart doth stand perilous near unto two rival holds, the House of the Poor and eke the Aysle of the Loony Ones, so that many seekers of the latter abode have oft been beguiled unto this castle unwittingly; some of whom, as soon as they perceived their error, departed hastily away, and some of whom yet remain.[31]

Other contributors were more on their guard, not just against their doctors or superiors, but against the British society they encountered on returning to Britain. The editorial of 1 September 1917 is one instance of this resentment:

> In this excellent concentration Camp we are fast recovering from the Shock of coming to England. For some of us were not a little

wounded by the apparent indifference of the public and the press, not indeed to our precious selves, but to the unmitigated durances of the fit fellow in the line. We were a little too piqued at the piquancy of smart women, and as for the dainty newspaper jokes concerning the men in the mud, we could not see them at all...[32]

The author's sourness towards press and society opinion in Britain is obvious. He was not alone. Other officers in 'this excellent concentration Camp' felt the same estrangement from those who ostensibly supported the war, but who could never comprehend combat or those who had experienced it. These officers felt set apart even further, from themselves and others, as casualties of war who were unable physically to demonstrate their injuries. Guilty relief at being out of danger temporarily nevertheless relieved their fear and shame.

The many letters of thanks written from officers at the Lennel to its leading light, Lady Clementine Waring, reveal the more intimate patterning of officers' shell shock experience according to social background and expectation.[33] The type of letter which an ex-convalescent officer would write to his erstwhile aristocratic 'hostess' is unlikely to reveal criticism of treatment, any more than a gentleman would complain about the service to the mistress of a house where he had spent a country weekend. What the letters do show is the type of social background many officers came from, and their keenness to abide by the conventions of polite society. Many of the letters discuss minor events and mutual acquaintances in a similar fashion, and they commonly followed the same ritualized, polite format:

I hope you will accept my apology for not writing previously... I am now back with my unit at the above place, and it is not a very charming place. Let me take this opportunity of thanking you very much indeed for all your kindness to me during my stay at Lennel, and thanks to your treatment I am feeling better now than I have ever felt... Could you also sell me any game?[34]

Considering these letters as well as some of the highly articulate and expressive articles in *The Hydra*, and the evidence on educational background from Lennel case notes, the experience of some shell-shocked officers was cocooned compared to that of the other ranks.

Staying at the Lennel was apparently a much happier experience for officers than Craiglockhart. 'Unpleasant' incidents sometimes punctuated even this genteel form of recovery however, as the following letter hints:

> ... I do sincerely hope that you will forgive me if I was the cause of any unpleasant situation or inconvenience and also should my martial temperament uncontrolled – have in any way have asserted itself to exceed the limits of propriety... I am *SOBER* once more – so doctor says – but still confined to bed with oft recurring beastly head-aches. I am being removed to Craiglockhart Hospital E'burgh tomorrow where I am to be boarded shortly and probably invalided out. 'Sic transit gloria spenceris'!... [35]

With the exception of a few such incidents, it appears that life at the Lennel largely remained within 'the limits of propriety'. Nevertheless, these soldiers were constrained by the requirements of behaviour among peers, while still suffering the traumatic effects of the war. At both the Lennel and Craiglockhart officers were happy to enjoy some sense of comradeship as fellow sufferers, but they were also bound to behave 'well' in the presence of so many others who had 'given in' to their nerves.

Soldiers of all ranks were subject to the same military, financial and administrative pressures as patients in wartime hospitals. Officers, however, received most public attention during the Great War, and they have continued to do so since the Armistice. As veterans, psychiatric casualties had equally diverse fates that were related more to their social and economic circumstances than their former rank. Part III examines the experience of war neurotic ex-servicemen from all ranks with particular attention to the larger non-officer group, and the unique reputation that shell shock acquired within British society through the twentieth century.

Part III
Legacies

8
Demobilization: On Returning Home

The demobilization of 'shell shock'

In medical language and Army policy 'shell shock' was always reluctantly tolerated. In 1917–18 the term was more fully replaced by the official therapeutic vocabulary of 'neurasthenia', 'neurosis' and 'psychosis'. This shift in terminology signified an attempt to downgrade wartime traumatic neurosis and its post-combat consequences; to enforce the demobilization of shell shock. Without the defence of active service and their role on the promotion of wartime medicine's efficiency, the notion of genuinely neurotic ex-servicemen came under increasing suspicion as veterans re-appeared in civilian life in the role of unproductive labourers claiming 'compensation neurosis' from the state. This sceptical outlook was built into the Ministry of Pensions' bureaucratic procedures for all war-damaged workers seeking compensation as claims were calculated according to a flexible percentage disability rating system. Thus the new techniques of mechanized labouring, substantially advanced by the war, were reinforced in the new peace, as the government administered its bureaucratic proced-ures to convert formerly unproductive ex-soldiers into newly industrious employees. The War Office attempted to put 'shell shock' behind it too, drawing a line under the episode with the findings of the War Officer Committee of Enquiry published in 1922. However, in employment ex-change and pensions' medical examinations, veterans, the general public and politicians continued their fascination with the mental disabilities thrown up by the recent conflict. Also, after the peace settlement the issue of war neurotic ex-servicemen provided a symbolic rallying call for those concerned with the proper treatment, cure and readjustment of all veterans.

The number and cost of war neurotic ex-servicemen increased in the years immediately after the Armistice. In 1920 there were 15 medical centres that could accommodate such men, and according to the official figures 63,296 (5.4 per cent of all pension holders) were in receipt of related pensions.[1] The *4th Ministry of Pensions Report* explained that the increase in claims was due not least to 'the patient's liability to relapse during a period of economic or domestic stress', and that 'the most successful and permanent results have been obtained by means of occupational treatment during a stay in hospital, especially if it is followed by the immediate return to employment on discharge'.[2] Poor economic conditions often made this impossible; by 1921 the number of treatment centres doubled from 15 to 29, 1,356 new hospital places were introduced, and 48 new specialist out-patient clinics were opened. In total there were 63,296 neurological cases under Ministry of Pension treatment.[3] By 1925 this number had risen to 74,289, and by 1929 the number had fractionally increased, by 578, to 74,867. The situation had stabilized and many of the curable cases had been processed, but the treatment of neurasthenia was still an important part of the work of the Ministry of Pensions as unemployment and adverse personal circumstances continued to make effective treatment and cure difficult.[4] Observing this trend, the Ministry placed new emphasis on long-term rehabilitation from the mid-1920s.[5] Between 1925 and 1930 the total number of in-patients receiving treatment fell from 11,795 to 1,729; likewise, the number of institutions treating 'neurasthenic, neurological [and] psycho-therapeutic' cases fell from 15 to seven.[6] However, the total figure for ex-combatants receiving pensions continued to increase. In March 1939, according to one medic writing after the Second World War, 120,000 war neurotic ex-servicemen were claiming war-related pensions, amounting to 15 per cent of all claims.[7]

This and the following chapter examine the formation and development of policy towards war neurotic ex-servicemen, the social and psychological problems they faced and the forces that shaped their post-combat life.[8] What follows is a study of a part of the wider community of veterans: of those soldiers who suffered traumatic neurosis during the war and did not recover by its end, and of those who developed such conditions in their post-combat lives. In practice it is almost impossible to separate the two.[9]

The War Office Report into Shell Shock

The reintegration of war neurotic ex-servicemen back into workplace and home was a significant political issue during the postwar years not least because newspapers and politicians were still absorbed with a cause which proved they were on the side of justice and the common man. The alleged wrongful wartime courts-martial and execution of shell-shocked soldiers was an especially troubling, controversial topic.[10] Thus speaking in favour of setting up the Enquiry on 28 April 1920 Viscount Haldane stressed the need to avoid 'injustice in criminal proceedings' but equally to protect the public from exposure to 'this terrible malady'.[11] Several of the speakers in this debate were also willing to admit what had often been denied during the war, that, as Lord Southborough put it, 'dreadful things may have happened to unfortunate men who had in fact become irresponsible for their actions'.[12] These were not the only issues under discussion. The misdiagnosis of 'war heroes' and their unjust incarceration in asylums, as well as the failures of the Ministry of Pensions treatment system, were also of continuing concern, and it was to counter the newspaper and political disquiet on all of these matters that the War Office Committee of Enquiry was established in 1920. The combat-related mental disorders of servicemen and ex-servicemen were most widely discussed in the immediate post-war years then, and especially in the two years between the establishment of the Enquiry in 1920 and its final report in 1922.

In the House of Commons in May 1921, for instance, John Davison MP questioned the efficiency of the Ministry of Pensions treatment network when he asked '[W]hether in any of the mental hospitals under his [the Minister of Pensions] control methods of treatment advised by medical officers have been withheld from patients, and, if so, on what grounds; whether schemes of employment suitable for patients are in operation in these hospitals; and, if not, whether such schemes will be instituted.'[13] The debate went far beyond the Parliamentary chamber though, to the extent that the popular myths and wayward opinions of self-appointed experts had to be publicly rebuffed. Thus also in 1921 William Robinson, Senior Assistant Medical Officer at the West Riding Asylum, Wakefield, felt compelled to write an article arguing that whatever public, politicians and journalists might believe, most ex-servicemen left in asylums were in truth potentially or actually psychopathic, and had to be locked up for their own safety and for the protection of the public.[14] These were the worst cases of 'feeble-minded lads, moral imbeciles and epileptics' allowed into the Army because of poor medical screening. Although not recruited to fight at the front, some nevertheless arrived there in the latter part of the war when the manpower shortage was at its most acute; later they were wrongly diagnosed as shell shock cases.[15]

After the war, these mistakes were compounded by the widespread public belief that all service patients in asylums could be cured by 'psycho-analysis', and when doctors stated this was not true, said the aggrieved Robinson, they were accused of pre-judging cases and of inflexible attitudes towards new treatments.[16] 'The forms of mental disorder from which the majority of service patients suffer seem to be only imperfectly understood by those from whom the greatest amount of outcry emanates,' the author concluded.[17] War neurotic ex-servicemen were of concern as well to the state since they were a potential burden on national finances, and since their effective treatment could save funds. Here again there was great public interest and misinformation, as Viscount Knutsford complained in a House of Lords debate in April 1919, 'everybody seemed to think that they could cure neurasthenia'.[18] This conclusion remained true against a background of growing public interest in Freudian ideas in the early 1920s, but psychoanalytic techniques remained controversial. In an exchange in the House of Commons on 21 July one MP, Mr Mills, suspiciously quizzed the Minister of Pensions, asking 'if he has any results that will justify the continuation of the treatment of ex-servicemen by the process known as psycho-analysis; whether he has received any protest from the men compelled to undergo this torture; how many people are under this treatment and what are the qualifications deemed to be necessary by the Ministry for those who are experimenting with shattered lives'.[19]

All such arguments, it was hoped, would be publicly laid to rest in the second half of 1922 by the publication in June of the *War Office Report*. In the event it resolved little, but did serve its purpose by officially shelving the subject. The range of opinion expressed during the Committee hearings showed that little had changed since the war. Some Committee witnesses continued to push the line that 'shell shock' was a convenient evasion of duty, if not disguised malingering.[20] The Committee acknowledged this point of view by recommending psycho-neurosis or mental breakdown should not be a ground for returning a soldier to Britain and should not be seen to provide 'an honourable avenue of escape from the battlefield'.[21] The Committee was equally conservative in its views on aetiology and treatment. High incidence rates, they concluded, could be prevented only by high morale and a 'no nonsense' approach to neurotic servicemen in the field: fear, synonymous with cowardice, desertion and dishonour could not be conclusively linked to shell shock, but nor could the connection be disproved. Treatment remained an awkward topic because it still seemed to legitimize fear; if there had to be treatment, the Committee recommended, it should consist of rest and recuperation.[22] '[G]ood results will be obtained in the majority by the simplest forms of psycho-therapy, i.e., explanation, persuasion and suggestion, aided by such physical methods as baths, electricity and massage. Rest of mind and body is essential in all cases.'[23] Despite the best efforts of some witnesses and committee members, the wartime military consensus prevailed; the final recommendations of the Committee addressed military interests, above all the most uncontroversial forms of prevention and cure. The thinking of the War Office Report did not pass unchallenged however, as the editor of *The Lancet*, among others, balked at the notion that the only difference between 'shell shock' and 'cowardice' was that those affected by the latter showed less willpower in the face of active combat.[24]

There was a final renewed wave of public discussion in the wake of the War Office Committee Report. One correspondent wrote to the *New Statesman* to denounce the government for its inefficiency and the veterans for their weak-willed capitulation to mental disorder: 'There are many hundreds of these nerve-racked ex-servicemen, scattered up and down the country. Some are in hospitals and other institutions of the Ministry of Pensions – some are "border-line" cases. Some are living at home – a burden to their friends and the local ratepayers. All are a burden to the state, since they are non-productive.' Not only were these men a burden to the state, their failure to re-enter the labour market amounted to a loss of valuable skills, knowledge and experience. 'They know they could never keep a job, and their knowledge is a constant deterrent to recovery. The hustling foreman at the factory would terrorise them, the impatient customer would flurry them, the keeping of an appointment would put them "all in a flutter", till they became again the dithering nervous wrecks that fill the neurological hospitals and clinics.'[25] Pensions policies and the question of responsibility to soldiers and disabled ex-servicemen had long troubled the state as well as members of the armed forces, and war neurotic ex-servicemen with such perplexing, inexact symptoms were especially troublesome to process. To understand why, it is necessary to know something of the development of the military pensions system before and during the Great War.

Ministry of Pensions practice

Following the earlier scandalous failure of the system at the time of the Boer War (1899–1902), by early 1914, the Armed Forces disablement pensions scheme had been reformed.[26] The Chelsea Commissioners were responsible for the pensions of the other ranks and all widows at the outbreak of the Great War, and in late 1914, the government appointed a Select Committee that recommended an increase in the existing rates. These changes included a new maximum disability pension of 25 shillings a week.[27] Allowances became available for 'aggravation' or worsening of what was seen as injury or disease acquired before service, as well as payment for disability that clearly resulted from the war. Unfortunately, the system was not designed with the needs of shell-shocked soldiers in mind, nor, as they became known, did it adapt to their special requirements. The most important drawback of the system, even following the introduction of the Special Medical Board in 1916–17, was that the criteria for assessing a physical disability and a mental disability were incompatible. In the case of a lost limb or debilitating illness the judgement was based on a chart that listed the percentage disability rating for the loss of a foot or an eye. These 'objective' criteria were supplemented by the doctor's on-the-spot opinion. There were no such criteria for the assessment of mental damage from war. Moreover, every doctor was aware that expenditure should be limited wherever possible, and as a consequence of both training and military experience, many medics were suspicious of shell-shocked men.[28] As the Chelsea Commissioners were not known for their generosity and many Special Medical Board tribunal doctors were RAMC professionals, the whole system was weighted heavily against the interests of war neurotic ex-servicemen. The combination of financial pressure and medical opinion against shell shock meant that the interests of the economy and the war disabled were best served, in the minds of state and medical authority, by judging symptoms subjective.[29]

Against a background of troubled reintegration for disabled and discharged soldiers returning to Britain with pensions, employment and work, Sir John Collie was uniquely positioned to shape the experience of war neurotic ex-servicemen.[30] Already President of the Special Medical Board for Neurasthenia and Allied Disorders, which came into operation as a branch of the Ministry of Pensions in April 1917, three months later Collie was assigned Director of Neurasthenic Institutions by the Ministry of Pensions, and in the following January, he became Director of Medical Services.[31] It was in this final year of the war too that the Ministry of Pensions took over full state responsibility for the treatment of special classes of disabled men, and the Institutional Committee of the War Office with its Red Cross advisers was disbanded. The function of the Special Medical Board was to examine all discharged soldiers with 'neurasthenia and functional nervous disease' and to accord gratuities or recommend pensions. The Board also had the job of periodically re-examining all men who were in receipt of temporary pensions after discharge and suffering from the same disorders. In 1918 the number of pensioners in this group was approximately 25,000.[32]

There are obvious reasons why Sir John was put in charge. While working as the Medical Examiner for the London County Council before the war, he had found time to write several tomes reflecting his special interest: the border areas between medicine and the law. In *Fraud and its Detection in Accident Insurance Claims* (1912) and *Malingering and Feigning Sickness* (1917), Collie explored the topics that later became so import-ant in making treatment and pensions decisions for war neurotic ex-servicemen. Unlike the academic doctors and psychologists who worked with war neurotics, Collie scorned treatments not dictated by his own 'common sense'; and like many doctors who treated war neurotics during and after the Armistice, he loathed anything that resembled psychoanalysis, considering it quackery.[33] Collie had also acquired a reputation by the start of the war for being suspicious of any patient who claimed to be ill, particularly claims of 'functional nervous dis-ease'.[34] As the newly appointed Director of the Army Medical Services section of the Ministry of Pensions in 1918, he explained his position on shell shock treatment. 'Personally,' he stated, 'I have always believed that hard work and continuous work is the only way to be really happy, and that in one form or another is the only salvation for those who are suffering from functional nervous diseases.'[35]

Collie's appointment proved divisive both with staff at the Army Medical Services section of the Ministry of Pensions and with veterans and their supporters. Staff and fellow medics at the Ministry accused Sir John of high-handed, spiteful careerism; ex-soldiers and activists ac-cused him of an obsessive interest in the detection of malingering.[36] An incident in the summer of 1918 illustrates both Collie's working methods and the response of interested parties.[37] Earlier, in June 1917, a discharged serviceman identified as 'John Johnson' was examined for a pensions award resulting from nervous disorder, with symptoms includ-ing partial paralysis and nervous tics. Although he was a known malin-gerer and the only proof of disability was his alleged functional symptoms, Johnson expressed surprise when his award was refused. In spite of appeals and requests he was not re-examined, and the Ministry declared the case closed. In the spring of 1918, unsatisfied with the treatment he had received, Johnson consulted a Harley Street specialist who provided a supportive medical report that testified his symptoms were impossible to fake. Thus armed, and by now with a considerable grudge against Sir John, Johnson went to his MP and the press to force recompense for his alleged disability. The public battle that followed led to questions in Parliament and a series of commentaries on the case in *John Bull*. Charles Rudy's description of *John Bull*, published in November 1918, is worth quoting here because it suggests how it was that the shell shock issue became so important to soldiers as well as the public and the politicians. *John Bull*, Rudy wrote, was 'the soldier's friend' *par excellence*.

> The influence of this journal is only short of phenomenal. The sometime wild prophesies of its editorial seer do not affect the estimation in which it is held – and why? Because in its pages Tommy is not treated as a blatant hero crying aloud for German blood, but as a man who, though he has certain duties to perform, possesses nevertheless certain rights which *John Bull* intends unflinchingly to protect in the face of *all* the powers-that-be; because it flatters him as a rational man, and champions – or seems to champion – his cause at the expense of any and every institution *however much it may hitherto have been hallowed by tradition.*[38]

John Bull had a scurrilous reputation then, but, as Rudy hints, it was notable for campaigning on behalf of veterans and their pension rights. On 29 June 1918, the magazine roundly condemned Sir John:

> Physicians of high standing – we except Sir John Collie, Medical Officer to L.L.C., who is less a specialist than a monomaniac – are agreed that 'shell shock' in its various forms is a painful and disabling affection. Unfortunately, Dr Collie has a 'pull' at the Ministry of Pensions; and in the case of John Johnson, of Brixton, recently noted in these columns, his influence has been exerted to rob a discharged soldier of a pension to which he is clearly entitled as if he had lost an eye or a limb. Despite the publicity given to the matter, no satisfactory steps have yet been taken towards meeting the man's indubitable claim; yet the Ministry are in possession of medical evidence which ought to outweigh the opinion of Sir John Collie, whose handling of the case and many others of the same character, has been grossly unsympathetic...[39]

Sir John was, however, apparently impervious to such criticism and Johnson's case was never reviewed. Perhaps he was right not to do so as there are several ways to interpret this incident. It might show the rank injustice and insensitivity of the Ministry, it might show too that obsessive and neurotic ex-soldiers sometimes felt themselves persecuted. In either instance, Johnson's case illustrates the strength of public feeling that pensions and shell shock issues might easily arouse.

It is equally clear, whatever view he took of individual cases, that Collie remained ignorant of developments in medical science even after the war. Shell shock, he continued to believe, was the result of physical concussion or of microscopic shell fragments; while neurasthenia and related mental disorders were to a large extent the result of personal inadequacy.[40] In a lecture to the Royal Institute of Public Health in the autumn of 1917, the doctor gave what can be taken as his definitive view of neurasthenia and its treatment.[41] Particular importance was placed on strong willpower and a good hereditary background in both the prevention and speedy recovery of cases. As for the remainder, they were unwilling or unable to be cured, much of their condition was self-induced and, like peacetime neurasthenics, they were prone to weak will and morbid introspection. The soldier's condition was self-sustaining because, like the malingerer, he did not want to recover. Treatment for Collie was the process of overcoming 'delusive feelings of inability to work' and correcting 'the perversion of mental outlook' that formed the basis of all neurasthenia.[42] This process of 're-education' as defined by Collie became the basis of the Ministry of Pensions' cure and rehabilitation policy from 1917 onwards; treatment depended on capturing the mind quickly after the onset of symptoms so that it would be 'set in the right mould'.

Treatments based on these suppositions were developed through 1917 at the First Home of Recovery at Golders Green, and before the war ended, similar regimes were installed in another eleven Ministry of Pensions centres in Britain.[43] 'The class of case we lay ourselves out for are men suffering from certain forms of paralysis, tremors, stammering, etc.,' said Sir John, describing the aims of Golders Green. 'We are hopeful that by the rapid cure of a few of the earlier and simpler cases we shall create in the institutions an atmosphere of confidence and cheerfulness which will unconsciously influence the trend of thought of these unfortunate men. After all our conduct in life is largely the result of suggestion. Our idea is that cheerfulness shall be the prevailing atmosphere of these homes.'[44] All Ministry of Pension Homes of Recovery stressed forgetting the experience of war and replacing it at least superficially with a more positive atmosphere and frame of mind. Leading doctors in these hospitals argued that staying 'cheerful' was the key to recovery and this should be combined wherever possible with a busy regime of outdoor work.[45] The parallels with pre-war treatment for neurasthenia are strongest in Ministry of Pensions methods, as Captain B. Williams revealed describing rehabilitation in summer 1917:

> Work and interest in extraneous life are the best cure for such cases. One of the worst services that can be rendered to them is to lavish injudicious sympathy upon them. From the nature of the disorder the man is apt to pity himself unduly and to welcome greedily well-meant but ill advised attempts to make him think himself incapable of exertion. Chiefly in order to save such men from their friends and to give them the bracing treatment they require, a home for neurasthenics discharged from the Army has recently been opened by the Pensions Ministry at Golders Green.[46]

Despite Collie's implementation of this type of regime at the Ministry of Pensions, and despite the unquestionable relief it gave to many ex-servicemen, the inadequacies of the system were apparent towards the end of the war.[47] By the summer of 1918, for example, the number of traumatic neurosis cases returning to Britain was far in excess of the facilities available. The Pensions Survey Board was examining a weekly average of 459 cases. The branch dealing with exceptional cases, alleged inadequacies of treatment, refusals of treatment and complaints against local Pension Boards was in addition attempting to deal with upwards of 300 cases a day, and this number was still increasing in August 1918.[48] Similarly, according to one specialist working for the Ministry of Pensions, many soldiers who might otherwise have been treated quickly and simply, remained disabled. Major A.F. Hurst had developed a straightforward technique for treating functional symptoms such as paralysis, tics or mutism, but other Ministry medics were unconvinced.[49] Hurst agreed with the widespread view that many patients were prone both to exaggerate symptoms and prolong treatment and hospitalization when given the opportunity, but the major differed from the Ministry's thinking in his belief that modified re-education together with persuasion and suggestion could help cure functional nervous disorders.[50] Hurst also noted how little many medics actually knew about such conditions. 'The great majority of soldiers sent to hospital on account of fits are really suffering from hysteria and not true epilepsy. This is unfortunately not very widely recognized, with the result that many have become pensioners and are given three doses of bromide a day for supposed epilepsy when a single dose of psychotherapy would have effected a cure.' Worse still, 'numerous soldiers have been invalided from service with a useless hand or arm which remains useless for the rest of their lives unless the functional nature of the incapacity is recognized'.[51] Collie's approach, sanctioned by both military and pension authorities, was then to have life-long, frequently damaging implications for shell-shocked servicemen as they tried to return to civilian life.

The trauma of return

There was a sense in which every soldier who had seen active combat and returned home thinking idealistically of his past peacetime life, was traumatized. Most soldiers naturally preferred to be at home living in peace and security rather than on the war front in combat and danger. At the same time, the experience of war separated the soldier from the past life he wanted to recapture, and from friends and family who had not shared his experiences. Later on, as he tried to cope with the intractable problems of housing, employment and family relations, or observed the apparent procrastination and hypocrisy of politicians and bureaucrats, the ex-combatant might easily have caught himself longing for life at the front.[52] The return from the war and the transition to civilian life strained the nerves of all returnees.

Evidence on the psychological experience of homecoming from the Great War for both healthy and psychologically disturbed veterans is patchy, but data from other follow-up studies on different countries and different wars can supplement our knowledge on British war neurotic ex-servicemen after the 1918 Armistice. Most useful are the American studies, mainly carried out following the Second World War, which include extensive research into the process of recovery and reintegration up to 15 years after the conclusion of hostilities. This body of evidence stresses the link between domestic conditions, employment and the continuation of mental conditions that began in the war.[53] There are, though, limits to the usefulness of this evidence in relation to British war neurotic ex-servicemen after the Great War: conditions of combat and social attitudes change according to time and place, and these changing conditions alter the experience of psychological disorder and the process of recovery for veterans. Furthermore, American ex-servicemen enjoyed substantial provision for employment training and education. In Britain, as we shall see, much less was available. Despite these limitations such sources provide a comparative yardstick and a useful perspective on the long-term effects of traumatic neurosis, and for this reason the American experience is useful in association with a larger body of specifically British evidence.

Two American psychologists, reporting on Second World War ex-combatants, carried out one of the first systematic examinations of returning soldiers.[54] In their survey of postwar readjustment Karpe and Schnap found that as well as idealization of the home situation and underestimation of the difficulties of readjustment, one of several scenarios commonly troubled soldiers. The most widespread of these was the return to an unhappy family situation or altered marital circumstances. Changes in the composition of the household by death, birth or marriage also forced the veteran to adapt more rapidly than would normally be required. Marriage or the near-prospect of marriage and the changes this entailed might also produce intense anxiety or stress. Lack of family support of any kind also made veterans more psychologically vulnerable. As well as these general circumstances, more immediate conditions could bring about a 'trauma of reunion'. Either the guilt of separation or the extreme discrepancies between the expectation and reality of return might rekindle old conflicts; job loss or a confrontation with a shop steward could break a man's self-confidence and belief in his ability to adapt to the complexities of civilian life. According to Karpe and Schnap, otherwise healthy soldiers often suffered emotional trauma and depression when faced with the reality of returning home. The common situations outlined by the authors give some indication of how difficult it must have been for many ex-servicemen returning from France in 1919. War neurotic ex-servicemen carried a still heavier psychological burden.

Norman Fenton, who worked at the American Expeditionary Force Base Hospital in France towards the end of the war, wrote the only English language follow-up study on the shell shock cases of 1914–18. With financial support from the New York National Committee for Mental Hygiene, Fenton surveyed all the American troops he could trace who were treated at the AEF hospital in France. In total 758 ex-soldiers replied to a survey in 1919–20 and most of the same group answered another questionnaire in 1924–25.[55] The central theme of *Shellshock and its Aftermath* (1926) was that readjustment and reintegration depended on social, economic and emotional support as much as degree of disability. An ex-serviceman with chronic fatigue, which could seriously affect his employment prospects, stood an excellent chance of recovery and successful reintegration with a supportive family and employer. An ex-serviceman who suffered nightmares or a slight stutter, which apparently posed no serious problem in many types of work, might cling to his symptoms for years if he had no emotional support or other motivation to encourage recovery, and no income of any kind other than his state compensation. Based on the 1919–20 survey, *Shell-shock and its Aftermath* divided war neurotic ex-servicemen into five groups. There is no suggestion that the British ex-soldiers of the Great War reacted identically, but Fenton's groups are worth describing in more detail because they map out the variety of ways war neurotic ex-servicemen probably adapted to civilian life after war.[56]

'Psychotic' men suffered both chronic and acute conditions including 'psychopathic personality', epileptic-type fits and 'dementia praecox'. All such ex-servicemen required constant supervision and institutional care and accounted for 1.3 per cent of all cases. 'Disabled' men did not require constant medical supervision and institutional care, but were effectively unemployable. They were also likely to require frequent re-hospitalization for 'psychoneuroses' or 'nervous breakdown'. Symptoms were less intense and did not last over extended periods of months and years, as in 'psychotic' cases. 'Disabled' veterans accounted for 20.4 per cent of all cases. 'Fatigued' men were able to take some employment where it was available, but were unable to do so without personal discomfort and probable relapse. Symptoms included fatigue following mild exercise or exertion, severe headaches, a lack of motivation or ambition, and bouts of severe depression. Where a wife or other family members were present, or the employer was especially considerate, members of this group were able to live with some degree of independence. 'Fatigued' cases accounted for 17.3 per cent of the total sample. 'Neurotic' ex-servicemen had full employment or were capable of full employment, but continually suffered from severe nervous difficulties and saw doctors either regularly or frequently. A common feature was difficulty in personal relationships. Symptoms included occasional fine tremors and tics, speech defects, insomnia, jumpiness, poor concentration, memory disorders and 'spells' of different kinds. Such ex-soldiers were capable of, and best suited to, light work or outdoor activities. Their symptoms were not in themselves a great handicap, but often resulted in minor injuries and less frequently serious accidents. Especially trying for 'neurotic' veterans were long hours of factory work with noisy machinery; agricultural activities were considered of greatest therapeutic benefit, especially in the prevention of moods or deep depression. 'Neurotic' ex-servicemen accounted for 22 per cent of cases in the survey. 'Normal' men were veterans who had returned to civilian life, work, homes and families, and were able to support themselves. Successful reintegration did not mean, however, that 'normal' ex-servicemen were fully recovered. Nervousness, headaches, memory lapses, dizzy spells and restlessness were common symptoms. A dropped screwdriver or a newspaper article could provoke an outburst of anger or excitement. The condition was latent: cured for the purposes of everyday living, but always with the possibility of relapse. In Fenton's survey, this group was by far the largest at 38.9 per cent.

In Britain, apart from disruption to family life or employment prospects the returning soldiers discovered that the government was ill-prepared for their arrival. Few arrangements were made to assist in the creation of an effective administrative framework for treatment or a coherent pension policy. Even after the introduction of the Ministry of Pensions in 1916–17, the type and extent of state provision for the war disabled as well as healthy veterans presented a huge task.[57] The special requirements of the rapidly mounting numbers of casualties of all types were largely ignored during the first two years of the war when there was minimal provision for rehabilitation. The requirements of the severely disabled such as the limbless or paralysed were met mostly from the work of voluntary associations and charities, who raised funds privately; consequently there were large gaps in both the pensions and rehabilitation systems.[58] Ministry of Pensions policy was shaped by a variety of objectives. These included: the desire to ensure pre-war social structures were not significantly changed, to minimize responsibility for the hugely successful recruitment pledges, and to retain and enhance levels of voluntary subscription. More than anything the state's financial obligations had to be limited. The introduction of conscription made nonsense of the argument that soldiers joined the armed forces at their own risk. Even so, the government persisted in its view that paternalism and charity should play an important role in assisting returnees. By the autumn of 1918 and on into 1919 war-disabled ex-servicemen and returning soldiers alike lost belief in the military and political handling of the war, in the public view of 'war heroes' and in the adequacy of pay and pensions. 'Apart from anything else,' wrote one commentator in November 1918, 'I consider that our real post-bellum danger lies in Tommy's loss of faith in the higher institutions of his country, coupled as it is with the determination to put an end to the slaving days of yore.'[59]

The grievances of healthy and disabled returnees included badly handled demobilization, low rates of pensions and gratuities, failure of coordination in handling soldiers' cases, and lack of housing. Veterans' radicalism reached its height in the summer and autumn of 1919, when there were demonstrations and marches, disruptions at peace festivals and discontent widely voiced over the government's apparent apathy.[60] This unrest is described in a Ministry of Pensions Report that followed a questionnaire investigating the reasons for the ex-soldiers' discontent. It was sent to the Regional War Pensions Committees in October 1919 at the request of the War Office, first, to discover if the ex-servicemen's protests were justified, and second, if so, to make suggestions on how the situation could be rectified. Among the suspected causes of soldiers' ill feeling, the Ministry of Pensions listed:

a. lack of co-operation between various departments working for the resettlement of ex-soldiers. b. apparent lack of sympathy on the part of departments, notably in failing to take a sympathetic and compre- hensive view of cases presented. c. failure on the part of officials concerned to interpret Government provisions in the widest sense, particularly in regard to training and financial grants. d. delay in arriving at a final decision or settlement of the case, resulting in unnecessary expenditure of money to the public, and dissatisfaction, anxiety and worry on the part of the applicant.[61]

Many of the local War Pensions Committees quickly confirmed these were important aspects of ex-soldiers' discontent and added their own comments.

Unanimously the Ministry was condemned for one mistake: dividing responsibility for individual soldiers to various government depart- ments. The Birmingham War Pensions Committee President spoke for many in a letter dated 5 October 1919:

I think the discharged men are fully justified in their complaint about lack of cooperation between various departments. To my mind it was a disastrous policy for the Ministry to delegate its responsibilities to other Government Departments ... A pensioner cannot be divided into so many bits. His pension, treatment, training and employment are inseparably inter-related, and any attempt to divide up the re- sponsibility amongst various authorities was bound to lead to the present situation.[62]

Other committees attacked the narrow-minded attitudes of local offi- cials and administrators, in the employment exchanges, for example. 'Men often disqualified through technical difficulty. (Portsmouth). A tendency to "get rid" of applicants rather than examine the case and offer all that the government can do. (Leicester). No allowance made for man's absence from training for good reasons (eg sickness or holiday); the date of completion of training is not accepted (as was formerly done by the Ministry of Pensions). (Luton).'[63] From the report of the Scottish regional HQ of the Ministry of Pensions on 11 October 1919 discontent was evidently deepest in the heavily populated urban districts: Glasgow, Dundee, Edinburgh and Leith. Here the uncooperative and distant Ministry of Labour aroused angry opposition:

> When the training was taken over by the Ministry of Labour the Officials did not appear to have even an elementary knowledge of the Regulations governing training, and consequently chaos reigned, and from what I hear things have not improved, when a man applies for training he usually finds that the scheme is filled, and no endeavour is made to suggest an alternative scheme. When he is fortunate enough to obtain training he is kept entirely in the dark as to what is going on, and soon realises that no interest is being taken in him. Again the conditions of training are continually changing, which confuses the man considerably. Delay on the part of the Pension Issue Office and civil Liability Department may be responsible for a certain amount of unrest, but undoubtedly the main cause is the training.[64]

Employment exchanges and training schemes were similarly inflexible and persistently treated ex-servicemen with 'barrack room' manners.

In the final War Office Report of March 1920, a sorry story emerged. Soldiers were met constantly with impersonal, petty-minded bureaucracy, with staff who were preoccupied by regulations and technicalities, and with a system that took no interest in the full facts of any individual case. Not surprisingly, ex-servicemen believed the state felt no sense of responsibility towards them, and they in turn became hopeless and discouraged.[65] Anticipating these findings government reforms were introduced at the end of 1919 which went some way to resolving these technical difficulties by giving statutory pension rights, by ensuring training and employment for the disabled and by giving preference to ex-servicemen in finding employment. Local Pensions Committees were also directed to include veterans as members, and private and public agencies were to assist wherever possible. Despite these efforts employees were, finally, at the mercy of economic conditions, and when the postwar boom ended many conscripts and volunteers who joined the Army from school found themselves without work and without the necessary skills to find any work.[66] For ex-servicemen who had idealized both their home and their future while in the trenches, poor treatment at the hands of the state and severely limited economic prospects made the return home a frustrating, difficult process. By the end of 1929, with 58 per cent of the total unemployed men who had served in the war, the prospects for war neurotic ex-servicemen were hardly better than in 1919.[67]

Disputed definitions after war

As a part of the wider group of ex-servicemen returning from the Western Front during and after the Great War, the experience of war neurotic ex-servicemen was affected by generalities like government legislation and specifics like the personality of Sir John Collie. As members of the wider group of returning veterans, they faced one problem that was common to all servicemen: readjustment to the world after war. Many returnees felt the experience of the trenches had permanently separated them from non-combatants, and civilian society only seemed to magnify this sentiment. Their hopes and ambitions quickly frustrated, ex-servicemen had little patience with the apparent procrastination and hypocrisy of politicians and bureaucrats. After anger, many fell into despair. In addition to these common predicaments, war neurotic ex-servicemen endured ineffective medical treatment and so many war-related psychological disorders were never fully treated. This situation was aggravated by the appointments and policies of the Ministry of Pensions. The treatment of traumatic neurosis in Britain was in large part forged by Sir John Collie, a medic whose outlook and practice developed under the influence of the Workmen's Compensation Acts, and by the theories of malingering, neurasthenia and race that were so influential in the formation of military policy in the years before the Great War.[68] If Collie's views were damaging, he was still a fair representative of the many Great War medics who were trained in one tradition before the war, then confronted by bureaucratic and political pressures as well as medical uncertainties, and required to treat a perplexing new disorder once the war had started. However, unlike most medics Dr Collie directed policy, and many available forms of treatment that might have helped war neurotic ex-servicemen were lost in favour of his 'common sense' approach. The 'common sense' definition of health for Collie was fitness for work; in the case of war neurotic ex-servicemen, this definition was misleading.

Putting the hurdles of poor medical judgement and ineffective treatment aside, the sheer number of cases presented was a further obstacle. The system for processing returnees was overloaded even before the war had finished; war neurotic ex-servicemen were obvious targets for government departments that had to cut expenditure because of short-age of funds after the Armistice. This makes it all the more remarkable that such a large proportion of veterans nevertheless did manage to reintegrate and adapt back into civilian society within a few months or years of their return from the front. Without support from family and employer, an apparently recovered ex-serviceman could quickly relapse; the rise in compensation neurosis through the 1920s and 1930s is poorly documented, but all too predictable given the poor economic conditions between the wars. The evidence that does exist for the postwar lives of war neurotic ex-servicemen is presented in the following chapter.

9
Veterans: War Neurotic Ex-Servicemen

Pensions in postwar society

While war neurotic pensioners in Britain were better off than their nearest peers on the Continent – in France there were no payments from the war, in Germany existing payments ceased in 1926 – many thousands of lives were permanently blighted by the war. One indication of the number is that there were 187 out-patient clinics in Britain treating mental disorders of all kinds by 1939, and that among their patients were many of the 120,000 in receipt of combat-related pensions.[1] The experience of war neurotic ex-servicemen can best be understood by seeing them both as part of the wider community of veterans affected by postwar social change, Ministry of Pensions policies and bureaucratic structures, and also as a particular instance whose claims were examined and reassessed by the Special Medical Board system. One viewpoint provides the common social context within which every veteran lived; the second makes available the particular details of assessed and reviewed pension claims for psychological debility that influenced the lives of the 114,600 pensioners who claimed awards between April 1919 and May 1929.[2] Doctors' case notes and memoirs illustrate the difficulties in which ex-soldiers found themselves as well as the bitter resentment that the work of the Ministry sometimes aroused. Pension case notes and administrative documents give a further insight into ex-servicemen's everyday lives and continuing neurotic conditions. The post-combat life patterns of war neurotic ex-servicemen are difficult to trace, especially into the 1930s, but it is possible to illustrate the variety of their experience through the interwar years.

For some men leaving the Army the Ministry of Pensions was no more than a bridge into the civilian world as they worked their neuroses out in the home, the office and the factory. For others, it decisively influenced how, and even if, they were able to return successfully from the war.[3] To the Ministry of Pensions, war neurotic ex-servicemen were part of a much wider group of injured or disabled veterans treated in the numerous TB annexes, paraplegic units, epileptic colonies, orthopaedic hospital annexes and other specialist treatment units across the country. Hard-pressed by financial constraints, inadequately staffed and constantly petitioned by the thousands of returnees who flooded the system, the Ministry wanted to reduce short-term costs by the development of quick, affordable treatments, and to reduce long-term costs by helping servicemen back to health.[4] Recognizing that the treatment of war neurotics was an important part of the Ministry's work – it believed a large proportion of cases could be improved or fully cured – a nationwide medical assessment system was set up in 1917. Fritz Kaufmann, Germany's foremost advocate of electric shock therapy during the war, described the dilemma that faced both German and British state authorities. Pensioning soldiers off, he wrote in 1916, 'leads to unpleasant consequences for the family in question. In addition, it leads to a loss in the living work force at the state's disposal. A by no means unimportant further consequence is the considerable burden put on the military treasury.'[5] Accordingly, the job of the Special Medical Boards was to evaluate and re-examine the claims of soldiers throughout the country and to send them on to one of the Ministry's various homes for borderline mental cases, treatment centres and outpatient clinics for neurasthenic cases, and homes of recovery. By 31 May 1918, in addition to the 58 convalescent homes and 266 general hospitals and infirmaries that might take such cases, 12 of the Ministry's 135 specialist centres dealt exclusively with neurasthenic and nervous disorder patients.[6]

The system was beset with problems because of poor economic conditions, a shortage of state funds and War Office thinking. Reports from around the country in 1921 document how unemployment and labour unrest compounded the troubles of veterans, among them war neurotic ex-servicemen. In the West Midlands 'difficulty is experienced with the employers, who are often unwilling to accept men after they have heard details of their [mental] disability. The present crisis of unemployment is complicating matters...' In Scotland '[t]here is a demand for hospitals and clinics for treatment and training. Labour unrest has made everything very difficult in Glasgow. There is much difficulty in getting men with pre-war disabilities back into work.' In the northern district the situation was made easier because 'the greater proportion of patients are miners and nearly always revert to their original employment'.[7] Nationally, then, and for all fit veterans except those in the essential heavy industries, the prospects for postwar employment were unpromising. Even before the war had ended however, unfit ex-servicemen found themselves at a disadvantage in the job market.

Both during the war and after a chronic shortage of effectively trained staff and proper facilities made the prospect of a return to full health and a final, fair pension settlement frustratingly elusive.[8] In December 1919, Sir John Collie described the networks' shortcomings. Writing to the Association of Local War Pensions Committees he stated that the problem 'is not so much on the side of providing accommodation as on the scarcity of medical men who have received the training necessary for the treatment of cases'.[9] Short courses in the specialist treatment and care of war-related mental disorders were introduced in response, but because there was a severe shortage of doctors, this small band had no discernible effect. One consequence of inadequate training, discovered only in 1921, was that different regions used different diagnostic criteria, and in some places into the 1930s, soldiers who suffered a condition resembling epilepsy were wrongly diagnosed and treated.[10]

War Office thinking, which strongly influenced the ethos and methods of Ministry treatment centres, also stymied the system. It was stressed, for example, that the personality of the staff helped create the right atmosphere for the recovery of well-being and healthfulness, that morality and willpower still mattered more than medical science. This was one of the conclusions of the 1922 *War Office Committee of Enquiry into 'Shell Shock'*, which equally rejected even the most modified forms of psychoanalytic treatment, and both medical and military authorities treating war neurotic ex-servicemen held the same opinion. In this view, a certain type of medic was desirable for work with the Ministry of Pensions both in its treatment centres and on its assessment boards. As one doctor put it, 'it seems to me that the class of doctor we require there is not so much a scientist of Psycho Therapy or a specialist in neurological cases, as a good fellow with a kindly eye and a good square chin – a man who can and will command the respect of the patients as a man'.[11] The promotion of manly self-respect was seen as an important therapeutic tool then: to be encouraged because it would ensure that as few veterans as possible were hospitalized and as many as possible were in occupational training and out-patient therapy. In rehabilitation, this notion displaced potentially more effective cures; in pension evaluation, moreover, it meant that many ex-servicemen's willpower and masculine assertiveness were in doubt.

The Special Medical Board system

The assessment system for mental casualties both during and after the war was also based on the assumption that willpower and moral initiative counted more than medical science. This distinction was first formalized in the wartime regulation, introduced in the autumn of 1916, which distinguished between soldiers whose shell shock was a physical 'wound' and soldiers who were suffering psychological 'shock'. From this point onwards only 'wound' cases were entitled to a wound stripe or badge, and, consequently, a pension.[12] To the Army this division was a matter of manpower and morale; to the Ministry of Pensions it was logical and cost saving; to ex-servicemen it was a demoralizing rejection of those who most required assistance. The culture of suspicion that filled the minds of Ministry of Pensions' doctors, as the temporary RAMC doctor Lieutenant Gameson stressed, also corrupted medical diagnosis. 'For the Ministry of Pensions between the two wars...I have the greatest contempt. Of course it had to exercise restraint in its disbursements, yet it was under no obligation automatically to regard almost every claim as suspect; which it did, summoning medical and surgical yes-men to help it wriggle out of its minimal responsibilities.'

As the recipient of a state pension B.M. Downes of the 9th Battalion Cameronians wrote scathingly of his own encounter with a Special Medical Board. The medics appeared to him to be previously retired men whose ideas were outdated and whose attitudes were narrow-minded, 'who assess what pension, if any, should be grudgingly given to a man crippled in service of his country'.[13] Describing his own case, he wrote, 'The Chairman of the board said they had assessed my hip and leg wounds at 20% disability but they were not giving me anything for the chest wound as in their opinion the symptoms I had described since receiving it were due to shell shock or "war neurasthenia" – "as we call it", he observed pretentiously and would disappear after a little while in civvy street.' Downes appealed and was given another examination, but the second result was no more to his satisfaction 'with a meagre 10% added to my wounds disability pension based originally in the 1914 cost of living when whisky was 3/6 a bottle'.[14] In his disappointment Downes possibly exaggerated the harm of this decision, yet his comments do show the intense feeling the issue of pensions could arouse as it seemed to him and his comrades that the major objective of the system was to cheat them of the reward they had rightfully earned fighting for their country.

The system that Gameson and Downes found so objectionable was established, according to the Director General of the Army Medical Department, Sir John Collie, to examine cases and award gratuities to those who were already discharged suffering from 'neurasthenia or functional nervous disease'. The first Special Medical Board was set up in London in the spring of 1917, and there were twenty boards across the country by the end of the year administering discharge and pension claims. Every Special Medical Board, empowered to recommend or approve a soldier's discharge and pension allowance, and to review all cases at six-monthly or yearly intervals, had the same structure: two civilian and two RAMC doctors, plus one Special Medical Board representative. The Director General explained how he thought Special Medical Boards ought to go about their work in a circular dispatched to every local centre:

> The prognosis of F[unctional]. N[ervous]. D[isorder]. is always diffi-cult, and the difficulty is much enhanced when it depends on accur-ately gauging the value of alleged subjective symptoms. What a patient alleges he feels is always very real to him, but unhesitatingly to accept statements and award Gratuities or Pensions at these exam-inations in the absence of physical corroboration would in many cases be to do an injustice to the State and harm to the individual.[15]

These notes became the basis of the examination procedure in the 1920s, and they lend credibility to Gameson's allegation that the Minis-try made every attempt to 'wriggle out of its minimal responsibilities': the culture of suspicion in the Special Medical Boards was fostered and encouraged by its Director General.

Even with good will, the accurate, fair assessment of how far a mental condition was due to war service was a particularly difficult task.[16] When medics were inexperienced, non-specialist or suspicious, and when patients were resentful, aggressive or uncommunicative, it became nearly impossible. As in wartime, ex-servicemen were quick to note the slights on character and record handed down by (often) non-combatant medics, and to reciprocate in their critical opinion of the Ministry. As in Downes' case, this bitterness was not related only to the Special Medical Boards; the Ministry of Pensions was thought a conveni-ent target for a more general critical attack on the ex-soldiers' situation.

Collie's rationale for these policies was the requirement to keep a tight rein on costs by limiting the number of potential claimants, and this objective must have seemed fully justified given the alarming acceler-ation of cases through the early 1920s.[17] For a variety of reasons, many

Special Medical Board medics were inclined to sympathize with these aims – medics like Major W.J. Adie of the RAMC special reserve for example, whose testimony to the War Office Committee of Enquiry into Shell Shock was noted earlier, and who served as a neurologist during the war in addition to serving as a Special Medical Board examiner afterwards. Like many others, Adie believed that during the wartime traumatic neurosis signified nothing more than the opportunity for large numbers of soldiers to evade their duty; after the war, it was a bid for pension entitlement. Another Ministry of Pensions official, Dr C. Stanford Read, Officer in Charge at 'D' Block Royal Victoria Netley, and author of *Military Psychiatry in Peace and War* (1920), made a different distinction between soldiers' and veterans' mental conditions.[18] 'When the Armistice came,' the witness said, 'the neurosis stopped, and psychoses went on, showing that they were different conflicts. Of the latter, the probability is that the men have drifted into various asylums.' Those service patients who were still in asylums and whose histories Dr Read had been able to follow, 'were nearly all suffering from Dementia praecox'. Both medics represented the opinion of many other Special Medical Board doctors; both, for different reasons, were disinclined to allow pensions to war neurotic ex-servicemen.

Post-combat lives

Given this attitude among the Special Medical Board doctors, and the certainty that ex-servicemen discussed and judged among themselves the Board's decisions, an examination would certainly have been a tense, unsettling ordeal. The Board decided, fairly or not, if a man was entitled to a pension; if and by how much that pension would be cut; if and when it would be stopped entirely, possibly leaving him and his dependants in poverty. In 1915 percentage rates were introduced to measure how far each serviceman's war injury reduced his earning power; in 1917, shortly after the Ministry of Pensions was established and the final compensation rates were fixed, Sir Alfred Keogh explained how he hoped the new system would work: 'Pensions rates for general cases, together with fixed rates for losses of limb, have now been settled, so far as any question of this kind can be adequately defined; but ample powers exist to consider the peculiar nature of wounds or other disabilities and their effect upon the earning capacity of the individual.'[19] This discretion allowed for scepticism as well as generosity.

To receive a pension it was necessary for each ex-serviceman to fill in the standard Ministry of Pensions form. There are about 40,000 skeletal files and 15,000 fuller files catalogued at the Public Record Office, including Army cases from the other ranks, in the main up to 1923. From an examination of 1,050 of these files, 59 appear to have suffered some form of mental disorder. The records detailed the applicant's age, civilian occupation and probable place of abode, as well as height and weight, and a brief pension and medical record up to 1923, along with contrasting ratings in and out of the Army. Designed to register the details of the physically wounded majority, these forms required doctors to record a 'date of origin' and they often described the incident and behaviour that preceded the diagnosis. The individual pension histories attached to each pension form show basic service record and details of the medical reviews that took place at six-monthly or yearly intervals. After each examination, the Special Medical Board recorded its opinion on any changes in the patient's condition, and noted any amendment in the percentage rating of his disability, together with details of treatment and time spent in hospitals. The percentage rating in each case and at each medical review shows the continued degree of injury. By comparing the criteria used for physical and psychological cases it is possible to describe the level of disablement; by analysing individual cases according to this percentage it is possible to gain an insight into the working of the pension system and the post-combat lives of veterans. What follows is a detailed exploration of some of these case notes, not offered as a representative sample, but as illustrative examples that highlight the varied experience of war neurotic ex-servicemen. Ministry of Pensions correspondence helps fill in the picture of what happened after 1922, when the medical case notes end.

Twenty per cent disability

Physically injured ex-soldiers given the lowest disability rating had lost the equivalent of two fingers of either hand, and received in 1917 a weekly pension of 8s. 6d. for a warrant officer class one or 5s. 6d. for a private class five.[20] Many men had a much higher rating when first admitted to hospital, but within six months, this was usually reduced. A 20 per cent rating for a traumatized soldier meant that while he might appear to function normally in society he lived with the probability of a sudden relapse: a bout of unpredictable behaviour or an emotional outburst might set him back months; unemployment or isolation might set him back by years. With support from sympathetic family members and an understanding employer, he integrated back into civilian society within a matter of months however, and worked if some relatively undemanding job were available.

Some veterans in this group received a rating below 20 per cent, some were initially given higher rates, but many Special Medical Board doctors seem to have believed that any mental complaint not accompanied by physical injury did not warrant any higher rating. Twenty per cent became the standard final settlement figure. Occasionally, medics flatly rejected claims of disability, more often they attributed continuing neurosis to non-war-related circumstances such as poor home environment, unemployment or heredity. Most ex-soldiers did not trouble to question their medical assessment, even when it clearly caused hardship. Private K., a farm labourer and the youngest of four orphaned children, who was passed fit for enlistment at a medical on 7 August 1914, aged just over 17, certainly falls into this category. Discharged as unfit for further military service in March 1919, with no trade and no prospect of employment, K. had served on active service throughout the war: he was in the Mediterranean Expeditionary Force from September 1915 to January 1916 (at Gallipoli), and in France from July to September 1916, as well as for long periods thereafter until December 1918. The total length of his service amounted to four years 235 days, and during that time, he had gained entitlement to wear two gold wound stripes and three blue chevrons. The pension notes describe a soldier who spent 118 days in various hospitals in 1916–17 suffering loss of speech [aphonia], as well as loss of sleep, memory and concentration, but afterwards returned to active duty. After the end of the war, however, his mental health deteriorated once again. In January 1920, the Gloucester Board examined him. 'Complains about general weakness and states that he has "turns" occasionally. Tremors of hands present. Pupil reaction normal . . . slight tremor of head present, mental development poor. His answers are vague and contradictory. It is not clear of what nature his "turns" are. 20 per cent.' A year later, in January 1921, K. complained of weakness. His condition was recorded as '1–5 per cent aggravation passed away', and his disability payments were stopped. The Board did note though that K. was '[c]ongenitally a man of poor mental equipment'.

Fifty per cent disability

A 50 per cent rating was given to physically injured men for amputation of the leg below the knee or the left arm below the elbow or loss of vision in one eye, and was worth 21s. 3d. to a warrant officer class one and 13s. 9d. to a private class five in 1917. For a war neurotic ex-serviceman 50 per cent rating still meant independent living and employment were in theory possible, but at the cost of extreme fatigue, even if suitable work was available. In the case notes there are several instances of recurrent symptoms attributable to financial and employment problems, as well as individual tragedies.

Two cases illustrate the struggle these moderately disabled soldiers faced as they tried to adapt to civilian society. Private M. had enlisted in 9 December 1914 at the age of 28 and served throughout the war, but became disturbed after an unrecorded incident in December 1918. M.'s doctor described him as 'melancholic'. At the time his case seemed routine, but after leaving the Army his mental health deteriorated rapidly as he became obsessed with the idea that he would be forced to go back into further military service. The doctor optimistically gave a 50 per cent disability rating in 1918 and noted 'dull, quiet, reserved fellow, shows no delusions of hallucination, now appt. conv. Bright and cheerful and sleeps well'. Examined again at Plymouth in November 1920, M.'s condition seemed to have worsened: 'Is at present in a demented condition. Nothing can be obtained. Relative states he shows no signs of violence, but has a delusion the Army wants him again. 50 per cent.' A final entry in March 1921 states '7-3-21 / Suicide . . . insane'. This instance appears to have been exceptional. Despite unemployment, relapse that sometimes led to re-hospitalization and intense mental distress in the years after the war, there are only eight recorded cases of war neurotic ex-servicemen taking their own lives up to 1921.[21]

By contrast, Private H., who had enlisted in 1904, and was diagnosed with 'neurasthenia' and 40 per cent disability following a shell explosion during a gas attack in June 1915, managed a good recovery. Discharged in March 1917, a year later he was still suffering anxiety and tremors and his disability rating had risen to 60 per cent. He was examined again at the Birmingham Neurological Clinic in November 1921. 'Patient rapidly adjusting himself and almost fit for discharge. His present trouble seems to be connected with existing economic conditions only, and will I believe disappear when he has established himself, as he is trying to do, at the G.P.O: in the meantime he is doing well as a pedlar. Disability less than 20 per cent (6–14). Treatment continuing.' Finally discharged in January 1922 H. still had no proper work but was no longer so anxious or depressed.

Eighty per cent disability

An 80 per cent physical disability rating was for the loss of both feet, the amputation of the leg at the hip or the right arm at the shoulder joint, or for the total loss of speech. For a warrant officer class one, this was worth 34s. 0d. and for a private class five 22s. 0d. in 1917. An 80 per cent rating for a war neurotic ex-serviceman meant he was disabled, largely unemployable, subject to intermittent periods of hospitalization for serious mental conditions, but not necessarily in full-time institutional care. Ex-servicemen rarely lasted more than six months with such a high rating. The following two instances, each of which details the case history of a regular soldier, illustrate some of the reasons rates were reduced.

Severely disabled ex-soldiers sometimes suffered conditions that were not caused by the war but were aggravated by it. According to the Special Medical Board, such men suffered constitutional disorders and were therefore beyond state responsibility – men like Private P., who joined up aged 21 in 1903 and was discharged in August 1915 as physically unfit, and whose case notes describe him as suffering '[n]ervous debility from childhood, aggravated by exposure, 75 per cent, discharged 12-8-15, physically unfit... Always has had head trouble. Chronic headaches, cannot concentrate. Indefinite history of fits.' In a subsequent examination at Chilsden in March 1916, his headaches and 'anaemic nervous symptoms' were still present. By December 1918, moreover, they seemed to have become worse: P.'s 'neurasthenia' still caused a 50 per cent disability; the headaches and nervous hand tremors persisted; 'traffic neurosis' and 'war dreams' were added to his list of symptoms. The end of the war seems to have coincided with a gradual improvement in P.'s condition, and perhaps a growing reluctance on the part of Special Medical Board doctors to continue his payments. Following two examinations within a few days at the end of April 1921, P. had his pension halved, and finally, in 1922, disallowed.

In other instances acute medical conditions subsided with the passage of years and disability allowance was correspondingly cut, but this hardly amounted to a recovery, as in the case of Private E. Born in 1882, medically examined in July 1916 and enlisted in September of the same year, E. remained in Britain until mid-April 1917, when he joined the B.E.F.; the date of origin of his complaint is recorded as September 1917. Diagnosed with 'neurasthenia', he returned to Britain to serve another six months before being discharged in April 1918 as physically unfit. In July of the same year he is described as 'Weak and Nervous. Unequal to sustained employment, cannot sleep, at times very tremulous'. By February 1919 he was somewhat improved, as his notes record. 'Sleep is disturbed. Sallow, thin, nervous, anxious expression... neurasthenia (Anxiety Neurosis). 50 per cent. States feels slightly improved, sleeping better, headaches not so frequent or severe, easily tires, restless.' From 1920 onward, he had severe depression, anxiety states and 'psycho therapeutic treatment'. E. was treated at the Ministry of Pensions Clinic for Nervous Disorders at Broad Street, Birmingham, and by August 1922, though he was pale and thin, and it left him weak, he was capable of sustained, heavy labour, and his mental condition was described as 'usual'. The final recorded diagnosis was 'Neurasthenia 1–5 per cent'. There are well-defined advances and retreats in E.'s mental health, not least a serious deterioration after the war's end. Technically, E. had regained his capacity for employment, but he was subject to relapse and could easily have found himself unemployable once again after 1922.

One hundred per cent disability

The 100 per cent rating was given for the loss of two or more limbs, total paralysis, lunacy, severe facial disfigurement or advanced cases of incurable disease. For this, a warrant officer class one was given 42s. 6d. and a private class five 27s. 6d. irrespective of service pension. Veterans with a 100 per cent mental disability rating for more than six months would have been chronically and acutely ill, psychotic and in need of constant institutional care and supervision. In practice, such instances appear to have been rare.

Sapper O., fully incapacitated for one month after his diagnosis of 'shell shock' in August 1917, was one soldier whose condition, the Pension Board agreed, was fully attributable to service. O. was reassessed annually until 1922: in April 1918 he suffered 'stutter, heartache, slight tremor, excited manner, dreams, sleeps badly – 70 per cent'; in June 1919, 'stammer much improved, sleep good, fit for work, now stammers badly – min. tremors... very nervous, 40 per cent'; in December 1920 'mild hand tremors, bad stammers, nervous, complains of headaches, palpitations, sweats, sinking feeling, medium tremble – 20 per cent'. Twelve months later 'stammering more than when enlisted, headaches, shaking and trembling on excitement, sinking feeling, medium tremor of hands and general shaking, bad hesitation of speech, nervous and excitable – 20 per cent'. In December 1922, he received a final settlement based on a diagnosis of 'shell shock (neurasthenia) (Agg.)'. O. complained of continuing weakness and headaches, and his examining doctor noted 'palpitations on exertion... speech hesitating'. In due course, he received a 15–19 per cent disabled and a final award of 7s. 6d. for 156 weeks, plus a £40 lump-sum settlement. Whether O. recovered and found employment before these payments ran out in 1925 goes unrecorded.

Private K. was one of the few soldiers to receive a 100 per cent disability rating for more than six months. A regular since 1905, his mental condition was associated with a head wound, which may account for the degree of leniency shown by his examining doctors. Before he became a soldier K. worked as a tailor, he served in India from 1905 to 1908, arrived in France on 22 August 1914, was injured in December, and returned to Britain in January 1915 to be discharged in April. K.'s case notes for that month describe him as follows: 'In action at Ypres 19-12-14. There is a grooved scare two inches long and half an inch wide at the upper and back part of the vortex of the head and which is still tender to touch. He complains of constant pain at the back of the head, with a sensation of dizziness and fullness of the head. These symptoms have not improved during past two months. General conditions are of neurasthenia. His memory is bad, sleeps badly and is in a very nervous state . . . probably permanent – totally prevents at present. (6.4.15)' K. continued to sleep badly and to endure nervousness, a 'tremulous' tongue, distress at any noise and memory loss. In March 1917, his rating fell to 75 per cent, and the examining doctor noted that he was 'mentally slow' but that he was also suffering severe depression and continued poor memory. From May 1920 to February 1922, the last entry in K.'s pension notes, he continued to have headaches, insomnia, bad dreams, defective memory, dizziness and blurred vision, nervousness and depression. His general condition was 'considered one of neurasthenia'. These acute and chronic symptoms had persisted for eight years, and may well have persisted for the remainder of K.'s life.

K. belonged to a significant sub-group of ex-servicemen who required long-term hospitalization for mental conditions after 1922.[22] Some of these men were mental defectives; others registered and re-registered with the Ministry of Pensions through the 1920s as their fortunes fluctuated in the outside world. Case reviews of the mid-1920s show that relapse and repeated breakdown often occurred after final pension settlements and lump-sum payments were used up; they also show that in many cases the Special Medical Board system failed: ex-servicemen relapsed because they had never been mentally fit to serve in the Army, had been discharged prematurely or were entirely unemployable. The number and variety of disorders among men consequently continued to grow after 1923, and was, as one official put it, 'quite disconcerting'.[23] 'Gross hysteria', psychosis, amentia (poor intellectual development) and dementia were among the conditions noted, and many such cases predated the war. One specialist at a care centre noted that alarming numbers of men experienced serious mental deterioration between medical exams over one to three years. What doctors had not been able to predict was the volatility of these conditions; as one official noted, 'assessment at that time [during and immediately after the war] may have been perfectly correct, but as a flat rate upon which to discharge the man is now hopelessly inadequate'.[24]

Employment could in theory assist successful reintegration, but here long-term war neurotic ex-servicemen found themselves at a further disadvantage. According to many veterans, the very name of their condition was enough to put off potential employers, and if the man in question had visible signs of mental disturbance, a bad stutter or a functionally paralysed hand, the stigma was greater and the chance of making a good impression all the more remote. Any neurotic ex-serviceman with a disability rating over 50 per cent was, too, as the Ministry eventually recognized, virtually unemployable.[25] Similarly, the longer their treatment lasted, especially for soldiers who were hospitalized soon after the end of the war or in the early 1920s, when stays could last from six months to three years, the less well equipped they were to resume responsibilities or readjust to the surroundings of civil life.[26]

There was also continuing pressure on the Ministry of Pensions to limit costs, and to achieve this cases were periodically reviewed and the number in expensive institutional care reduced. In 1923, for example, many incurable but uncertifiable men were discharged to long-term colonies requiring nominal specialist medical facilities or staff, as were the 'chronic neurasthenics', 'uncertifiable border-lines' and 'cases of mild mental disorder of an incurable kind'.[27] The mid- and late 1920s saw a shift too away from making soldiers fit for employment: those capable of health had achieved it, at least according to Ministry of Pensions criteria. The remaining task, then, was to take care of chronically disturbed ex-servicemen.[28] In 1925, the Ministry of Pensions identified a large and increasing group of 'post war inefficients'. Beyond the help of training or treatment, either mentally defective or neurotic, these men were relatively young and therefore likely to be a public liability for many years to come. The question for the Ministry of Pensions was where to put them.[29] Finally, it was agreed that one or more specialist centres should be established for such cases; the reasons for this move were identified in a 1923 letter from the Ministry of Pensions to the Treasury Secretary. 'It has been the constant experience of the Ministry that if such men are discharged from treatment they prove quite unable to adapt themselves to the ordinary conditions of social life, their condition begins immediately to deteriorate, a breakdown takes place, and readmission to an institution again becomes necessary.'[30] These attempts to 'shake out' those who would benefit from further treatment were only partly successful though, as the number claiming from the state continued to grow, and the whole process had to be repeated again in 1926 and in 1931.[31]

It was clear too by the mid-1920s that the earlier work of the Special Medical Boards had been flawed, ineffective and even counter-productive. The full examination of every lengthy case had been impossible because of the pressure of numbers, 'complete investigation of each case is almost impossible and errors of judgement inevitable'. Moreover, the Boards had consistently underestimated disability pension ratings:

> The neurasthenic is often both suggestible and self centred. The summons to a board is in effect a warning to him that the amount of his pension is to be considered and may be reduced... Boards are fully aware of this and unless they can find gross physical signs compatible with the man's complaint they are prone largely to discount the latter because they have no standard by which to check them.[32]

Inexperience and the culture of scepticism compounded the problem, as did the number and novelty of war neurotic ex-servicemen, but there were further difficulties.

Sometimes soldiers became increasingly neurotic and disabled as time passed, and it was only then that they were considered seriously or reassessed by the Ministry. 'Epilepsy aggravated – 40 per cent final award. Aged 32. Ten months pre-armistice service in France. Received a slight G.S.W. forearm necessitating 7 days in hospital. First fit January or February 1920. Epilepsy rejected by the ministry as N.A.N.A. Aggravation conceded by P.A.T. Now 70 per cent disabled. In-patient since July 1927.'[33] As the war receded it also became more important and more difficult to judge the extent of wartime aggravation, as in the following instance, also reviewed in 1931:

> Aged 45. Neurasthenia with fits – attributable – 30 per cent... Seven months in France – not up the line. First fit, according to the man's statement, after one month in France in 1917 and the next in 1923. Described by Medical Boards as a constitutional neuropath. Diagnosis now established as epilepsy. Totally disabled. In-patient at Maghull since December 1926. This case has been recently boarded... and the board have recommended as assessment of 100 per cent... M.S.I. is now being asked to consider what entitlement, if any, should be given for epilepsy, and what part of the condition should be ascribed to the effects of war service.[34]

Post-combat life patterns

On the evidence presented here, there were three clearly discernible life patterns for war neurotic ex-servicemen. First were those affected by the war but able to recover relatively quickly, at the latest by the early 1920s. Private A.L. is one such soldier, an ex-other ranker, who, on 27 May 1918, had become 'shaken in his nerves and tremulous' after being buried, losing consciousness and being taken prisoner.[35] A.L. returned to England in January 1919; his condition quickly deteriorated. 'One night he seemed to be in action again as on the day in which he was buried and he woke up in wild excitement...In June 1919 he had a similar attack.' He was sent first to the General Hospital Winchester and then to the Ashurst, Oxford where he was treated by hypnosis, but he was difficult to hypnotize and gained no benefit from the treatment. A private cure was no more effective. He arrived at Queen Square in January 1920, age 24, occupation 'ex-soldier'. A.L. had already been ill for one year nine months when Dr Saunders gave him a diagnosis of 'neurasthenia following shell shock'. 'He can sleep in the day time,' wrote Dr Saunders, in his medical report,

> [but] the least noise or excitement may cause him to tremble all over or jump out of bed. He has pains in his head and a feeling that his head is going to burst. He often has hot and cold feelings in his back and 'bubbly, airy' feeling as if there was a lot of hair hanging down the front of his face. He has sometimes a rising or falling sensation of a few seconds duration. This also occurs in dreams when it lasts much longer. In his dream he is either falling or gasping for breath or something equally distressing.

After treatment, his condition 'improved'. On the evidence of this case, the soldiers who recovered and reintegrated did not necessarily suffer slight symptoms then, but many men such as A.L. did successfully find their way back into civilian life.

Second were the veterans less able to shed their symptoms or re-enter civilian life, and who either never recovered from the war or suffered a severe relapse some years afterwards. Supporters saw them as chronic and acute victims; medical examiners tended to believe these were cases of 'compensation neurosis'. One example illustrates how many men who ought to have successfully recovered instead lapsed back into illness. In 1921, an ex-serviceman from the other ranks received a 20 per cent 'attributable' final award. Since he had not finished his apprenticeship before joining up he was unable to get regular employment; instead he decided to start his own tobacconist's business, but this failed within two years. At the same time his father died, and being ineligible for work training or unemployment relief, he was readmitted as a long-term hospital case to a special Ministry of Pensions centre in 1924. In a general shakeout two years later, his file was reviewed. 'Case No.113 – given less than 20% attributable final award – pre-war apprentice at joiner (time not completed owing to enlistment) post war work on and off as joiner... he has always been ineligible for training as his assessment was less than 20% and he is now ineligible for the dole and has no prospects of employment.'[36]

Such cases were common through the 1920s.[37] In 1923 T.A. Ross, the psychoanalytically-minded Director of the Cassel Hospital for Nervous Diseases (set up in 1921 to treat civilian and war neuroses) described how such symptoms and circumstances conspired against the recovery of war neurotic ex-servicemen.[38] Ross noted particularly that while a pensioner was ill he was drawing a disability allowance, which, if he had a family, would keep that family in the necessities of life. If he got well his personal allowance would drop considerably and the family allowance would disappear. 'The man therefore who was getting well became, *ipso facto*, the prey of the most distressing thoughts imaginable. The streets were full of unemployed: what chance had he, with his long record of illness, to get a job by which he could earn a living? He must have known that he had none. To become well meant literally that he and his family would starve; to get well, therefore, was the greatest tragedy that could happen to him...'[39]

Third were cases of men who left the services apparently healthy, but whose mental condition later deteriorated; some of these are among the 40,000 pension claims made for mental disorders after the Armistice, but many others were without pensions and reluctant to acknowledge their own condition. As noted earlier, this was because many of the doctors who had treated shell shock cases went on to deal with war neurotic ex-servicemen, and continued to believe slow recovery signalled moral bankruptcy, and so, like all neurasthenics and malingerers before or during the war, they deserved no compensation for their illness. The Ministry of Pensions was often of the same opinion, but although many war neurotic ex-servicemen in this third group were denied pensions and therefore do not appear in the official figures, their conditions persisted.[40] This was the situation with one ex-lieutenant at the Cassel whose mild neurotic symptoms had deteriorated into 'borderline psychosis' by 1926. During the war E., who had served with the Royal Flying Corps and later in the infantry in Salonica, had become alcohol-dependent and had shown the kind of reckless self-confidence that was sometimes associated with officers close to traumatic neurosis.[41] The only note on treatment during the war, however, states that he was 'put in a darkened room by himself...for one month'. After the war, failing to adapt to civilian society, E. voluntarily withdrew from almost every contact with daily life.

Cut off from ordinary society and effective medical treatment for the first half of the 1920s, his case was only properly reviewed on 27 July 1925, when the Bristol Ministry of Pensions Board decided that these symptoms were directly attributable to the war. The Board report described his condition. 'Flushing of head, neck, etc. Nervous depression, headaches, insomnia. Has been in hospital 13 months to 5 weeks ago. Waiting to go to Cassel's Hospital...Condition profound obsession amounting almost to borderline psychosis. Recd. Admission to Cassel's Hospital...100% [disability payment] for 6 months.'[42] On the day of the patient's discharge from the Cassel, Dr Ross wrote to Sir Maurice Craig describing the results of the hospital's treatment: 'E., whom you sent here in the early Spring on account of morbid blushing, left today after about five months' stay, and I am glad to say he is feeling to all intents perfectly well. You may remember that he was unable to go into company, take any meals in public, and had latterly got into the habit of going out at night only. The symptoms had been present for nearly five years. He is now able to do everything with comfort. The only trouble about him is that he is now over thirty years of age, and has no profession and no job of any kind to go to.'[43]

Writing in 1943, the American medic D.A. Thom summed up what had been learned about traumatic neurosis since the First World War. 'The economic aspect of the problem is appalling when one considers the money spent on treatment, training and compensation. It can be said that the war neuroses begin early. They are long drawn out, they are difficult to treat, and they tend to increase for at least twenty-five years after the cessation of hostilities.'[44] As American ex-servicemen had the advantage of extensive facilities and treatment, such cases certainly persisted throughout the lives of the less privileged British war generation.[45] Clearly many war neurotic ex-servicemen were cured and re-entered normal family and working life. Many others did not. How men outside the official treatment network survived has largely gone unrecorded, though one suggestion is that their distressed mental state converted into physical symptoms such as debility, anaemia, gastritis or rheumatism.[46]

Of greater long-term importance, as the mental conditions of war became physical complaints, so the cultural significance of shell shock was transformed by imagination and memory. Siegfried Sassoon hinted at both these changes, more fully explored in the next chapter, in his description of war neurotic ex-servicemen in the 1930s:

> Shell shock. How many a brief bombardment had its long delayed after effect in the minds of these survivors, many of whom had looked at their companions and laughed while inferno did its best to destroy them. Not then was the evil hour, but now; now, in the sweating suffocation of nightmare, in paralysis of limbs, in the stammering of dislocated speech. Worst of all, in the disintegration of those qualities through which they had been so gallant and selfless and uncomplaining – this, in the finer type of man, was the unspeakable tragedy of shellshock; it was thus that their self-sacrifice was mocked and maltreated – they, who in the name of righteousness had been sent out to maim and slaughter their fellow man. In the name of civilisation these soldiers had been martyred, and it remains for civilisation to prove that their martyrdom wasn't a dirty swindle.[47]

10
Recall: The Great War in the Twentieth Century

The meaning of 'shell shock' (I)

Always an imprecise term, 'shell shock' attracts new layers of meaning with its growing distance in time and memory from the Great War.[1] In the last year of the hostilities, E.A. Mackintosh could show the condition straightforwardly as a horrifying, uncontrollable madness. In *War, the Liberator* (1918) he describes it as follows: 'The Corporal... collapsed suddenly with twitching hands and staring, frightened eyes, proclaiming the shell-shock he had held off while the work was to be done.'[2] Here, shell shock is synonymous with the most destructive images of industrial battle: bombardment in the trenches of the Western Front, the supposed passive suffering and obliteration of soldiers in the line, the long-term damage to the psyche and the spirit that the war inflicted on its participants. Twitching, staring and terror signify too the negative image of shell shock: the common fear of lunacy and the asylum that was also an important part of the condition's public profile in these years, as were the implicit military associations with cowardice, malingering and degeneracy. At the same time, Mackintosh allows sympathy and suggests heroic effort. Despite his strict devotion to duty, the awfulness of the war swamps the corporal's mind; moreover, the horror of the incident shows the severity of his sacrifice: losing his mind was just as terrible an injury as losing his face or legs.

By the mid-1920s, however, the growing public interest in Freudian ideas that so irritated Ministry of Pensions medics allows a more neutral discussion; 'psycho-neurosis' was now subject to strict, scientific analysis. Hence Fraser and Gibbon's comment in *Sailor and Soldier Words* (1925): 'Shell shock... Since the war, the term has been officially abolished, in favour of the technical term "Psycho-neurosis".'[3] Scientific

159

analysis was distant, though, from popular memory, in which the neurotic ex-serviceman stood on a street corner, twitching, with a sign around his neck, which stated: 'shell-shocked'.[4] By the mid-1930s, the bitterness and poverty that came with the slump give the condition another meaning. Now even a professional soldier writing with hindsight reflects the harsh judgement that the war generation handed down to 'the generals'. 'The most rapid way to shell-shock an army,' J.F.C. Fuller wrote in *Generalship* (1933), 'is to shell-proof its generals; for once the heart of an army is severed from its head the result is paralysis.'[5]

At the outbreak of the Second World War, neither troops nor generals had illusions about the destructive capacity of modern combat. Consequently, more psychologists were available to the troops, and psychological medicine, which had moved forward since 1918, was taken more seriously. This was in part because the treatment of traumatic neurosis had led doctors further towards the idea of industrial psychology, which in turn was used to assist the recruitment and at times questionable training techniques for soldiers in the Second World War.[6] Hence Graham Greene's 'There's not a finer shell-shock clinic in the country' in *Ministry of Fear* (1943), which demonstrates that by the mid-1940s, and in the midst of a major military conflict, in popular imagination shell shock was acknowledged and tolerated as a part of modern combat. At the same time, it is apparent from other sources that military leaders remained sceptical.[7] After 1945, shell shock recedes from the front line and back towards the home front taking on new, less military associations. In S. Kauffman's *The Philanderer* (1953), it is a distant echo of suffering, and perhaps a badge of victimhood, as in 'An unfortunate rambling man, supposed to have been shell-shocked in the war'.[8] While to *The Listener* (168/2, 9 February 1978) sixty years after the Armistice, a piece of bad news has the same destructive force as the explosion of a Howitzer 5.9 shell. 'Seeking relief from this shell-shock, I phoned a screenwriter friend.'[9]

The associations and implications of the term 'shell shock' have continued to change, especially during the revival of interest in the Great War after 1989. In the early 1980s, the British government agreed to give medical assessments to former Far Eastern prisoners of the Second World War. It was only after 1986, when the Ministry of Defence recognized post-traumatic stress disorder as a legitimate medical condition thereby making the state liable for the treatment and pensions of veterans of both Northern Ireland and the Falklands War, that a wider public debate became possible.[10] Recent discussion of 'post-traumatic stress disorder' and 'traumatic memory' has thus led to a recasting of shell shock as a form of these later conditions. Since then, just as interest in post-traumatic stress disorder and the revival of traumatic memories of childhood sexual abuse have allowed an examination of the moral values of modern society, so shell shock has become a mirror on the past reflecting back issues of contemporary concern: gender roles, class relations and human rights.

Between the 'strong' use of the term 'shell shock' to describe the worst destructive effects of the war, and the 'weak' use to describe an unpleasant emotional surprise or physical fatigue, there is a history of transmission through British culture that reaches from the Great War to the present day, a fragment of the fading collective memory. The postwar history of shell shock, which derives from imagination and memory, and remakes the condition after the Armistice through the work of memoirists, filmmakers, novelists and poets, is the subject of this chapter. Terms and histories overlap and interact with one another in this history. The meanings that we ascribe to shell shock today are difficult to disentangle from the events that took place during the war, and from the criss-cross of meanings that have grown through the years. This account begins, then, with the period when Great War traumatic neurosis acquired most of its meanings: the interwar years, then considers the conflicting images of the war from 1945 to 1989, and finally proceeds to the modern-day revival of interest in the Great War. To consider how shell shock is remembered following the three major turning points of the century, 1918, 1945 and 1989, is to understand one aspect of the memorialization of the First World War as it adapts itself, in Raphael Samuel's phrase, to 'the urgencies of the moment'.[11]

After 1918

The most heated debates during and after the First World War took place between 1917, when public knowledge and concern grew over possible miscarriages of justice, and 1923, when there was widespread public discussion following the *Report of the War Office Committee of Enquiry into 'Shell Shock'*. The military and political leaders who were largely responsible for the report had finessed shell shock during the war by naming it a 'special' disorder, by portraying psychological casualties as an unusual kind of war hero who deserved particular sympathy, and by remaining silent on the subject when it looked as if it might threaten military discipline. Towards the end of the war and afterwards though, ex-combatants, poets and novelists began exploring the wider cultural implications of shell shock. It is at this time that the condition starts its association with war disillusion and the refined, poetic sensibilities of Siegfried Sassoon and Wilfred Owen, with the brutalities of military injustice that were a part of (in Sassoon's words) the 'dirty swindle' of the war, and with the radical questioning of masculine identity and ideals taken up by Rebecca West and Virginia Woolf. All these ways of seeing shell shock became fruitful genres of war memory in later years.

The public's first concern during and after the war, which prompted in part the setting up of the War Office Committee of Enquiry, was the fully justified suspicion that soldiers were being court-martialled and executed as 'cowards' and 'malingerers' instead of receiving medical treatment. From time to time, relatives objected to the injustice of a court-martial, and these cases were publicized and raised by Members of Parliament such as Philip Snowden as well as by servicemen's magazines, especially *John Bull*. One such notorious court-martial decision was made in the case of Sub-Lieutenant Edwin Dyett, whose deranged behaviour at the time of his arrest did not prevent him from becoming, in 1917, a very rare instance of a shell-shocked officer executed for desertion.[12] Aggrieved relatives were only one group with an interest in the condition at this time. Postwar medical specialists such as C.S. Myers understood that, in retrospect, shell shock was a first step towards the new study of industrial psychology.

Fictional and poetic accounts take an interest in shell shock too, and in literary circles the condition symbolized the wider rejection of and revulsion against the war, especially as it was presented early on in heroic rhetoric. One example of a combatant's rejection of war that invokes shell shock is *Naked Warriors* (1919), Herbert Read's collection of poems published just months after the end of the conflict; others include A.P. Herbert's *The Secret Battle* (1920) and Wilfred Owen's *Collected Poems* (1920).[13] *Naked Warriors* is one of the bleakest accounts of war's destructive effects on the human body and spirit. In 'Kneeshaw goes to war', the protagonist, blank and thoughtless, joins up, trains, encounters the horrors of war and loses a leg. This injury gives Kneeshaw self-awareness, but at the cost of immense bitterness and pain. In 'Killed in action', a soldier, exhausted by the endless cruelties of the war, commits suicide in no man's land. In 'The execution of Cornelius Vane' Read describes the mental confusion of a soldier who tries to flee the front, is caught, and executed for desertion:

> But Cornelius sprang to his feet, his pale face set.
> He willed nothing, saw nothing, only before him

Were the free open fields:
To the fields he ran.[14]

This account articulates the already well-established resentment against
the injustices and ironies of the war among some groups of writers and
intellectuals. Yet if the despair of this account did not yet fit the wider
mood of British society as it tried to come to terms with its damage and
escape from its gloom, nor did A.P. Herbert's more careful approach.
According to Winston Churchill, who wrote a preface to *The Secret Battle*,
thoughts of the war were 'a little swept aside by the revulsion of the public
mind for anything to do with the awful period just ended'.[15] Nevertheless, Herbert's view of shell shock had something in common with the
opinion of aggrieved relatives, newspaper editors and campaigning re-
formers who argued that psychological casualties were brave men pushed
beyond endurance by a combination of military incompetence and medical ignorance. The narrator of *The Secret Battle* argues his case at the
conclusion of the novel: 'This book is not an attack on any person, on
the death penalty, or on anything else, though if it makes people think
about these things, so much the better. I think I believe in the death
penalty – I do not know. But I do not believe in Harry being shot. That is
the gist of it; that my friend was shot for cowardice – and he was one of the
bravest men I ever knew.'[16]

The Secret Battle presents the case of a man unjustly executed for cowardice, and to ensure the appearance of fairness, Herbert neatly summarizes all sides of the shell shock debate around 1920. The story, narrated by
his comrade and friend Benson, concerns Harry Penrose, an officer who
serves at Gallipoli and then on the Western Front. Herbert's study, based
on the case of Sub-Lieutenant Edwin Dyett, recounts a series of incidents
that lead Penrose to doubt his own bravery, especially when men under
his command die.[17] As he loses his belief in the romance of war and
comes to see it as 'a disgusting business, to be endured, like a dung-hill',
Penrose determines to keep up appearances, despite suffering dysentery
and nervous exhaustion.[18] Leaving the Dardanelles, Harry returns to
England, recovers and gets married, but once back in the war, this time
in France, one incident after another increases his fear of being caught
under fire after dark. Harry describes his recurring dreams to Benson:

I dream of them [explosions] every night...usually it's an enormous endless plain, full of shell-holes, of course, and raining like hell,
and I walk for miles (usually with you) looking over my shoulder,
waiting for the shells to come...and then I hear that savage kind of

high-velocity shriek, and I get into a ditch and lie down there ... and then one comes that I know by the sound is going to burst on top of me ... and I wake up simply sweating with funk. I've never told anybody but you about this, not even Peggy, but she says I wake her up sometimes, making an awful noise.[19]

Throughout, Harry's behaviour is honourable, but events constantly undermine his determination; Herbert makes it obvious that while there were many ways for men to avoid disaster, injustices did occur.

Harry's next misfortune, which leads to his eventual execution, is to come under the command of Colonel Philpot, who suffers all the worst vices of the 'old men' running to war: Penrose is temporary, youthful, capable and competent; Philpot is a regular, elderly, slothful and obtuse. Colonel Philpot's malice turns a relatively minor incident into a court-martialling offence when Penrose is accused of running back from the lines under heavy fire; when he tells the truth about his condition, he is ignored. After the brief court-martial Penrose is found guilty and the decision is passed up to higher military authorities, but before the final verdict Benson and the other men in the company discuss the case, as the narrator says, 'to show the kind of feeling there was in the regiment – because that is the surest test of the rightness of these things'.[20] One soldier speaks against Penrose and for the honour of the regiment; another distinguishes between fear and yielding to fear; a third points to the success of the Australian troops without the death penalty. The consensus, though not unopposed, is that shell shock '*is* a medical question, really. Only the doctors don't seem to recognise – or else they aren't allowed to – any stage between absolute shell-shock, with your legs flying in all directions, and just ordinary skrim-shanking'. It should be described therefore not with the loaded phraseology of morality or discipline, but with the neutral terminology of medical science. Whatever its causes, 'the doctors ought to be able to test when a man's really had enough'.[21]

Herbert makes his case cautiously, so as not to alienate conservative readers, as the question of military mistreatment of war traumatized soldiers was still pressing when *The Secret Battle* was published. Even by 1920 though, the issue was less urgent, slowly becoming a 'lesson' of the war and a symbol of its cruelty. In fiction the shell-shocked survivor quickly becomes a stock figure too, a sign of destroyed manhood back from the war and struggling to survive in the 1920s and 1930s. Shell-shocked men now began to appear in genre fictions such as Gilbert Frankenau's wartime romance *Peter Jackson, Cigar Merchant* (1920) and the detective novels of Dorothy L. Sayers such as *Whose Body?* (1923) and *Busman's Honeymoon* (1937).[22] Like H. Read, A.P. Herbert, with his sensitive story of the effects of traumatic neurosis on family life, tries to locate the psychological disturbances of 1914–18 on the Home Front as well as the Western Front. Two other remarkable works of fiction, both of which have become defining accounts, do the same; complex and ambiguous, they explore the effects of the war on the male psyche, and the social pressures that influenced war neurotic ex-servicemen.

Rebecca West's *The Return of the Soldier*, initially published in serial form starting in January 1918, then as a complete work in June 1918, has been reworked twice in later revivals of interest in the Great War: in 1928 as a play by Jay Van Druton, and in 1982 as a feature film by Alan Bridges, starring Alan Bates and Julie Christie.[23] Set during the war, but at the furthest possible remove from the front, in a Thames valley English country house with no male inhabitants, West's novel contrasts the imperfectly expressed womanly spirit of nurturing and life-giving with a manly respite from the destruction and death of the war, showing how both men and women could shrug off the roles assigned to them by society, but only momentarily. Chris Baldry is the officer who comes back from the Western Front to Baldry Court, where his wife Kitty and his cousin Jenny, the narrator, await him. Chris's 'shell shock' comes in the form of amnesia which blocks out all memory of his married life with Kitty and leads him back instead to Margaret Allington, with whom he had an affair fifteen years earlier. West's version of 'shell shock' is not concerned therefore with clinical details, but with masculinity, femininity and relations between men and women.

With the help of Margaret and the psychoanalytically-minded Dr Anderson, and partly against their better judgement, Chris is brought back to the terrors of his war experience and in returning he is forced to give up both his decency and his innocence, to become again the fighting man society expects him to be. Chris's return takes him from one state in which 'He would not be quite a man' to another, where manliness means fighting and the knowledge of death.[24] Jenny's conclusion is that both men and women are trapped, and both are victims of the war:

> He [Chris] walked not loose-limbed like a boy, as he had done that very afternoon, but with a soldier's hard tread upon the heel. It recalled to me that, bad as we were, we were yet not the worst circumstances of his return. When we had lifted the yoke of our embraces from his shoulders he would go back to that flooded trench

in Flanders under that sky more full of flying death than clouds, to that No Man's Land where bullets fall like rain on the rotting faces of the dead...[25]

In another consideration of the meaning of shell shock, however, the soldier chooses not to return. Rather than accept the values of proportion (seeing the self in the light of wider social demands) and conversion (submitting to authority), Smith chooses suicide. It would be misleading though to single out Septimus Smith as the only aspect of *Mrs Dalloway* (1925) related to the war and its meaning, especially in a novel that is spun on the intricate web of connections between human lives. Virginia Woolf's portrait of the world after war has much wider ambitions, but one of the novel's achievements is an intimate understanding of mental disorder and its treatment.[26]

In particular, Woolf's portrait of shell shock shows close attention to the public debates of the early 1920s. The author very likely knew of the *Report of the War Office Committee of Enquiry into 'Shell Shock'*, which was presented to Parliament and discussed widely in the press in August 1922, shortly before she conceived the character of Smith in October 1922.[27] Woolf had also reviewed Siegfried Sassoon's wartime collections of poetry *The Old Huntsman* (1917) and *Counter-attack* (1918) and met the author in 1924. The character of Smith seems to draw on this too. For example, Sassoon's horrifying vision of dead bodies on the streets of London echoes in Smith's hallucinations.[28] Woolf's account of shell shock and its cure also derives from what she herself knew of depression: Smith's symptoms resemble those of depression as much as traumatic neurosis; his treatment is a composite of Woolf's experiences with Dr George Savage and Sir Maurice Craig, both of whom were in some way involved in the treatment of traumatic neurosis during the war.[29] *Mrs Dalloway* can hardly be reduced to a piece of social criticism or a source of historical evidence, but in the context of a discussion of the developing meanings of the Great War in British society, it has some defining features. Already, for example, shell shock is associated with officers, not men from the other ranks. Moreover, it is associated with the poetic sensibility of Siegfried Sassoon, whose initials are also those of Septimus Smith, while Smith is described as a sensitive 'poet from Stroud'. *Mrs Dalloway* marks, therefore, a strengthening of the association between shell shock and poetic sensibility, the officer ranks, postwar disillusion and the feminist debate on masculine identity.

The story of Owen and Sassoon also turned shell shock into an artistic rite of passage, giving authority to the words of both poets. The publication of Owen's collected poems introduced by Siegfried Sassoon in December 1920 reinforced these associations, as did Owen's draft preface.[30] The reviews of December 1920 were quick to take up Owen's advice to look at war's pity rather than war's poetry, all the more powerful because it came from beyond the grave. One reviewer in *The Athenaeum* took up this theme: 'The vehemence and the agony which they [the poems] manifest are, and compel, conviction. None but the most sincere philosophy could express itself so. There is no other philosophy in modern war, with its monstrous attacks doomed to failure nine times out of ten, its brutalising standstills with slow mental and sudden physical butcheries.'[31] Written a matter of weeks after the second Remembrance Day ceremonies, these words show how Owen's work managed eventually to capture and define the nation's mood, first as it was experienced, and a decade or more later as it was recalled. Similarly, *The Observer's* reviewer also stressed the theme of remembering the war: 'But the world turns aside from that which makes it feel uncomfortable, uncertain whether after all any idea justifies the mutual inflicting by human individuals on human individuals ... suffocation by gas, death by gangrene, castration, blindness, and insanity. For that is what war is.'[32] While Rupert Brooke's *Collected Poems* sold 300,000 copies and Owen's first volume sold just 730 copies, it was Owen's vision of the war that eventually prevailed.[33] The discontent of the postwar world finds its voice in Owen's words, as poets, critics and readers all came to recognize. One reviewer wrote, as he surely could not have done a year earlier: 'In reading the twenty-three poems now collected it is almost impossible to conceive of any other point of view.'[34] Owen's growing reputation was no accident. It came about because of the quality of his poems, but also through the advocacy of his fellow soldier-poets, especially Edmund Blunden and Siegfried Sassoon.

Edmund Blunden's 'Memoir', published as a part of the preface to the 1931 revised edition of Owen's collected poems, further advances his reputation and influence through the 1930s. Blunden begins his account of Owen's life by emphasizing his subject's credentials as a poet, who because of the misfortune of his times was destined to make war his most important subject. 'Twelve years of uneasy peace have passed since the war, among its final victims, took Wilfred Owen, and ten years since the choice edition of his poems by his friend Siegfried Sassoon revealed to lovers of poetry and the humanities how great a joy has departed.'[35] Blunden then moves Owen rapidly towards Craiglockhart and 'the friendship of Mr Sassoon' that 'supplied the answer to the petition for a poet's companionship' and in these experiences 'The trial brought out his greatness and directed his passion. With a clear and spacious view of the function of poetry, he rapidly produced the poems which have made him famous.'[36] Thereafter Owen grows closer to Sassoon's circle of friends and plans a collection of poems, but by late July 1918, he is shortly to go abroad again, only to die just before the war's end. However, Owen's soldierly experience and his poetic vision, his life, work and death, Blunden explains, have a continuing and special relevance:

> In the coming race there will be a multitude of mirage-builders, and the business which now engages the heart and brain of so many leaders in every country is how to save them from the normal consequences of their own illusions, of those who, for whatever purpose, encourage and exploit them. Here Owen will be found achieving his object of pleading; being dead he speaks. He speaks as a soldier; as a mind, surveying the whole process of wasted spirit, art, and blood in all its instant and deeper evils; as a poet, giving his reader picture and tone that wherever they are considered afford a fresh profundity, for they are combinations of profound recognitions.[37]

Against the background of anti-war demonstrations, the rise of fascism and the widespread influence of left-wing political belief in the Britain of the 1930s, the suffering, dissidence and vision of Sassoon and Owen made them attractive figures to the younger generation who grew to maturity in the years after the Great War. It is certainly at this time that they come to be seen as 'anti-war'; that 'anti-war' is conflated with pacifism in movements like the Peace Pledge Union; and that Owen in particular attracts the admiration of the leading poets such as Cecil Day Lewis, W.H. Auden and Stephen Spender.[38] The continuing power of Sassoon's vision is illustrated in Gilles MacKinnon's film *Regeneration* (1997), where his 1937 sentiments are projected back to 1917 and in an argument – an imaginary exchange with W.H.R. Rivers – the poet describes the war as a 'dirty swindle'. The memory of the war, and shell shock as a prominent part of it, took shape, then, between 1918 and 1945, but like war neurotic ex-servicemen themselves, the harshest recollections were slowly fading back into the fabric of British society.

After 1945

Between 1945 and 1989 the British view of the Great War changed from a subject for old soldiers in their bar-room reminiscences and their published memoirs to a subject for serious academic debate; from a vivid reality that still shaped the lives of ex-servicemen and their families to a fading remnant of collective memory, brought back to mind only by the Armistice Day celebrations or thoughts about the licensing laws. The accounts published on the war between 1945 and 1989 reflect this in their type and number. They range from the late memoirs and fictions of old soldiers still published into the 1960s, to versions of the Great War shaped by the anti-nuclear and anti-Vietnam war movements, to the later pioneering academic studies. All these have changed the various meanings of shell shock.

One account that perhaps rightly belongs to the interwar period is *Siegfried's Journey* (1946), the final part of Sassoon's second version of his life story, this time casting aside the transparent fictionalization of the earlier *Sherston Trilogy*.[39] *Siegfried's Journey* is noteworthy because unlike the earlier trilogy, the protagonist becomes Sassoon the poet, and the author is thereby able to describe his own recollections of Owen during the war. This is an 'authentic' voice from the war then, and because of Sassoon's reputation and the interest of the younger generation, it is an authoritative voice. This is also an account already inflected by the reworked collective memory of the slump. Written twenty-five years or more after Sassoon first met Owen, it is also a notable attempt to make Owen live up to his steadily growing reputation. Sassoon is especially keen to limit the extent of his own influence. He claims, for example, that his contribution was to lend a copy of Barbusse's *Le Feu*, 'which set him alight as no other book had done', and then to pass on a few 'technical dodges' and 'simplifying suggestions'.[40] Furthermore, Sassoon freely admits that between 1917 and 1946 his own understanding of his meeting with Owen changed drastically. Initially, he did not recognize the author's particular genius, nor did he realize until later 'that Wilfred had endured worse things than I had realised', but in retrospect he, like later generations, would look back on Owen differently:

His face – what would it have become? While calling him back in memory I have been haunted by the idea of the unattainable features of those who have died in youth. Borne away from them by the years, we – with our time troubled looks and diminished alertness – have submitted to many a gradual detriment of change. But the young poet of twenty-five years ago remains his word-discovering self. His futureless eyes encounter ours from the faintly smiling portrait, un-conscious of the privilege and deprivation of never growing old, conscious of the dramatic illusion of completeness that he is destined to create.[41]

This is the voice of the war generation ageing and yet unable to forget the dead who could not grow old; and of Owen becoming that generation's noblest example of anguish and loss, both physical and mental.

After 1945, the smoke and noise of more recent wars further obscures the memory of the Great War, as does the struggle for survival in the later 1940s and early 1950s, and it is not until the late 1950s that public interest in the Great War begins to grow once more. This renewal of interest is partly due to the nearing of the fiftieth anniversary of the outbreak of the Great War, in 1964, but the dominant images of the war at this time, of lively, first-hand recollection by the many participants still living, as well as the cruder view of mud and blood and bungling generals, were also influenced by more recent developments. One such development was the renewed awareness of working-class life in British society that separated 'us' the soldiers from 'them' the generals; another was the teaching of the war poets in state schools; finally there was the anti-war movement of the later 1950s and early 1960s and especially the huge support among teenagers, women and many others for the Campaign for Nuclear Disarmament. Because of this, and because they tapped into soldier's memories and civilian's recollections, which were both critical and affectionate, works like *In Flanders Field* (1958) by Leon Woolf, *The Donkeys* (1961) by Alan Clark, and the Theatre Workshop's production of *Oh What a Lovely War*, first performed at the Theatre Royal, Stratford, in March 1963, appealed to a wide audience.[42] *Oh What a Lovely War*, for example, used the conventions of music hall variety performance to escape the already over-familiar 'realism' of the war poets, and to recall life in Britain during the war years. The play used songs, pierrot-actors and slide projections of photographs, newspaper advertisements and propaganda posters to portray the conflict as the war generation and its children remembered. The satire boom of the early 1960s, with its disdain for the supposed hypocrisy of political and religious leaders, and its suspicion of figures of authority, is a part of the backdrop to the production. So too is the attack on 'the establishment' of the time – the political, business and military leaders who had, it was believed, brought the nation to its state of postwar ruin. Several scenes highlight the apparent conspiracy of interests that worked against the citizen soldier. For example, at a grouse-shooting party British, French, German and American munitions manufacturers talk about their interest in continuing the war and the 'peace scares' they want to avoid.[43]

Similarly in *The Donkeys* Alan Clark gives an account of the destruction of the professional Army, which was 'machine-gunned, gassed and finally buried in 1915'.[44] In the final pages of *The Donkeys*, Clark pictures 'The Generals' enjoying their lively New Year 1915 celebration in London, while in the trenches the troops sing 'I don't want to die / I want to go home'.[45]

Old soldiers were still writing too, but their attitude was increasingly at odds with the prevailing images of horror and irony, and in the case of Theatre Workshop, class antagonism and gallows humour. In *Soldier From the Wars Returning* (1965) Charles Carrington stresses how remote this new view of the war seemed from the memory of participants:

> The craze for war-books died down in 1931 and did not reappear until a generation had arisen who scarcely remembered the Second World War. By this time, we veterans of the First were so far removed from the correct modes of thought as to be relics of antiquity, buried beneath many historical strata. Not only did the pacifist mood of the early nineteen-thirties conceal our true character, but the bellicose traditions of the Spanish Civil War and the Second World War had overlaid it with new conceptions of military ethic.[46]

Carrington's memory, unlike some other re-creations of the First World War in the 1960s, was not of existential horror, farce and mental derangement, but of a war that gathered men together, made them newly aware of themselves and their world, and created unforgettable high points in their lives. But then, as Alan Clark noted in *The Donkeys*, the Great War had become by 1961 'as remote as the Crimea'.[47]

As veterans' voices gradually faded in the 1970s and 1980s, other influences began to reshape recent understandings of shell shock. The Second World War and the Vietnam War both produced their own experiences of war neurosis and their own crops of war neurotic ex-servicemen. However, while the soldiers who suffered 'combat fatigue' in the Second World War were in many cases apparently able to re-adapt to civilian society, American ex-servicemen from the Vietnam War, suffering both psychological disorder and social disorientation, were not. Robert Jay Lifton brought the condition of Vietnam veterans to the public's attention in his book *Home from the War* (1973). Lifton and veterans' rights activists lobbied throughout the 1970s for the acceptance of what they termed 'Post-traumatic Stress Disorder', and with the official acceptance of PTSD in 1980 by the American Psychiatric Association came the popularization of traumatic memory.[48]

This affected powerfully the perception of all groups of psycho-logical casualties; retrospectively their experience during and after the various conflicts of the twentieth century began to look quite different. One example of this is the case of French conscripts in the Algerian War between 1954 and 1962. After veterans commissioned a psycho-logical report in the early 1980s to discover the extent of post-traumatic stress disorder, state authorities were forced to recognize the damage done to men in combat zones that never officially existed.[49] Meanwhile in Britain following the Falklands conflict in 1982 the authorities discovered during a reassessment of surviving British prisoners of war from the Far Eastern camps that up to 60 per cent continued to suffer post-traumatic stress disorder.[50] Influenced too by the growing problem of psychological disorders in veterans from Northern Ireland and the Falklands the Ministry of Defence recognized PTSD as a legitimate diagnosis in 1986.[51] The British veterans did not have a film-maker of the calibre of Bertrand Tavernier to make a documentary like *The Undeclared War* (1992); nevertheless, the later themes of memory and trauma now began to affect the recollection of the Great War.

After 1989

The post-1989 revival of interest in shell shock as a metonymic symbol of the war may also be illustrated by the French historian Pierre Nora's belief that the mechanisms of social memory most strongly found in 'primitive' societies are disappearing from the post-industrial West, and depend increasingly on the officially organized recollection of museums and monuments, archives and anniversaries.[52] Hence the reconsider-ation prompted by the six-year cycle of remembrance, beginning in September 1989 and ending in August 1995, which marked the passage of five decades since the Second World War. Within this cycle fell several other significant dates including the 100th anniversary of Wilfred Owen's birth in March 1993 and the 80th anniversary of the start of the Great War in August 1994. These anniversaries signalled important events in the national past, but it was not inevitable that they should ignite such public interest nor that they should provoke such wide-spread discussion. One explanation for this apparently new concern with public commemoration is that it marks an attempt to create a new sense of 'temporal coherence' within the collective memory at a time when older identities such as the nation state are apparently be-coming less important.[53]

In this view it has been possible to reaffirm national and personal British identities, and to address current concerns by looking again at those most prominent moments of national unity: the First and the Second World Wars. This in turn led to the revival of interest in shell shock in both popular memory and literature after 1989 as one of many ritually repeated themes considered since the Great War that continues with each re-examination to provide new connections between past and present. Alistair Thompson's work on the public and private memories of the ANZAC troops who fought at Gallipoli is suggestive here.[54] He argues that as the public myth of the campaign was used to promote the idea of Australia's birth, it became remote to some participants, who in turn recomposed their recollections of the war to match popular memory. Films such as Peter Weir's *Gallipoli* (1981) also changed the soldier's view of what he had experienced. There is no evidence on whether British shell shock veterans were similarly affected by Sassoon's writing on the war, or, to give just one example, by Alan Bridges' 1982 version of *The Return of the Soldier.*

The 1990s saw the publication of a number of accounts of shell shock, witnessing a revival of interest in the subject. These include one by the lawyer Anthony Babbington, whose main concerns are military history and military injustice; another by the journalist Wendy Holden, based on the Channel 4 television series, which concentrates on medical treatment and patient experience; a third by the historian Hans Binne- veld, on the development of military psychology.[55] Each of these ac- counts traces the psychological disorders of warfare through the twentieth century, each argues that although there may be variations according to time and place, shell shock is a universal disorder that appears wherever the mind is placed under severe stress. Moreover, these accounts all provide a roughly similar picture of the condition, mentioning the opposition between techniques used by Dr Yealland and Dr Rivers, the injustices done to soldiers who were falsely accused of cowardice and malingering, and the wrongful execution of certain men as a result. These are important issues, but as I have tried to show, they give a restricted and in some ways skewed picture, a view based on powerful communal memories of the Great War. To understand better how these cultural memories function in the present, I will discuss here Pat Barker's *Regeneration Trilogy*, a popular, widely praised fiction that may stand in for the wider debate on the meaning of the Great War in recent years.[56]

Set between July 1917, the date of Sassoon's 'Declaration', and November 1918, when Owen was killed in action on the banks of the

Sambre-Oise canal, *The Regeneration Trilogy* takes W.H.R. Rivers as its major true-life protagonist. Its reworking of the Great War tells several stories, including those of Owen, Sassoon, Rivers and Yealland, and in doing so it reinterprets one of the most powerful myths of the war for a modern audience. The trilogy became one of the bestsellers of the 1990s; and the third volume, *The Ghost Road*, won the Booker Prize in 1996; *Regeneration* became a big budget motion picture directed by Gilles Mackinnon (1997) and starring Jonathan Pryce as Rivers (interestingly, a film version of *Mrs Dalloway*, directed by Marleen Gorris, was also released in the same year). Barker's work is therefore responsible in part for triggering the revival of interest in shell shock in the 1990s, although it is also a part of the wider resurgence of interest in the Great War that began after 1989. In addition to the true-life historical characters Barker is concerned with the social issues that are of interest to a modern audience: shell shock treatment and military justice as human rights issues, women's involvement in the pacifist movement during the war, and the temporary shifts in gender and class relations within Home Front society between 1914 and 1918. In describing the details of shell shock treatment and in outlining its meaning Barker follows the historian Eric Leed and the feminist critic Elaine Showalter. It was Leed who argued that modern identity was remade by the experience of the war, and Showalter who believed shell shock to be an epidemic of male hysteria that helped redefine the gender roles of men and women in wartime and postwar British society. Within this format of mixed fact and fiction therefore, Barker is able to revive the question that has always been asked about shell shock: what does it show about human nature, and particularly masculine identity?

Symbolized by the nerve regeneration experiment that Dr William Rivers carried out before the war with his colleague Dr Henry Head, her answer is in the theme that unifies the trilogy. Together the two scientists mapped out the regrowth of nerves which they had observed in cases of accidental injury using Head as their experimental subject; in doing so they made the distinction between the 'protopathic' and the 'epicritic' sensibilities, a division that Rivers comes increasingly to question.[57] The first sensations of early nerve regeneration, Rivers and Head found, were primitive, intensely painful, 'all or nothing' – protopathic; the later renewal of sensation was refined, discriminating and sensitive – epicritic.[58] *The Regeneration Trilogy* describes this division not only within Rivers but also in all the major characters; it chronicles the ways in which the war upsets the balance in each of them and their attempts to reorient themselves. The injury that the war does to the nerves of each man leads to a painful regrowth that should arm them to manage in their new environment; sometimes, however, it proves inadequate.

In Rivers, as the doctor whose job it is to uphold the values of state and collective society, this duality is expressed as increasing doubts about his work, which is to heal the patient's mind so that he might return to killing and being killed.[59] Owen and Sassoon are also divided against themselves: both are 'sensitive' poets who object to the way the war is conducted and yet believe that their moral authority is based on continued participation. Stressing the divisions within human nature that the war brought out, Barker shows both aspects of Owen: an active killer as well as suffering victim:

> I [Prior] saw him [Owen] in the attack, caped and masked in blood, sieze a machine-gun and turn it on its previous owners at point-blank range. Like killing fish in a bucket. And I wonder if he sees those faces, grey, open-mouthed faces, life draining out of them before the bullets hit, as I see the faces of the men I killed in the counter-attack. I won't ask. He wouldn't answer if I did. I wouldn't *dare* ask.[60]

The reinterpretation of male trauma during the First World War, initially articulated by West and Woolf shortly before and after the Armistice, and revived by Showalter in the 1980s, thus makes a dramatically successful reappearance in the 1990s. *Regeneration* is distinguished not least by its vivid retelling of the encounter between Owen and Sassoon. The story has been told repeatedly since 1917, and in one sense Barker can add little to it; several set-piece scenes are therefore dramatic re-creations of other accounts. For example, *Siegfried's Journey*, which includes Sassoon's own version of events at Craiglockhart, and Yealland's notorious description of treatment in *Hysterical Disorders of Warfare*, contrasted somewhat misleadingly with the proto-Freudian techniques of Rivers reported in his paper 'The Repression of War Experience'.[61] Barker enlists shell shock as a part of a wider questioning of social values: the war matters because it prompts its participants to reconsider their beliefs, to question the difference between health and sickness, loyalty and betrayal, civilization and savagery. At the centre of this radical questioning of normative values is the issue of gender identity, so for Barker, shell shock signals the repression of men, their status as victims of, and rebels against, imposed gender roles. In part then, the author of *Regeneration* is remaking the oldest recollections of shell shock.

The meaning of 'shell shock' (II)

Looking back across the twentieth century, in one sense, the meanings of the Great War viewed through the prism of shell shock have remained wholly stable. The injustice of the capital courts-martial becomes the injustice of the Great War itself; the 'unmanned' warriors of wartime become the unemployed, poverty-stricken and neurotic ex-servicemen of peacetime; the desperate, neurotic, compensation claimant becomes the symbol of lifelong war damage inflicted on millions of veterans. All these images pass down from the Great War and revive at times when they find new relevance in contemporary public debate. In another sense, though, the memory of shell shock is an entirely unstable condition. Like the symptoms of traumatic neurosis, it slips from one part of the collective mind to another, changing its name and its form as surrounding conditions and expectations alter. The memory of shell shock has remained potent too, because it has become the first and most powerful expression of the destructive effects of industrial warfare on the mind, of the war generation's tragedy.

11
Conclusion

In the second decade of the twentieth century a number of European poets and writers, members of artistic movements including the Futurists, Imagists and Dadaists, declared in their manifestos the limits and inadequacies of language.[1] In 1912, for instance, the Russian Futurists invented the term 'zaum', which expressed 'the crisis of confidence suffered by language when confronted with the modern world'; two years later British soldiers on the Western Front invented another term which described that same emergency.[2] Yet while 'zaum' was a metaphor, audible in the artist's salon and a public performance hall in Moscow or St Petersburg, 'shell shock' was a bodily collapse of reason and language to be heard first in the trenches of the Western Front, and later, by private appointment only, in the consultant's clinic or in the veteran's suburban home. It was in these shut-off spaces that the stutterers, gaggers and forgetters of the First World War failed to articulate their trauma, and demonstrated more eloquently than any artistic statement the modern era's failure of words.

The soldiers' experience of shell shock during the Great War was a function of the modern industrial society that these men had lived in well before 1914. Labourers had long been accustomed to having their activities measured and regulated precisely, to working by strict schedules and orders, and to specializing in various kinds of intense physical activity. With this industrialization of life and labour came new mental states, and in turn, this led to the greater number and visibility of trauma, hysteria, neurasthenia and mental fatigue cases. The men who suffered these conditions were examined and treated as a function of their work, they were judged by the criteria of employment fitness and non-employment compensation, and they were found wanting. Forty years or more before the Great War then, medical, military and political professionals began to set out the cultural expectations and practical routines that would shape the appearance of shell shock; these conditions were the prerequisite to its arrival.

British medical practitioners were wary of the new male hysteria, shell shock, just as they had been circumspect with the earlier women's hysterias like neurasthenia. They initially saw it either as a variation on such pre-war disorders, or as a form of invisible physical injury. Doctoring such patients was in any case a low priority, and although there were some well-known hospitals, the majority of psychological casualties were treated by non-specialists in small hospitals spread throughout Britain. Here, recovery was often slow, discharge premature, cure incomplete. The medical profession made some important advances in the theory of traumatic neurosis treatment and they were able to put these into practice and share them in their own specialist medical community, but this did not translate into better treatments or standards of care for the majority of soldiers, members of the other ranks. The approach of professional Army doctors and military leaders was determined by military need and, indirectly, eugenic theory. Although they were important for their moral stand against the predominant view, dissenting medics in the field were the rare exception; although they were important for their theoretical contribution and for the soldiers they treated, progressive and academic psychologists were far outnumbered. The majority of doctors were Army traditionalists, alienists, insurance and malingering experts, or inexpert general practitioners. For these medics, the traumatic neuroses of war only ever received partial recognition: a physical wound was still necessary to call a soldier a true casualty of war.

Shell shock was the subject of widespread debate and concern throughout the war both in France and in Britain. The military view remained that it was a threat to manpower, an excuse for lack of discipline or evasion of duty. Especially prominent among higher ranking officers and professional regular RAMC doctors was the opinion that the complaint resulted from fear and ignorance, which led to widespread panic and cowardice. This view meant that Army medical policy was preoccupied with discrediting and subverting the very idea of combat-related psychological disorders. The main groups advocating policy change were journalists and politicians who advocated soldiers' rights in Britain and military leaders who responded to the startling numbers of psychological casualties recorded in the second half of 1916 in France. In Britain shell shock caught the public imagination early in the war; superficially, it was a simple, comprehensible condition which, experts argued, could be quickly and simply cured with the correct treatment. Its imaginative and emotional appeal resulted in political controversy, especially in the latter part of the war when courts-martial procedure and form of treatment came under close scrutiny. By the Armistice a significant difference already existed between the personal experience and the popular perception of the complaint.

Shell shock was made as opposing definitions and interests clashed, as each interest group promoted its own cause: Home Front morale was encouraged using shell shock treatment as an example of the remarkable achievements of wartime medicine, and by fund-raising campaigns; state expenditure was confined through administrative policy; the betterment of soldiers' welfare came through political and newspaper campaigning. Exchanges between patient and doctor were oppositional in character, but also collaborative, though the patient was usually in a weaker position. Army doctors often blocked departure from the field; many soldiers, traumatized or not, agreed that this was the best 'cure'. While some soldiers felt sorry for such men, war neurotic servicemen were also ridiculed and distrusted as cowards, lunatics and malingerers. Soldiers of all ranks, but especially officers, censured themselves for the sake of their comrades and for the sake of appearances. There were no significant changes in attitude or policy during the war. Improvements, usually the result of isolated efforts by individual doctors working on the Western Front, were local and minimal.

On the Home Front treatment varied dramatically in both type and quality. While public and medical campaigns and publications tried to stress that psychological casualties were the equal of wounded soldiers, those in charge of treatment only begrudgingly acknowledged such opinions. For their own part, some soldiers resented the cures they received, but most appear to have accepted them, sometimes reluctantly and in full awareness of their paradox. Many mentally unfit men were allowed into the Army and then abandoned after they broke down; most doctors associated shell shock with physical concussion or a particular event such as an explosion. Most cases were traced back to the experience of combat, though not to disillusion with the war. Pro-war and anti-German sentiments meant soldiers were often distressed that they could not continue in the front line.

Many of the best-known sources on shell shock detail the experience of officers; the majority of shell-shocked soldiers were from the other ranks. The conditions in which officers worked and the nature of their work meant in part that they suffered different stresses. Much of the distinction between officers and the other ranks was the product of tradition and social convention, as treatments, hospital regimes and the attitudes of medics and patients show. After the war this often put officers in a much better position to recover. War neurotic ex-servicemen without financial, family and employer support were far more likely to remain unemployed, to be in hospital or to claim money and medical assistance from the state. The poorly arranged demobilization, the inadequate treatment of ex-servicemen and the outdated policies of the Ministry of Pensions all blighted the lives of war neurotic ex-servicemen. As with many other groups of disabled ex-servicemen, issues of morality, heredity and parsimony continued to guide policy.

Even as the war ended shell shock was entering the culture and quickly establishing itself as a symbol of the war. With the changed mood of the postwar period, the silences and reassessments that came in the 1920s, shell shock transcended the experience of the individual soldier and became a symbol of the anguish the troops suffered and the betrayal they endured after the Armistice. The memory of shell shock has therefore been remade many times to suit the mood of the moment, but there are also some enduring themes. First, shell shock represents the experience of all soldiers in the war, and the mental distress of the few is taken as a symbol of the suffering of all. Second, shell shock has associations with Sassoon and Owen and through them with ideas of anti-war sentiment and disillusion with the war. Third, from the beginning, shell shock was seen as a redefinition of the relationship between men and women, and especially as a crisis of heroic masculine identity. None of these ideas was much evident during the war, nor did they enter rapidly into the culture after the war.

The shell shock episode resonates through Britain's twentieth century not only because of this artistic, cultural legacy. The medical investigation of traumatic neurosis that was partly stimulated by the failure of shell shock treatment harboured an equally important development: the search for more efficient ways to manage mass emotions rationally, especially fear, in the service of the state. With the expansion of total war to include civilian as well as service populations after 1939, and with the increasingly destructive capabilities that the new industrial war machine displayed, there was a new urgency to this objective.[3] It derived in part from the need not to repeat the failures of 1914–18: the punishment of soldiers who should have been hospitalized; the admission and consequent financial responsibility for large numbers of mentally defective men; the suggestive labelling of mental disorders that encouraged the notion of sickness; the unwitting reward of traumatic neurosis with discharge and financial compensation.[4]

To achieve this medics now incorporated the new developments in the mental sciences during the 1920s and 1930s, which shifted away from moral exhortation and hot baths towards chemical and surgical techniques, as well as a wider acceptance of, or at least familiarity with, the methods of psychoanalysis. Thus William Sargant, in charge of the Belmont Emergency Hospital in Surrey, one of the most important reception centres during the Second World War, experimented with barbiturate sedative drugs such as sodium amytal, coma-inducing insulin injections, electroconvulsion therapy and surgical intervention by leucotomy.[5] Meanwhile at the Northfield, near Birmingham, the largest British wartime centre, opened in 1942, many of the same techniques were used, while Michael Foulkes, a psychoanalytically-minded German émigré, also introduced discussion group sessions.[6] By these means, medicine was meant to play a central role in bringing about the modern bureaucratization and standardization of experience.

However, just as efforts to control the hysteria epidemic of the Great War failed, so in the Second World War the high rates of mental disorder indicate the state was signally ineffective in its disciplinary efforts. Despite a greater toleration of military psychiatrists, awareness of the mistakes made during the Great War, and selective recruitment procedures, the breakdown rates among the British soldiers of the Second World War remained high: in the active phase of the Battle of France, 10–15 per cent; in the first ten days of the 1940 Normandy Battle, 10–20 per cent; in the first two months of the 1942 Middle East campaign, 7–10 per cent; in the first two months of the Italian campaign, 11 per cent.[7] Moreover, the state's ability to coerce its citizens into active warfare was limited in April 1930 when the Army and Air Force Act ended the death penalty for the military offences of cowardice and desertion.

The events of 1939–45 and 1914–18 nevertheless between them define that unique invention of the twentieth century – total war. In this sense, the Second World War marks an expansion and an intensification of the techniques, logic and consequences of the First. Civilian populations are the prosecutors and targets of war, fear is channelled to serve the state's interests in war, languages of imaginative and literal expression fall into incoherence and silence. Genocide is announced by the Armenian massacre of 1915; likewise, the premonition of the twentieth century's later mass traumas is to be intuited in the making of shell shock.

Bibliographical Note

The recent interest in shell shock during the Great War partly finds its origins in two notable studies of the 1970s: *The Great War and Modern Memory* (1975) by Paul Fussell, and *No Man's Land* (1979) by Eric Leed.[1] These studies were among the first to relate the soldier's cultural knowledge and social experience to his feelings and thoughts on active combat. Paul Fussell wanted, for example, 'to understand something of the simultaneous and reciprocal process by which life feeds materials into literature while literature returns the favour by conferring forms upon life'.[2] Fussell's concerns were the experience of the Western Front: the transactions between literary form and real life; the ways it was remembered, conventionalized and mythologized. The sources he used were not notably new, nor unfamiliar, but they were reworked to trace common themes such as the labyrinthine world of the trenches and the 'homoerotic tradition' running through many soldiers' memoirs.[3] Examining the immediate scene of trench warfare and the broader cultural background, the author traces the images and perceptions that shaped a variety of responses to the war. One result was a realization of the richness and variety of soldiers' lives in the trenches as they sought to understand and cope with the complexities of their own experience. By examining the transaction between literary traditions and real life, *The Great War and Modern Memory* opened up the subject of how soldiers experienced war.

Eric Leed, like Paul Fussell, attempts to interpret and relate the experience of war to the culture of its participants, 'to produce a cultural history of the First World War *through* men who participated in it, by tracing their discoveries and reversals'.[4] By the interpretation of a whole set of cultural repertoires, such as the new symbols and conventions that emerged from active participation, Leed maps out the transformations in combatants' personal identity. The thesis of *No Man's Land* is that for many Europeans the pressure to escape from modern industrial society was a major driving force behind participation in the war, but that far from affording an escape from industry and modernity, the new combat was more intensely industrialized than peacetime society. For Leed the war thus effected a major contribution to the definition of modernity by changing the personality and expectations of its participants.

Elaine Showalter in her 1987 study of hysteria *The Female Malady: Women, Madness and English Culture, 1830–1980*, conceived of 'a feminist history of psychiatry and a cultural history of madness as a female malady' which would provide 'a gender analysis and feminist critique missing from the history of madness'.[5] In this view, only a feminist interpretation can decode the physical symptoms and psychotherapeutic encounters that resulted from this unique outbreak of large-scale male hysteria thereby allowing an examination of the conflicting meanings of masculinity within a specific historical context.[6] Developing Eric Leed's argument, Showalter argues that the psychological casualties of the Great War signify a widespread crisis of sexual identity: male hysteria suggested feminine behaviour; psychological damage and the taint of cowardice implied effeminate or homosexual tendencies; social emasculation and sexual impotence were widespread.[7] This argument is, I believe, overstated. It is certainly true that military authorities – both doctors and generals – failed to distinguish between medical and moral conditions in the minds of soldiers. True too that the authorities accused soldiers of cowardice when they suffered traumatic neurosis. However, Showalter's evidence for widespread impotence is circumstantial, it comes from German surgeries on the Western Front and from the clinics of Budapest, and is said to reflect a vaguely defined general climate; Ben Shepherd has more recently cited Dr Marie Stopes in support of this argument, but again the connection between postwar malaise and wartime traumatic neurosis seems tenuous.[8] Furthermore, there is nothing in the medical literature or case notes to support the idea that impotence was widespread. The evidence for the claim that soldiers experienced emasculating anxiety in large numbers, or that military doctors viewed feminine behaviour as characteristic and significant in psychological casualties at best awaits further research.[9]

Also considering the Great War in the context of its wider culture, *War Machine* (1993), by Daniel Pick, places the conflict against the backcloth of mechanized slaughterhouse techniques, rationalized factory methods and standardized railway time; and in parallel he catalogues the use of the 'war is a machine' metaphor in pre-1914 European thought.[10] Pick notes, for instance, how the expansion of the rail network and the increased number of locomotive accidents provided some of the first examples of the mental trauma that comes with industrial technology, and how the growth of state welfare systems, work insurance and legal compensation set in place the medical practices that shape shell shock treatment.[11] Industrialization also meant that when the European nations went to war in 1914 their civilian and military leaders became a kind of senior management: making, justifying and enforcing policy decisions. Similarly, soldiering goes from the use of pre-industrial Napoleonic strategies through a phase of deskilled labour in the middle years of the war, to become finally a series of highly specialized tasks within a mass production system for the manufacture of mutilation and death.[12] This type of study marks a move towards a social history of industrial and military medicine, especially in the context of the historical appearance of trauma in the American Civil War, in railway accidents and, later, in the context of the Great War.[13] Similarly specialized, and equally compelling, are recent studies in the social history of medicine, where the generalities of cultural commentary are rejected in favour of a much more closely focused examination of 'modernity' based on the implementation of bureaucratic procedures of organisation and management.[14]

Our understanding of the environment of war and of the place of medicine within that environment has expanded greatly in recent years, but it remains difficult to say what exactly it was like to suffer the trauma of industrial warfare. Although more narrowly focused within the context of war studies, Omer Bartov's work on *The Eastern Front 1941–45, German Troops and the Barbarization of Warfare* (1985) comes close to the themes of the present work, examining the effects of the combat environment on the conduct of warfare and the welfare of troops in Russia during the Second World War.[15] There are similarities here too with Ashworth's (1980) study of the trench warfare system, or Trevor Wilson's *The Myriad Faces of War* (1986). John Keegan's *The Face of Battle* (1976) still stands out for its discussion of the war environment and the nature and extent of combat motivation.[16] Recently, innovative studies have also been published on morale, Army politics and changes in the methods of warfare.[17] Detailed studies of the postwar experience are also emerging, although here the coverage remains very patchy.[18] Growing interest in the social and medical history of trauma, hysteria and post-traumatic stress disorder in recent years has led to several general studies.[19] Two of these are especially noteworthy. Allan Young's *The Harmony of Illusions* (1995) challenges the notion of traumatic memory and argues that post-traumatic stress disorder and its historical variants are bound together by clinical practices and the mutual negotiations of medic and patients. Ben Shepherd's *A War of Nerves: Soldiers and Psychiatrists 1914–1994* (2000) offers a perceptive account of the medical men who shaped the definition and treatment of psychiatric casualties, and their patients.[20] Research on 'hysterical men' in the French and German Armies during the Great War has also dramatically expanded our knowledge, although these studies still tend to look at doctors and their published writing rather than medical records or the personal experience of soldiers.[21]

Jay Winter takes up the theme of the continuity between war and peace in his study of remembrance and commemoration, *Sites of Memory, Sites of Mourning* (1995). This comparative cultural history questions the view put forward by Paul Fussell and later developed by Samuel Hynes that the war was a disruption of mass, intellectual and artistic life.[22] Exploring memorials, ceremonies and spiritualism, Winter concludes that survivors and mourners alike interpreted and understood death and destruction by reference to the past: to tradition, to mythology and to the Bible. My own view is that although many participants and relatives came to understand their experience by reference to the past, a profound disruption of consciousness did nevertheless take place during the Great War. It is prefigured in the growth of urban industrial society as witnessed by Georg Simmel, and it is embodied in the paralysis and mutism of the Great War's psychological casualties.

Notes

Chapter 1

1 *The Times History of the War*, VII (London: Times Publishers, 1916), p. 317.
2 *OED*, XV, 293, 2a; 194.
3 G. Simmel, 'The Metropolis and Mental Life', in C. Harrison and P. Wood, *Art in Theory 1900–90* (Oxford: Blackwell, 1992), pp. 323–4.
4 Here I am indebted especially to Roy Porter's suggestive essay 'The Body and the Mind, the Doctor and the Patient: Negotiating Hysteria', in S. Gilman et al., *Hysteria beyond Freud* (Berkeley: University of California, 1993), p. 229.
5 See, for example, M. Evans and P. Lunn, eds., *Memory and War in the Twentieth Century* (Oxford: Berg, 1997).
6 R. Samuel and P. Thompson, *Myths We Live By* (London: Routledge, 1990).
7 The most accessible extracts are to be seen in episode 5 of the BBC documentary *1914–18* (London: BBC, 1997).
8 PRO, MP 15/56, 'Dr Wallace on the Diagnosis of Neurasthenia'; T. Lewis, *Soldier's Heart and the Effort Syndrome* (London: Shaw, 1918); A. Young, *The Harmony of Illusions* (Princeton: Princeton University Press, 1995), pp. 52–3; B. Shephard, '"The Early Treatment of Mental Disorders": R.G. Rows and Maghull 1914–18', in H. Freeman and G.E. Berrios, eds., *150 Years of British Psychiatry*. Vol. 2: *The Aftermath* (London: Athlone, 1996), p. 451; J.D. Howell, ' "Soldier's Heart": The Redefinition of Heart Disease and Specialist Formation in Early Twentieth-century Great Britain', in R. Cooter, M. Harrison and S. Sturdy, eds., *War, Medicine and Modernity* (Stroud: Sutton, 1999), pp. 85–105; M. Stone, 'Shellshock and the Psychologists', in W.F. Bynum, R. Porter and M. Shepherd, eds., *The Anatomy of Madness*, vol. 2 (London: Tavistock, 1985), pp. 242–71.
9 See, especially, M. Thomson, 'Status, Manpower and Mental Fitness: Mental Deficiency and the First World War', in Cooter, Harrison and Sturdy, eds., *War, Medicine and Modernity*, pp. 149–66.
10 C. Stanford Read, *Military Psychiatry in Peace and War* (London: H.K. Lewis, 1920), p. 102; C.S. Myers, *Shell Shock in France* (Cambridge: Cambridge University Press, 1940), p. 82. Both quoted by Thomson, 'Status, Manpower and Mental Fitness', p. 152.
11 W. MacPherson et al., eds., *Medical Diseases of War*, vol. 2 (London: HMSO, 1923), p. 32.
12 G.M. Smith and T.H. Mitchell, *History of the Great War Based on Official Statistics*. Volume 7, *Medical Services, Casualties and Medical Statistics* (London: HMSO, 1931), pp. 115–16.
13 P. Lerner, 'Hysterical Men: War, Neurosis and German Mental Medicine' (PhD thesis, Columbia University, 1996), 1; M. Roudebush, 'Battle of Nerves: Hysteria and its Treatments in France during World War One' (unpublished paper, 1997), 1; D.M. Hiebert, 'The Psychological Consequences of War and Demobilisation in Germany 1914–29' (unpublished paper, 1985) puts the

official German figure for 'disorders of the nerves', including both pre-war and psychotic cases, at 613, 047.

14 'Recent Developments and Editorial Notes', *Recalled to Life*, III (April 1918), 322.

15 Young, *The Harmony of Illusions*, p. 5.

Chapter 2

1 See especially W. Schivelbusch, *The Railway Journey: The Industrialization of Time and Space in the 19th century* (Berkeley: University of California Press, 1986).

2 J.E. Erichsen, *On Concussion of the Spine* (London: Longmans, Green, 1872).

3 H. Page, *Injuries of the Spine and Spinal Cord without apparent Mechanical Lesion* (London: J. and A. Churchill, 1885).

4 See, for example, S.V. Clevinger, *Spinal Concussion* (New York: F.A. Davis, 1889); A.M. Hamilton, *Railway and other Accidents* (New York: Baillière Tindall, 1906).

5 J.J. Putnam, 'Recent Investigations into Patients of So-Called Concussion of the Spine', *Boston Medical and Surgical Journal*, CIX (1883), 337.

6 G.M. Beard, *American Nervousness: Its Causes and Consequences* (1881), ed. A.D. Rockwell (New York: Arno, 1972); *Sexual Nervousness: Its Hygiene, Causes, Symptoms and Treatment* (1884), ed. A.D. Rockwell (New York: Arno, 1972); *A Practical Treatise on Nervous Exhaustion* (1905), ed. A.D. Rockwell (New York: Kraus, 1971).

7 A. Rabinbach, *The Human Motor: Energy, Fatigue and the Origins of Modernity* (New York: Basic Books, 1990), p. 154.

8 W. Haymaker, 'Wier Mitchell (1829–1914)', in W. Haymaker and F. Schiller, eds., *Founders of Neurology* (Springfield, Ill.: C.C. Thomas, 1970), pp. 479–83.

9 Schivelbusch, *The Railway Journey*, p. 146.

10 M.R. Trimble, *Post-Traumatic Neurosis* (Chichester: John Wiley, 1981), p. 59.

11 Sir John Collie, 'The Effects of Recent Legislation upon Sickness and Accident Claims', *Practitioner*, XCVII (July 1916), pp. 1–2, in J. Bourke, *Dismembering the Male: Men's Bodies, Britain and the Great War* (London: Reaktion, 1996), pp. 88–9.

12 On hysteria, see M.S. Micale, *Approaching Hysteria. Disease and its Interpretations* (Princeton, NJ: Princeton University Press, 1995).

13 M. Micale, 'Charcot and the Idea of Hysteria in the Male', *Medical History*, XXXIV (October 1990), 363–411.

14 M.J. Clark, 'The Rejection of Psychological Approaches to Mental Disorders in Late Nineteenth-century British Psychiatry', in A. Scull, ed., *Madhouses, Mad-Doctors and Madmen: the Social History of Psychiatry in the Victorian Era* (Pennsylvania: Pennsylvania University Press, 1981), pp. 271–312.

15 G.H. Savage and E. Goodall, *Insanity and Allied Neuroses* (London: Cassell, 1907). There is little written on Savage, except: S. Trombley, *'All That Summer She Was Mad': Virginia Woolf and her Doctors* (New York: Junction Books, 1981), pp. 107–58. On more academically-minded medics, see, for example, R. Slobodin, *W.H.R. Rivers* (New York: Columbia University Press, 1978);

R. Verin-Bora and L. Lotari, with W. McDougall, *William McDougall: Explorer of the Mind* (New York: Gerrett, 1967).

16   Savage and Goodall, *Insanity and Allied Neuroses*, pp. 96–7.
17   See, for example, J.A. Ormerod, 'Hysteria', in T.C. Allbutt and H.D. Rollestone, eds., *A System of Medicine*, vol. 7 (London: Macmillan, 1910), p. 724.
18   Micale, 'Charcot and the Idea of Hysteria in the Male', 385–93.
19   B. Shephard, *A War of Nerves: Soldiers and Psychiatrists 1914–1994* (London: Cape, 2000), p. 12; p. 98.
20   Roudebush, 'Battle of Nerves', pp. 51–62.
21   H. Oppenheim, *Die Traumatischen Neurosen nach den in der Nervenklinik der Charite in den 8 Jahren 1883–1889 gesammelten Beobachtungen* (Berlin: Hirschwald, 1889. Revised and updated 1893).
22   G. Eghigian, 'Hysteria, Insurance, and the Rise of the Pathological Welfare State in Germany, 1884–1926' (unpublished paper, 1993).
23   Lerner, 'Hysterical Men', pp. 111–47.
24   Van Creveld, 'Technology and War to 1945', p. 179.
25   Ibid., pp. 187–8.
26   A. Babbington, *Shell Shock* (London: Leo Cooper, 1997), p. 14; p. 18; H. Binneveld, *From Shell Shock to Combat Stress* (Amsterdam: Amsterdam University Press, 1997), p. 31.
27   R.L. Richards, 'Mental and Nervous Diseases During the Russo-Japanese War', *Military Surgeon*, XXVI (1910), pp. 178–9.
28   J. Terrain, 'The Substance of War', in Cecil and Liddle, eds., *Facing Armageddon*, p. 3.
29   See: E.T. Dean, Jr., '"We Will All Be Lost and Destroyed." Post-Traumatic Stress Disorder and the American Civil War', *Civil War History*, XXXVII (1991), pp. 138–59; G. Rosen, 'Nostalgia – A Forgotten Psychological Disorder', *Psychological Medicine*, IV (1974), pp. 340–54.
30   Richards, 'Mental and Nervous Diseases During the Russo-Japanese War', 178–9.
31   Major H.E.M. Douglas and Captain St M. Carter RAMC, 'Notes and Observations made during the Serbo-Bulgarian War, 1913'. Wellcome Contemporary Medical Archive RAMC Historical Collection 446/6.
32   *Graves Dictionary of the Vulgar Tongue*, in Trimble, *Post-Traumatic Neurosis*, p. 57.
33   H. Gavin, *On Feigning and Factitious Diseases Chiefly in Soldiers and Seamen* (London: J. Churchill, 1843).
34   A. Summers, *Angels and Citizens: British Women as Military Nurses, 1854–1914* (London: Routledge and Kegan Paul, 1988), p. 291; M. Sutphen, 'Striving to be Separate? Civilian and Military Doctors in Cape Town During the Anglo-Boer War', in R. Cooter et al., eds., *War, Medicine and Modernity* (Stroud: Sutton, 1999), p. 58.
35   *RAMC Training Manual*, 1911, p. 148; 2. Wellcome Contemporary Medical Archive RAMC Historical Collection.
36   J. Bourne, 'Total War 1: The Great War', in C. Townsend, ed., *The Oxford Illustrated History of Modern Warfare* (Oxford: Oxford University Press, 1997), pp. 102–4.
37   D. French, 'The Meaning of Attrition, 1914–16', *English Historical Review*, CIII (1988), pp. 385–905.

38 Lord Kitchener, Esher Diary, 9 October 1914, Esher MSS 2/13. Quoted in D. French, 'The Meaning of Attrition, 1914–18', pp. 387–8.

39 G. Cassar, 'Kitchener at the War Office', in Cecil and Liddle, eds., *Facing Armageddon*, pp. 46–7; French, 'The Meaning of Attrition, 1914–16', pp. 386–95.

40 Lieut.-Col. J.H. Boraston, ed., *Sir Douglas Haig's Despatches* (London: J.M. Dent, 1919), p. 346; French, 'The Meaning of Attrition, 1914–16', pp. 385–405.

41 See also J. Terrain, *White Heat: The New Warfare 1914–18* (London: Sidgewick and Jackson, 1982), pp. 146–8; T. Wilson, *The Myriad Faces of War* (Cambridge: Polity, 1986), pp. 122–5.

42 French, 'The Meaning of Attrition, 1914–16', p. 392.

43 Terrain, *White Heat*, pp. 146–8.

44 T. Wilson, *The Myriad Faces of War*, p. 125; C. Crutwell, *A History of the Great War 1914–18*, second edn (Oxford: Clarendon, 1936), p. 151.

45 PRO MH 106/2101. Sergeant C.; PRO WO 95/3941. Diary of the 1st Seaforth Highlanders, January–June 1915.

46 WO 95/3941. Diary entry 10 March 1915.

47 MH 106/2101. Medical case sheet, Sergeant C., 19 March 1915 and following entries.

48 See T. Ashworth, *Trench Warfare 1914–18. The Live and Let Live System* (London: Macmillan, 1980).

49 J. Bourne, 'The British Working Man in Arms', in Cecil and Liddle, eds., *Facing Armageddon*, pp. 336–52.

50 Bourne, 'Total War 1: The Great War', pp. 113–15.

51 E. Junger, *The Storm of Steel. From the Diary of A German Storm Troop Officer on the Western Front* (London: Chatto and Windus, 1929), pp. 167–8. See also T. Nevin, 'Ernst Junger: German Stormtrooper Chronicler', in Cecil and Liddle, eds., *Facing Armageddon*, pp. 269–77.

52 P.J. Campbell, *In the Cannon's Mouth* (London: Hamish Hamilton, 1979), p. 80.

53 P. Dubrille, in R. Holmes, *Firing Line* (London: Jonathan Cape, 1985), p. 232.

54 C. Edmonds, *A Subaltern's War* (London: Peter Dains, 1929), p. 35.

55 Quoted in M. Middlebrook, *The Kaiser's Battle* (London: Allen Lane, 1978), p. 161.

56 C.E. Montague, in Holmes, *Firing Line*, p. 115.

57 O. Bartov, *The Eastern Front 1941–45* (London: Macmillan, 1985), pp. 26–7.

58 Edmonds, *A Subaltern's War*, pp. 134–5.

59 See Chapter 3 for fuller discussion of this incident.

60 Lieutenant G.N. Kirkwood, RAMC (T), Medical Officer to the 97th Brigade of the 11th Border Regiment, 32nd Division, Statement to a Court of Enquiry, July 1916. Wellcome Contemporary Medical Archive RAMC Historical Collection 466/11.

61 G. Sheffield, 'Officer–Man Relations, Discipline and Morale in the British Army of the Great War', in Cecil and Liddle, eds., *Facing Armageddon*, p. 414.

62 C. Carrington, *Soldier from the Wars Returning* (London: Hutchinson, 1965), p. 76.

63 Sheffield, 'Officer–Man Relations', p. 421.

64 S. Audoin-Rouzea, 'The French Soldier in the Trenches', in Cecil and Liddle, eds., *Facing Armageddon*, p. 223.

65   Ibid., p. 221.
66   L. Smith, 'The French High Command and the Mutinies of Spring 1917', Cecil and Liddle, eds., *Facing Armageddon*, pp. 79–92.
67   H. Strachan, 'The Morale of the German Army 1917–18', in Cecil and Liddle, eds., *Facing Armageddon*, pp. 383–98.
68   R. Graves, *Goodbye to All That* (London: Penguin, 1960), pp. 83–92.
69   Peter Liddle Archive, tape 218–219; Gunner Sturdy, Ms Account, Imperial War Museum, p. 41; Captain L. Gameson, RAMC (T), Memoirs, Imperial War Museum, p. 163.
70   Fussell, *The Great War and Modern Memory*, pp. 114–54.
71   'Anonymous Written Account by a Shellshocked Officer', Wellcome Contemporary Medical Archive RAMC Historical Collection 739/2/13.
72   M.R. Habeck, 'Technology and the First World War: The View from Below', in J. Winter et al., eds., *The Great War and the Twentieth Century* (New Haven: Yale University Press, 2000), pp. 99–131.
73   T. Ashworth, 'The Sociology of Trench Warfare', *British Journal of Sociology*, XIX (1968), pp. 407–20.

Chapter 3

1   Editorial, *The Hydra*, 1 September 1917. See also Peter Liddle Archive, Dr W. Hills, Written Recollections as Neurologist with the 4th Army, March 1918–January 1919; Letter dated 21 August 1915, pp. 3–4.
2   PRO WO 93/49. Summary of First World War Capital Court Martial Cases.
3   Peter Liddle Archive, taped interview no. 678/679; taped interview no. 218/219, and 1917 *Diary*; Captain H.W. Kaye, 'A Very Complete Diary of an MO in France from September 1914 to August 1916, 43 Field Ambulance, 14 Div. 8th CCS'. Wellcome Contemporary Medical Archive RAMC Historical Collection 739/2/13.
4   H. Cushing, *From a Surgeon's Journal 1915–18* (London: Constable, 1936), in Cecil and Liddle, *Facing Armageddon*, pp. 451–65.
5   K. Simpson, 'Dr James Dunn and Shell Shock', in Cecil and Liddle, eds., *Facing Armageddon*, p. 505.
6   R. Cooter, 'Malingering in Modernity: Psychological Scripts and Adversarial Encounters during the First World War', in R. Cooter et al., eds., *War, Medicine and Modernity*, p. 131.
7   The War Diary of J.H. Dibble, 27 September 1914, p. 37, in C. Herrick, 'Of War and Wounds: The Propaganda, Politics and Experience of Medicine in World War One on the Western Front' (unpublished PhD thesis, University of Manchester, 1996), pp. 346–7.
8   J.H. Dibble, 9 August 1915, p. 121, in Herrick, 'Of War and Wounds', p. 370.
9   Archives du Musée du Service de Santé des Armées (AMSSA) Neurologie et Neuro-psychiatrie C/223 (Neuro-Psychiatrie: Conférences, Réunions). J. Grassett, 'Les Nevroses et psychonevroses de guerre', 27 November 1916, in Roudebush, p. 88.
10   Roudebush, 'The Battle of Nerves', PhD thesis, p. 83. This and later comments draw on Roudebush.
11   Binneveld, *From Shell Shock to Combat Stress*, p. 140.

12   Grassett, 'Les Nevroses et psychonevroses', p. 4, in Roudebush, 'The Battle of Nerves', p. 98.
13   See J. Babinski and J. Fromet, *Hysteria or Pithiatism, and Reflex Nervous Disorders in the Neurology of War*, trans. J.D. Rolleston, ed. E. Farquhar Buzzard (London: London University Press, 1918).
14   Ibid., pp. 216–18; Roudebush, 'The Battle of Nerves', pp. 111–13.
15   Ibid., pp. 134–5.
16   Grassett, 'Les Nevroses et psychonevroses', p. 3, in Roudebush, ibid., p. 153; pp. 171–2.
17   K. Singer, 'Prinzipien und Enfolge der aktiven Therapie bei Neurosen', *Zeitschrift für physikalisher und diadetische Therapie*, XXII (1918) 275, in Lerner, 'Hysterical Men', p. 228. This and later comments draw on Lerner.
18   Gaupp to K. Sanitatsamt, Tubingen, 23 September 1918. Universitatsarchive, Nervenklinik Collection, Eberhard-Karls-Universitat, Tubingen [UA Tubingen] 308/89, in Lerner, p. 270.
19   G. Liebermeister, 'Verhutung von Kreigsneurosen', *Medizinisches Correspondentzblatt des Wurttembergischen arzlichen Landsvereins*, 88, 1918, p. 308, in Lerner, 'Hysterical Men', pp. 273–4.
20   Gaupp, no title, 6. Tubingen, 18 May 1918. UA Tubingen, 308/89, in Lerner, 'Hysterical Men', p. 275.
21   Peter Liddle Archive, Letter dated 21 August 1915, pp. 4–5.
22   Letter, pp. 4–5.
23   WO 93/49 Summary of First World War Capital Court Martial Cases. Trial of Lance-Sergeant Walton, 12 March 1915, in A. Babbington, *Shell-Shock: A History of Changing Attitudes to War Neurosis*, pp. 3–6.
24   Hiram Sturdy, Ms. Account, Imperial War Museum, p. 111.
25   Ibid., pp. 40–1.
26   Claire Elise Tisdall, VAD, in L. MacDonald, *The Roses of No Man's Land* (London: Macmillan, 1984), p. 216.
27   Peter Liddle Archive, Letter dated 21 August 1915, pp. 4–5.
28   Anonymous written account, in Captain Kaye, 'A Very Complete Diary of an M.O.', Wellcome Contemporary Medical Archive RAMC Historical Collection, ref. 739/2/13.
29   Ibid., p. 1.
30   Anonymous written account, p. 2.
31   Ibid.
32   Ibid.
33   Ibid.
34   See E. Showalter, *The Female Malady* (London: Virago, 1985).
35   See Binneveld, *From Shell Shock to Combat Stress*, pp. 91–5.
36   2nd Lieutenant A.H. Crerar, letters dated 27 October 1916, Imperial War Museum.
37   Crerar, 30 October 1916; J.D. Crerar, letter to the author, 27 June 2001.
38   Gameson, Memoirs, 145.
39   On cases on the Somme, see Major-General Sir W. Macpherson *et al.*, eds., *Medical Diseases of War*, Volume 2 (London: HMSO, 1923), p. 32. On public debate, see, for example, J. Collie, 'War Shaken Men. The Treatment of the Neurasthenic', *The Times*, 27 November 1916, 7a; 'Shell-Shock Sufferers', *The*

Times, 3 October 1917, 3c; 'Procedure of Courts-Martial', *The Times*, 15 March 1918, 12c.

40 *'Shell Shock' – Proceedings of a Court of Enquiry. July 1916*, RAMC Historical Collection, 466/11; W.D. Chambers, 'Mental Wards with the British Expeditionary Force: A Review of Ten Months' Experience', *Journal of Mental Science*, LXV (1919), pp. 152–80.

41 *'Shell Shock' – Proceedings of a Court of Enquiry. July 1916*. Remarks by Commander 97th Infantry Brigade, Brevet, Lt.-Col. (Temp. Brig General) J.B. Jardine, CMG., DSO., 5th Lancers.

42 G. Oram, *Worthless Men: Race, Eugenics and the Death Penalty in the British Army during the First World War* (London: Francis Boutle, 1998), pp. 84–101.

43 Shephard, *A War of Nerves*, p. 101.

44 Peter Liddle Archive, Dr W.H. Hills, Written Recollections, March 1918–January 1919.

45 *'Shell Shock' – Proceedings*. Wellcome Contemporary Medical Archive RAMC Historical Collection, 466/11; Statement of Captain H.C. Palmer, 2nd KOYLE, Acting Officer-in-Command, 11th Border Regiment.

46 *'Shell Shock' – Proceedings*. Statement of Captain H.C. Palmer. Copy of the certificate given by Lieutenant Kirkwood, MO.

47 *'Shell Shock' – Proceedings*. Remarks by Brigadier General Jardine.

48 Major General Sir T.L.N. Morland, forwarding minute; Major General Sir H. De la P. Gough, Instructions; Lt.-Col. P. Evans, ADMS 3rd Division, minute; Surgeon General Sir A.T. Sloggett, DGMS, minute.

49 *'Shell Shock' – Proceedings*. Remarks by Brigadier General Jardine.

50 Forwarding Minute to X Corps by Commander 32nd Division.

51 Surgeon General Sir A.T. Sloggett, DGMS, minute.

52 'The Death Penalty in the Army', *The Times*, 1 October 1917, 8c.

53 WO 93/49. Trial of Private H.J. Farr, 10 October 1916; WO 71/509. Judge Advocate General's records Courts Martial.

54 WO 93/49. Trial of 2nd Lieutenant E.S. Poole, 21 November 1916. WO 71.1027. Judge Advocate General's records Courts Martial.

55 On Poole, see also Oram, *Worthless Men*, pp. 98–100.

56 WO 93/49. Trial of Private J. Seymour, 12 January 1918; Trial of Private J. Bateman, 30 August 1918; Trial of Private P. Murphy, 19 August 1918.

57 Gameson, Memoirs, p. 347.

58 Ibid., p. 349.

59 Peter Liddle Archive, tape interview 678/679.

60 Ibid.

61 Peter Liddle Archive, diary and taped interview ref. 218/219.

62 1917 Diary, 14 April.

63 1917 Diary, 2–3 and 19 May.

64 1917 Diary, 29 June.

65 1917 Diary, 14–15 September.

66 Peter Liddle Archive, Written Recollections, Dr W.H. Hills, Neurologist with the 4th Army. March 1918–January 1919.

67 Chambers, 'Mental Wards', pp. 152–80.

68 Dr Hills, Recollections.

69 Ibid.

70 Ibid.

71 Ibid.
72 Chambers, 'Mental Wards', p. 152.
73 See Chapter 2 on Savage and the *Journal of Mental Science*.
74 Chambers, 'Mental Wards', p. 170.
75 Ibid., p. 154.
76 Ibid., p. 179.
77 Ibid., p. 154.
78 Ibid., p. 179; Myers, *Shell Shock in France 1914–18*, pp. 87–8; Gameson, Memoirs, pp. 81–2; W.A. Turner, 'Nervous and Mental Shock – A Survey of Provision', *British Medical Journal* (1916) 82–3.

Chapter 4

1   *The Times*, 12 August 1916, 9.
2   On the symbolism of wartime medicine and wounding, see C. Herrick, 'Of War and Wounds', PhD thesis, University of Manchester, 1996.
3   *The Times History of the War*, vol. VII (London: Times Publishers, 1916), p. 317.
4   Ibid., p. 319.
5   These two aspects of shell shock constantly recur in the press coverage, for example: 'Battle Shock. The Wounded Mind and its Cure', *The Times*, 25 May 1915, 11c; 'Soldier Shot for Cowardice', *The Times*, 19 December 1917, 8c.
6   C.S. Myers, *Shell Shock in France 1914–18* (Cambridge: Cambridge University Press, 1940), p. 14.
7   See Chapter 5, and T.W. Salmon, 'The Care and Treatment of Mental Diseases and War Neuroses in the British Army', *Mental Hygiene*, I (1917) 509–47.
8   PRO WO 95/192. War Diary of Surgeon General W.G. Macpherson, Director General of Medical Services, 1st Army, Vol. II, 1–31 January. Entry for 12 January 1915.
9   W.A. Turner, 'Arrangements for the Cure of Nervous and Mental Shock Coming from Overseas', *Lancet* (1916) 1073–5; 'Nervous and Mental Shock – A Survey of Provision', *British Medical Journal* (1916) 830–2.
10 'The Wounded at the Front. Need for an Extended Organization. Red Cross and RAMC', *The Times*, 13 October 1914, 4b.
11 Fripp, Oyston, Perry and Hoarder, 'Memorandum on Army Medical Services to December 1915'. RAMC Historical Collection, Wellcome Library for the History and Understanding of Medicine.
12 'Memorandum', 1.
13 Ibid., 3.
14 Ibid., 4.
15 Ibid., 3.
16 J.M. Winter, *The Great War and the British People* (London: Macmillan, 1985), pp. 53–4.
17 G.S. Savage, 'Mental Disabilities for War Service', *Journal of Mental Science*, LXII (1916), 653–7.
18 Gameson, Memoirs, pp. 347–9; *Report of the War Office Committee of Enquiry into 'Shell Shock'* (London: HMSO, 1922), pp. 21–2.

19 Myers, *Shell Shock in France 1914–18*, p. 79.
20 2nd Lieutenant A.H. Crerar, Letter dated 20 October 1916, Imperial War Museum.
21 Savage, 'Mental Disabilities for War Service', 656.
22 Macpherson et al., eds., *Medical Diseases of War*, vol. II, p. 32; Myers, *Shell Shock in France 1914–18*, pp. 87–8.
23 Myers, ibid., pp. 93–4; 101.
24 Gameson, Memoir, p. 80.
25 Ibid., pp. 81–2.
26 General Routine Order no. 2384, 19/6/17; Gameson, Memoirs, p. 178; *4th Army Adjutant General Notes*, second edn (1918), pp. 13–14; 29.
27 Gameson, Memoirs, p. 179.
28 Ibid.
29 'Lord Knutsford's Appeal', *The Times*, 4 November 1914, 5b.
30 'Lord Knutsford's Appeal', *The Times*, 12 November 1914, 9d.
31 'Lord Knutsford's Appeal', *The Times*, 13 November 1914, 9d.
32 'A Kensington Hospital for Officers. Visit by Queen Alexandra', *The Times*, 18 January 1915, 4e.
33 'Obsession and Fraud. Studies in Diseased Personality. Sir J. Collie's Lecture', *The Times*, 27 January 1915, 5a.
34 'Cases of Shock from the Front', *The Times*, 6 February 1915, 5b.
35 On continued interest in Palace Green, see, for example, Lord Knutsford, 'Battle Shock', *The Times*, 26 May 1915, 11e; 'Officers and Nervous Shock', *The Times*, 31 January 1916, 9e.
36 Macpherson et al., *Medical Diseases of War*, II, p. 9.
37 *The Times History of the War*, VII, p. 327; *House of Commons, Parliamentary Papers, 1914–16*, III, pp. 15–18.
38 'Medical Notes in Parliament', *British Medical Journal*, 22 May 1915, 905.
39 'Battle Shock. The Wounded Mind and its Cure', *The Times*, 25 May 1915, 11c.
40 'Nerve Shaken Soldiers', *The Times*, 27 July 1915, 7f and 8a.
41 Viscount Knutsford, 'Neurasthenia and Shell-Shock', *The Times*, 16 April 1919, 16a. PRO PIN 15/55. Press Cuttings. *Nursing Times*, 30 October 1920; *The Lancet*, 30 October 1920.
42 Sir John Collie, 'War Shaken Men. The Treatment of the Neurasthenic. Plea for Institution', *The Times*, 27 November 1916, 7a. On changing medical specialist views in 1916, see: M.D. Eder, 'An Address on the Psycho-Pathology of the War Neurosis', *Lancet*, 12 August 1916, 264–8; C.S. Myers, 'Contribution to the Study of Shell Shock: (2). Being an Account of Certain Cases Treated by Hypnosis', *Lancet*, 8 January 1916, 642–55; R.G. Rows, 'Mental Conditions following Strain and Nerve Shock', *British Medical Journal*, 25 March 1916, 441–3.
43 Collie, 'War Shaken Men'.
44 'For War Shaken Men. Treatment of Neurasthenics', *The Times*, 28 December 1916, 3c.
45 Sir John Collie, 'War Shaken Men. An Institution for the Neurasthenic', *The Times*, 1 February 1917, 9d.
46 'News in Brief', *The Times*, 28 February 1917, 3f (last paragraph).
47 Lord Knutsford, 'Shell Shock Hospitals. A Red Cross Arrangement', *The Times*, 29 September 1917, 9e.

48 'Cure of Shell Shock. Organisation of Homes of Recovery. Sir J. Collie's Scheme', *The Times*, 14 June 1917, 3a; Sir John Collie, 'The Management of Neurasthenia and Allied Disorders Contracted in the Army', *Journal of State Medicine*, XXVI (1918) 2–17; 'Neurasthenia and Allied Disorders', *Recalled to Life*, 2 September 1917, 234–53.

49 'Cure of Shell Shock', *The Times*, 14 June 1917, 3a.

50 *Joint War Reports of British Red Cross/St John 1914–18*, 'Part XII – After Care of Disabled Men. Neurasthenia', 240–3; 'The First Home of Recovery. Golder's Green', *Red Cross Journal*, July 1917, 94–5; 'Treatment of Shell Shock', *The Times*, 5 April 1917, 4b; 'News in Brief', *The Times*, 4 May 1917, 3f (second paragraph); 'Ulster and the Wounded. Sir E. Carson on Glory in the Trenches', *The Times*, 23 July 1917, 8d; 'A Shell Shock Hospital. Generous Gift to the Nation', *The Times*, 21 August 1917, 3c; 'Shell Shock Hospitals', *The Times*, 22 August 1917, 9c.

51 T. Lumsden, 'Nerve Shattered Pensioners. A Scheme for Treatment', *The Times*, 27 August 1917, 8b.

52 See, for example: J.L. Carr, *A Month in the Country* (Harmondsworth: Penguin, 1980).

53 T. Lumsden, 'Nerve-Shattered Pensioners', *The Times*, 27 August 1917, 8b.

54 L. Stephens, 'Nerve-Shattered Pensioners', *The Times*, 4 September 1917, 12e.

55 Sir John Collie, 'Special Medical Board', *The Times*, 5 September 1917, 7d.

56 F. Milner, 'Insanity and the War', *The Times*, 29 September 1918, 8b.

57 'Shell Shock and Desertion', *The Times*, 20 February 1918, 8b.

58 'Procedure in Courts-Martial', *The Times*, 15 March 1918, 12c.

59 'Shell Shock Sufferers', *The Times*, 3 October 1917, 3c.

60 'Discharge of Shell-Shock Cases', *The Times*, 18 January 1918, 3b.

61 'Pensions and Red Tape', *The Times*, 18 March 1918, 5b.

62 G. Elliot Smith, 'Neurasthenic Pensioners', *The Times*, 22 March 1918, 8f. See also: E. Smith and T.H. Pear, *Shell-Shock and its Lessons* (London: Longmans Green, 1917).

63 C. Drummond, 'Neurasthenic Cases', *The Times*, 28 March 1918, 9e. See also W. Draper, 'Village Centres for Cure and Training', *Recalled to Life*, 3, April 1918, 342–57.

64 C. Drummond, 'Neurasthenic Cases. Patients to be Removed from Golders Green', *The Times*, 14 May 1918, 3a.

65 'The Treatment of Neurasthenics', *The Times*, 15 May 1918, 10a; C. Drummond, 'Golders Green Hospital', *The Times*, 16 May 1918, 9d.

66 'For Shell Shock Cases. 15 Curative Institutions', *The Times*, 5 November 1918, 3d.

Chapter 5

1 T.W. Salmon, 'The Care and Treatment of Mental Diseases and War Neurosis ("Shellshock") in the British Army', *Mental Hygiene*, I (1917) 519.

2 'Cases of Shock from the Front', *The Times*, 6 February 1915, 5b.

3 T.W. Salmon, 'The Care and Treatment of Mental Diseases and War Neuroses in the British Army', 520.

4   W. Vincent, 'Use of Asylums as Military Hospitals', *Journal of Mental Science*, LXII (1916) 174–8.

5   W.A. Turner, 'Nervous and Mental Shock', *British Medical Journal*, 10 June 1916, 831.

6   D.G. Thomson, 'A Descriptive Record of the Conversion of a County Asylum into a War Hospital for Sick and Wounded Soldiers in 1915', *Journal of Mental Science*, LXII (1916) 123–4.

7   H. Binneveld, *From Shellshock to Combat Stress: A Comparative History of Military Psychiatry* (Amsterdam: Amsterdam University Press, 1997), p. 138.

8   'Lord Knutsford's Appeal', 'Special Hospital for Officers', *The Times*, 9 January 1915, 9d.

9   PROMH 106 1887–1890, Admission and Discharge Registers Craiglockhart War Hospital, October 1916–February 1919; Scottish Record Office, GD1 \677\1 Medical Case Sheets, Lennel Private Convalescent Home for Officers.

10 L.S. Hearnshaw, *Short History of British Psychology 1840–1940* (London: Methuen, 1964), p. 287.

11 F.W. Mott, *War Neurosis and Shell Shock* (London: Hodder and Stoughton, 1919); 'Chadwick Lecture: Mental Hygiene in Shell Shock, during and after the War', *Journal of Mental Science*, LXIII (1917) 467–88; 'Neurasthenia: The Disorders and Disabilities of Fear', *Lancet*, 28 January 1918, 127–9; 'Special Discussion of Shell Shock without Visible Signs of Injury', *Proceedings of the Royal Society of Medicine, Sections of Psychiatry and Neurology*, XI (1916). On Mott's pre-war work, see 'The Neuropathic Inheritance', *Journal of Mental Science*, LIX (1913) 222–63.

12 E.E. Southard, 'The Effect of High Explosives upon the Central Nervous System', *Mental Hygiene* (1918) 397–401.

13 Ibid., 397.

14 Ibid., 401.

15 R.Weichbrodt, 'Zur Behandlung Hysterischer Storungen', *Archiv für Psychiatrie*, LVII (1917) 519–25. See also Lerner, 'Hysterical Men', 212–14.

16 Roudebush, 'A Battle of Nerves', 1.

17 J. Goldstein, *Console and Classify: The French Psychiatric Profession in the Nineteenth Century* (Cambridge: Cambridge University Press, 1987); I.R. Dowbiggin, *Inheriting Madness: Professionalization and Psychiatric Knowledge in Nineteenth-Century France* (Berkeley: University of California, 1991).

18 M. Laignel-Lavastine and P. Courbon, *Les Accidentés de la guerre: leurs ésprit, leurs réactions, leurs trantement* (Paris: Baillière, 1919).

19 Roudebush, 'A Battle of Nerves', 24.

20 Lerner, 'Hysterical Men', 110.

21 F. Kaufmann, 'Die Planmässige Heilung komplizierter psychogener Bewegungsstörungen bei Soldaten in einer Sitzung', *Münchener Medizinische Wochenschift, Feldärztliche Beilage*, LXIII (1916) 802–4.

22 See Lerner, 'Hysterical Men', 132–48.

23 Ibid., and 'Hysterical Cures: Hypnosis, Gender and Performance in World War One and Weimar Germany', *History Workshop Journal*, XLV (1998) 79–101.

24 Lerner, 'Hysterical Men', 161–2.

25 Among the most important publications are the following: E.D. Adrian and L.R. Yealland, 'Treatment of Some Common War Neuroses', *Lancet*, 9 June

1917, 867–72; F.W. Mott, *War Neurosis and Shell Shock* (London: Hodder and Stoughton, 1919); F.W. Mott, 'Chadwick Lecture: Mental Hygiene in Shell Shock During and after the War', *Journal of Mental Science*, LXIII (1917) 467–88; C.S. Myers, 'A Contribution to the Study of Shellshock: (1) Being an Account of 3 Cases of Memory, Vision, Smell and Taste, Admitted to the Duchess of Westminster War Hospital, Le Toquet', *Lancet*, 13 February 1915, 317–20; 'A Contribution to the Study of Shellshock: (2) Being an Account of Certain Cases Treated by Hypnosis', *Lancet*, 8 January 1916, 642–55; W.H.R. Rivers, 'The Repression of War Experience', *Lancet*, I (1918) 173–7; E. Smith and T.H. Pear, *Shell-Shock and its Lessons* (London: Longmans Green, 1917); L.R. Yealland, *Hysterical Disorders of Warfare* (London: Macmillan, 1918).

26 Leed, *No Man's Land*, p. 170.
27 For the original case, see Yealland, *Hysterical Disorders of Warfare*, pp. 5–23. For comments and reworkings of the case, see Leed, *No Man's Land*, pp. 174–5; Showalter, *The Female Malady*, pp. 176–8; Binneveld, *From Shellshock to Combat Stress*, pp. 111–14; Holden, *Shell Shock*, pp. 50–2. For Barker's fictionalized version, see *Regeneration*, pp. 201–5.
28 Showalter, *The Female Malady*, p. 176.
29 Ibid., p. 178.
30 See G. Holmes, *The National Hospital Queen Square, 1860–1948* (Edinburgh: Livingstone, 1954).
31 'Cases of Shock from the Front', *The Times*, 6 February 1915, 5b.
32 National Hospital Queen Square, Medical Notes and Records 1915–24.
33 Adrian and Yealland, 'The Treatment of Some Common War Neuroses', 867.
34 Dr Taylor, Queen Square Notes and Records, 1916.
35 Dr Tooth, 1916–17.
36 Dr Tooth, 1916.
37 Ibid.
38 Dr Turner, 1915–18.
39 PRO MH 106/2101. Mental Illness and Neurasthenia Case Notes.
40 Dr Taylor, 1918.
41 Dr Tooth, 1916.
42 Dr Taylor, 1916.
43 Ibid.
44 Only Binneveld, *From Shell Shock to Combat Stress*, pp. 111–14 reports this final response as well as the subsequent conversation.
45 Dr Taylor, 1918.
46 Dr Taylor, 1916.
47 Dr Russell, 1916.
48 Dr Michael Yealland (son), quoted in Holden, *Shell Shock*, p. 52.
49 See, for example, W. Brown, 'The Revival of Emotional Memoirs and its Therapeutic Value I and IV', *British Journal of Psychology*, Medical Section, I (1920) 16–19; 30–3; W. McDougall, *An Outline of Abnormal Psychology* (London: Methuen, 1926); C.S. Myers, *Shell Shock in France 1914–18* (Cambridge: Cambridge University Press, 1940); W.H.R. Rivers, *Instinct and the Unconscious* (Cambridge: Cambridge University Press, 1920).
50 A. Costall, 'Dire Straits? Relations between Psychology and Anthropology after the Cambridge Anthropological Expedition of 1898' (unpublished paper, 1998), 4.

51　On the background to the 'School', see C. Crampton, 'The Cambridge School: The Life and Influence of James Ward, W.H.R. Rivers and Sir Frederick Bartlett', PhD thesis, University of Edinburgh, 1978.

52　T.H. Pear, 'Reminiscences' (unpublished MS, 1959). On Maghull, see especially B. Shephard, ' "The Early Treatment of Mental Disorders": R.G. Rows and Maghull 1914–18', in H. Freeman and G.E. Berrios, eds., *150 Years of British Psychiatry*. Vol. II: *The Aftermath* (London: Athlone, 1996), pp. 434–64.

53　Pear, 'Reminiscences', 14.

54　A. Costall, 'Pear and his Peers: The Beginnings of Psychology at Manchester' (unpublished paper, 1998).

55　See, for example, G.E. Smith and T.H. Pear, *Shell Shock and its Lessons* (Manchester: University of Manchester Press, 1917); E. Jones, 'Recent Advances in Psycho-Analysis', *British Journal of Psychology*, Medical Section, I (1920) 47–71.

56　Rivers, *Instinct and the Unconscious*, p. v.

57　Shephard, 'The Early Treatment of Mental Disorders', 445–6.

58　H. Crichton Miller, *Functional Nerve Disease* (London: Hodder and Stoughton, 1920); C. Stanford Read, *Military Psychiatry in Peace and War* (London: H.K. Lewis, 1920).

59　McDougall, *An Outline of Abnormal Psychology*, p. xi.

60　Ibid.; on Netley, see also Stanford Read, *Military Psychiatry in Peace and War*.

61　J.K. Rowlands, 'A Mental Hospital at War' (unpublished paper, 1985), 11; PRO MH 106.1887–1890, Admission and Discharge Registers, Craiglockhart War Hospital, October 1916–February 1919.

62　McDougall, *An Outline of Abnormal Psychology*, p. 286.

63　M. Stone, 'Shellshock and the Psychologists', in W.F. Bynum, R. Porter and M. Shephard, eds., *The Anatomy of Madness*, vol. 2 (London: Tavistock, 1985), pp. 242–71; Shephard, 'The Early Treatment of Mental Disorders', 447.

64　M. Stone, 'Military and Industrial Roots of Clinical Psychology in Britain 1900–45', unpublished PhD thesis, University of London, 1985, 159.

65　W.H.R. Rivers, 'Freud's Theory of the Unconscious', *Lancet*, I, 1917, 912–14.

66　Shephard cites the experience of Millias Culpin, in 'The Early Treatment of Mental Disorders', 449.

67　Yealland, *Hysterical Disorders*, p. xi; Adrian and Yealland, 'Treatment of Some Common War Neuroses', 867–72.

68　S. Sassoon, *Sherston's Progress* (London: Faber, 1983), p. 14.

Chapter 6

1　Sir A. Keogh, 'The Treatment of the Disabled', *Recalled to Life*, I (June 1917) 9.

2　E. Bramwell, 'Physical Treatment', in H. Crichton Miller, ed., *Functional Nerve Disease* (London: Hodder & Stoughton, 1920), pp. 27–37.

3　J.A. Hadfield, 'Treatment by Suggestion and Persuasion', in ibid., pp. 61–87.

4　Ibid., pp. 79–81; p. 87.

5　M. Nicholl and J. Young, 'Psycho-analysis', in Crichton Miller, ed., *Functional Nerve Disease*, pp. 129–52.

6　W.H.R. Rivers, 'The Repression of War Experience', *Lancet*, I (1918) 173–7.

7   'Nerve Shaken Soldiers', *The Times*, 27 July 1915, 7f and 8a; 'Soldiers in Asylums. New Arrangements by Pensions Ministry', *The Times*, 12 October 1917, 3c.

8   'For Shell Shock Cases. 15 Curative Institutions', *The Times*, 5 November 1918, 3d.

9   'Cases of Shock from the Front', *The Times*, 6 February 1915, 5b; C. Drummond, 'Neurasthenic Cases', *The Times*, 28 March 1918, 9e; 'Neurasthenic Cases. Patients to be Removed from Golders Green', *The Times*, 15 May 1918, 10a; 'Golders Green Hospital', *The Times*, 16 May 1918, 9d.

10   J.K. Rowlands, 'A Mental Hospital at War' (unpublished paper, 1985), 2.

11   Pear, 'Reminiscences', 13; 18.

12   B. Shephard, ' "The Early Treatment of Mental Disorders": R.G. Rows and Maghull 1914–18', in H. Freeman and G.E. Berrios, *150 Years of British Psychiatry*. Vol. II: *The Aftermath* (London: Athlone, 1996), p. 435.

13   Pear, 'Reminiscences', 13.

14   Rowlands, 'A Mental Hospital at War', 11.

15   Shephard, 'The Early Treatment of Mental Disorders', 457.

16   Ibid., 443.

17   Rowlands, 'A Mental Hospital at War', 10.

18   Pear, 'Reminiscences', 15.

19   G.N. Smith and T.H. Mitchell, *History of the Great War*. Volume 7, *Medical Services, Casualties and Medical Statistics* (London: HMSO, 1931).

20   PRO MH 106 2101 and 2102.

21   WO 95 1664. War diary of the Second Battalion of the Queens Royal West Surrey Regiment, January–June 1915; MH 106 2101. Medical Case Notes, Cpl S.L., July–September 1915.

22   MH 106 2101. Medical Case Notes, Cpl S.L., July–September 1915.

23   MH 106 2102. Medical Case Notes, Private H.R., January 1915.

24   WO 95 1613. War Diary of the 17th Brigade 6th Division and 3rd Rifle Battalion, September–December 1914; MH 106 2102. Medical Case Notes, Private C.D., January–February 1915.

25   MH 106 2102. Medical Case Notes, Private E.M., February 1915; WO 95 1269. War Diary of the 2nd Brigade 1st Division and 2nd Battalion Royal Sussex Regiment, January–February 1915.

26   MH 106 2102. Medical Case Notes, Private E.M., February 1915.

27   WO 95 1496. War Diary of the 1st Battalion, the Rifle Brigade, August 1914–December 1917.

28   WO 95 1469. War Diary. 25 December, and 4 to 28 January 1915.

29   MH 106 2101. Medical Case Notes, Private C.D., January–February 1915.

30   MH 106 2101. Medical Case Notes, Private F.G., July–September 1915.

31   MH 106 2102. Medical Case Notes, Private J.C., March 1915.

32   MH 106 2101. Medical Case Notes, Private F.F., May–September 1915.

33   MH 106 2102. Medical Case Notes, Rifleman W.B., August 1916.

34   MH 106 2102. Medical Case Notes and Documents, Sergeant D., July–September 1915.

35   ' "The Entertainment Bureaus." Night Effects arranged for the Amusement of a patient suffering from Nervous Breakdown.' *3rd London General Hospital Gazette*, I, 7 April 1916, 177; 'Shell-Shock – Who'd be a Night Nurse?', *Craigleith Hospital Chronicle*, VI, XXXVI, Spring 1919.

36   Chas. A. Watts, 'Shell Shock', *Springfield War Hospital Gazette*, February 1917, 9.
37   Sgt. P.R. Croft RAMC (T), 'Shell Shock', *3rd London War Hospital Gazette*, II (2 November 1916) 41; Gunner McPhail, 'Just Shell Shock', *The Springfield War Hospital Gazette*, September 1916; 'Medical Boards', *The Springfield War Hospital Gazette*, June 1917, 24.
38   K.W.S., 'In Shell Shock Land', *Springfield War Hospital Gazette*, May 1917.
39   Ibid.
40   Gunner McPhail, 'Just Shell Shock', *The Springfield War Hospital Gazette*, September 1916, 14.

Chapter 7

1   On officers at Maghull and elsewhere, see, for example, J.K. Rowlands, 'A Mental Hospital at War' (unpublished paper, 1985), 5–6; R.P. Graves, *The Heroic Assault, 1895–1926* (London: Weidenfeld and Nicolson, 1986), pp. 173–4; 'Shell Shock Hospitals. A Red Cross Arrangement', *The Times*, 29 September 1917, 9e.
2   PRO MH 106 1887–1890. Admission and Discharge Registers Craiglockhart War Hospital. October 1916–February 1919; National Archives of Scotland GD1\677\1. Medical Case Sheets from the Lennel Private Convalescent Home for Officers, Coldstream, Scotland; NAS GD1\677\2. Letters to Lady Clementine 1915–18; NAS GD1\677\3 Admission and Discharge Registers 1916–17; Wilfred Owen Collection, *The Hydra. The Magazine of the Craiglockhart War Hospital*, April 1917–June 1918.
3   Macpherson, Herringham, Eliot and Balfour, eds., *Medical Diseases of War*, volume 2 (London: HMSO, 1923), p. 32.
4   S. Sassoon, *Sherston's Progress* (London: Faber and Faber, 1936), p. 23.
5   'Craiglockhart Military Hospital 1916–19', *The Buckle* (Edinburgh, 1968), pp. 28–38.
6   'Craiglockhart Military Hospital 1916–19', p. 34.
7   PRO MH 106 1887–1890. Admission and Discharge Registers Craiglockhart War Hospital, October 1916–February 1919.
8   NAS GD1\667–690. Lennel Admission and Discharge Registers 1916–17; PRO MH 106 1887–1890 Craiglockhart Records 1916–19; *The Hydra*, 21 July 1917; 4 August 1917, 16 (admission figures).
9   W.H. Bryce, 'The Management of the Neurotic-Institution', in H. Crichton Miller, ed., *Functional Nerve Disease: An Epitome of War Experience for Practitioners* (London: Hodder and Stoughton, 1920), p. 158; p. 162.
10   Ibid., p. 160.
11   Ibid., p. 161.
12   'Craiglockhart Military Hospital 1916–19', pp. 35–6.
13   MH 106 1887–1890. Craiglockhart Admission and Discharge Registers 1916–19; WO 95. Various. For the later findings of Craiglockhart medics, see: A.J. Brock, *Health and Conduct* (London: Le Play House, 1923); W. Brown, 'Hypnosis, Suggestion, and Dissociation', *British Medical Journal*, I (1919) 734–6; W. Bryce, 'Some Considerations in Psycho-Therapy', *Journal of Mental Science*, LXVII (1921) 195–205; W.H.R. Rivers, *Instinct and the Unconscious* (Cambridge: Cambridge University Press, 1920).

14 NAS GD1\677\1. Medical Case Notes from the Lennel Private Convalescent Home for Officers, Coldstream, Scotland.

15 NAS GD1\677\3. Lennel Admission and Discharge Registers 1916–17.

16 NAS GD1\677\1. Medical Case Notes. Major E.P., May 1917.

17 NAS GD1\677\1. Medical Case Notes. Lieutenant E.S., August 1917.

18 NAS GD1\677\1. Medical Case Notes. Captain J.N., May–July 1917.

19 WO 95 3009. War Diary of the 175th Brigade 58th Division and 2/12th Battalion of the London Regiment, 27 April–27 May 1917; MH 106 1887. Craiglockhart Admission and Discharge Register 27 October 1916–13 November 1917.

20 NAS GD1\677\1. Medical Case Notes. Major P.I., July–September 1917.

21 NAS GD1\667\1. Medical Case Notes. Major W.P., November 1917.

22 NAS GD1\677\1. Medical Case Notes. Lieutenant P.H.

23 NAS GD1\677\1. Medical Case Notes. Lieutenant H.C., October 1916–February 1917.

24 NAS GD1\677\1. Medical Case Notes. Lieutenant W.T., July–November 1917.

25 'Lord Knutsford's Appeal', *The Times*, 4 November 1914, 5b.

26 'Lord Knutsford's Appeal', 'Special Hospital for Officers', *The Times*, 9 January 1915, 9d.

27 'Battle Shock. The Wounded Mind and its Cure. A Special Hospital', *The Times*, 25 May 1915, 11c.

28 Ibid.

29 Lord Knutsford, 'Officers and Nervous Shock', *The Times*, 31 January 1916, 9c.

30 'To be Stared At', *The Hydra*, 8, New Series, June 1918, 12. Oxford English Faculty Library, Wilfred Owen Collection.

31 'Extract from ye Chronicles of Wilfred de Salope, Knight', *The Hydra*, 15 September 1917, 14.

32 Editorial, *The Hydra*, 1 September 1917.

33 NAS GD1\677\2. Letters to Lady Clementine, 1915–18.

34 NAS GD1\677\2. B.W. to Lady Clementine, letter dated 16 January.

35 NAS GD1\677\2. W.S. to Lady Clementine, letter dated 12 April.

Chapter 8

1 Ministry of Pensions, *2nd Annual Report: 31 March 1918–31 March 1919* (London: HMSO, 1920), p. 70; Ministry of Pensions, *3rd Annual Report: 1 April 1919–31 March 1920* (London: HMSO, 1920), pp. 52–7.

2 Ministry of Pensions, *4th Annual Report: 1 April 1920–31 March 1921* (London: HMSO, 1921), p. 9.

3 Ibid., pp. 32–4.

4 Ministry of Pensions, *8th Annual Report: 1 April 1924–31 March 1925* (London: HMSO, 1926), p. 24. Ministry of Pensions, *13th Annual Report: 1 April 1929–31 March 1930* (London: HMSO, 1930), p. 14.

5 Ministry of Pensions, *8th Annual Report*, p. 6.

6 Ministry of Pensions, *8th Annual Report*, p. 31; pp. 27–30. Ministry of Pensions, *13th Annual Report*, p. 20; pp. 17–19.

7   R.H. Ahrenfeldt, *Psychiatry in the British Army in the Second World War* (London: Routledge and Kegan Paul, 1958), p. 10.

8   There is still relatively little on this subject; see Leed, *No Man's Land*, pp. 186–92; R.D. Richie, 'One History of "Shellshock"' (San Diego: University of California, unpublished PhD thesis, 1986), pp. 421–45; P. Lerner, *Hysterical Men* (New York: Columbia University, 1996), Chapters 6 and 7.

9   Leed, *No Man's Land*, p. 189.

10   *Report of the War Office Committee of Enquiry into Shell Shock* (London: HMSO, 1922). See also T. Bogacz, 'War Neurosis and Cultural Change in England, 1914–22: The Work of the War Office Committee of Enquiry into Shell Shock', *Journal of Contemporary History*, XXIV (1989) 227–56.

11   *Hansard*, 28 April 1920, 1106.

12   Ibid., 1096.

13   PIN 15/55. House of Commons questions, 31 May 1921.

14   W. Robinson, 'The Future of Service Patients in Mental Asylums', *Journal of Mental Science*, LXVII (1921) 40–8. See also House of Commons question on shell shock cases in asylums, 12 July 1921, *The Lancet*, 23 July 1921, 208; House of Commons questions on the number of shell shock cases, and on the types of treatment available, 28 July 1921. Both reported in *The Lancet*, 6 August 1921, 310.

15   Robinson, 'The Future of Service Patients in Mental Asylums', 40–1.

16   Ibid., 48.

17   Ibid., 47.

18   Viscount Knutsford, 'Neurasthenia and Shell-Shock', *The Times*, 16 April 1919, 16a.

19   PIN 15/56. House of Commons question, press cutting. July 1921.

20   *Report of the War Office Committee of Enquiry into Shell Shock*, pp. 17–18.

21   Ibid., p. 191.

22   Ibid.

23   Ibid., p. 192.

24   '"Shell Shock" and "Cowardice"', *The Lancet*, 19 August 1922, 399–400. See also Bogacz, 'War Neurosis and Cultural Change in England, 1914–22', 250.

25   C.E. Thwaites, 'Colonies for the Insane', *New Statesman*, 21 October 1922. Press cutting from PRO PIN 15/57.

26   A. Summers, *Angels and Citizens* (London: Routledge and Kegan Paul, 1988), pp. 205–37.

27   'Pensions and Allowances', *The Times*, 12 November 1914, 9d.

28   PIN 15/571. Entitlement to Pensions 1917–19.

29   See the following chapter for details on the practice of the Special Medical Boards, also: 'A Defence of Chelsea Hospital. Delays due to the System', *The Times*, 22 August 1916, 3d; 'Payment of Pensions. Official Explanation of the System', *The Times*, 24 August 1916, 3d.

30   PIN 15/54. Notes by Sir John Collie on the Treatment of Neurasthenia.

31   'Appointment for Sir John Collie', *The Times*, 7 July 1917, 6d; *The Times*, 4 January 1918, 7b.

32   J. Collie, 'The Management of Neurasthenia and Allied Disorders Contracted in the Army', *Journal of State Medicine*, XXVI (1918) 11.

33   Ibid., 2–26.

34 'Obsession and Fraud. Studies in Diseased Personality. Sir J. Collie's Lecture', *The Times*, 27 January 1915, 5a.

35 Collie, 'The Management of Neurasthenia', (1918)11.

36 See early correspondence in PRO PIN 15/4. Medical Boards 1917–22.

37 Full details are recounted in PRO PIN 15/1431. Examination of Cases or Suspected Cases of Malingering 1917–18.

38 C. Rudy, 'Concerning Tommy', *Contemporary Review*, November 1918, 549.

39 'A Painful Case. Baseless Charge against Disabled Soldier', *John Bull*, 29 June 1918. Press cutting in PIN 15/1431.

40 Collie, 'The Management of Neurasthenia', (1918) 3; 6.

41 This was published in 1917 and again in 1918 as J. Collie, 'The Management of Neurasthenia and Allied Disorders Contracted in the Army', *Recalled to Life*, II (September 1917) 234–53; J. Collie, 'The Management of Neurasthenia and Allied Disorders Contracted in the Army', *Journal of State Medicine*, XXVI (1918) 2–17.

42 Collie, 'The Management of Neurasthenia', (1918) 5–6. See also 'Cure of Shell Shock. Organisation of Homes of Recovery. Sir John Collie's Scheme', *The Times*, 14 June 1917, 3a.

43 Sir John Collie, 'Restorative Treatment', *Reveille*, I (August 1918) 42–4.

44 Collie, 'The Management of Neurasthenia', (1918) 15.

45 See, for example, Lieut.-Col. William Turner, Preface to J. Collie's 'Neurasthenia and Allied Disorders', *Recalled to Life*, II (September 1917) 251–3; W. Draper, 'Village Centres for Cure and Training', *Recalled to Life*, III (April 1918) 242–357; Major A.F. Hurst, 'Nerves and the Men', *Reveille*, II (November 1918) 260–8.

46 Captain B. Williams, 'Pensions', *Recalled to Life*, I (June 1917) 127.

47 See, for example, 'Nerve Shattered Pensioners. A State Scheme for Treatment', *The Times*, 22 August 1917, 9c; W. Draper, 'Village Centres for Cure and Training', 342–57.

48 Collie, 'Restorative Treatment', 52–3; PRO PIN 15/54. Special Medical Board Case Reviews 1917.

49 On Hurst, see especially A.F. Hurst, 'Cinematographic Demonstration of War Neurosis', *Proceedings of the Royal Society of Medicine, Neurology Section*, XI (1917–18) 39–42; 'Observations on the Etiology and Treatment of War Neuroses', *British Medical Journal*, 29 September 1917, 409–14; 'Nerves and the Men (The Mental Factor in the Disabled Soldier)', *Reveille*, II (November 1918) 260–8; *The Psychology of the Special Senses and their Functional Disorders* (Oxford: Oxford University Press, 1920).

50 Hurst, 'Nerves and the Men', 260–1.

51 Ibid., 264–5.

52 See, for example, Leed, *No Man's Land*, pp. 188–9.

53 See, for example, N. Fenton, *Shellshock and its Aftermath* (New York: Henry Kimpton, 1926); G. Massoneau, 'A Social Analysis of a Group of Psychoneurotic Ex-Servicemen', *Mental Hygiene*, XI (1922) 575–91; H. Archibald, D.M. Long, C. Miller and R. Tuddenham, 'Gross Stress Reaction in Combat – A 15-Year Follow-up', *American Journal of Psychiatry* (1962) 317–22.

54 R. Karpe and I. Schnap, 'Nostopathy – A Study of Pathogenic Homecoming', *American Journal of Psychiatry*, CIX (1952–3) 46–51.

55 N. Fenton, *Shellshock and its Aftermath* (London: H. Kimpton, 1926), p. 73.

56 Ibid., pp. 91–4.
57 See, for example, PIN 15/421. Unrest amongst Ex-Soldiers: Administration of Labour Exchanges, etc. 1918–19. Also Ward, 'Great Britain: Land Fit for Heroes Lost', in S.R. Ward, ed., *The War Generation* (London: Kennikat Press, 1975), pp. 10–13.
58 See, for example, 'Moral and Military Pensions. Revolt of the Towns', *The Times*, 20 July 1916, 9c; 'Disabled Soldiers Pensions', *The Times*, 1 March 1916, 9f and 10a.
59 Rudy, 'Concerning Tommy', 550.
60 PRO PIN 15/421. Ministry of Pensions Report on 'Unrest Amongst Ex-Soldiers', 31 March 1920.
61 PIN 15/421. Ministry of Pensions questionnaire to Regional War Pensions Committees 1-10-19.
62 PIN 15/421. Birmingham War Pensions Committee to Ministry of Pensions 5-10-19.
63 PIN 15/421. Report on 'Unrest Amongst Ex-Soldiers', 31 March 1920.
64 PIN 15/421. Scottish Regional H.Q. to Ministry of Pensions, 11-10-19.
65 PIN 15/421. Report on 'Unrest Amongst Ex-Soldiers', 31 March 1920.
66 S.R. Ward, 'Great Britain: Land Fit for Heroes Lost', in S.R. Ward, ed., *The War Generation* (New York: Kennikat, Port Washington, 1975), pp. 11–37.
67 R.C. Davidson, *The Unemployed* (London: Longmans Green, 1929), p. 94.
68 G. Oram, *Worthless Men* (London: Francis Boutle, 1998), pp. 84–101.

Chapter 9

1 B. Shepherd, *A War of Nerves: Soldiers and Psychiatrists 1914–1994* (London: Jonathan Cape, 2000), pp. 165–8.
2 G.M. Smith and T.H. Mitchell, *The Official History of the Great War*, vol. 7 (London: HMSO, 1931), chart opposite p. 328.
3 Major A.F. Hurst, 'Nerves and the Men', *Reveille*, 5 November 1918, 261–2; PIN 15/58. Treatment of cases of Neurasthenia in Special Neurological Hospitals. Cases at Maghull, 31 August 1931.
4 'Recent Developments and Editorial Notes', *Recalled to Life*, 3 April 1918, 332. On the Medical Services Department see also 'Bird's-Eye View of the Activities of the Medical Services Department, Ministry of Pensions', *Recalled to Life*, 3 April 1918, 445.
5 F. Kaufmann, 'Die planmässige Heilung komplizierter psychogener Bewegungsstörungen bei Soldaten in einer Sitzung', *Münchener Medizische Wochenschrift*, 30, Mai 1916, Feldärztliche Beilage 22, 354–7, in H. Binneveld, *From Shell Shock to Combat Stress: A Comparative History of Military Psychiatry* (Amsterdam: Amsterdam University Press, 1997), p. 108.
6 'Treatment Centres on 31 May 1918', *Reveille*, I, August 1918, 54.
7 PRO PIN 15/56. 'Treatment of Neurasthenia 17/6/21. Regional Reports on Occupational Treatment'.
8 See, for example, PRO PIN 15/56. 'Treatment of Neurasthenia. Arrangements for Provision, Accommodation, etc. Memo on Conference 17/6/21'; 'Provision of Treatment for Neurasthenia 25-11-21'.

9 PRO PIN 15/55. Sir John Collie (Director General of Medical Services) to the Association of Local War Pensions Committees, 18 December 1919.

10 PRO PIN 15/56. 'Treatment of Neurasthenia. Arrangements for Provision, Accommodation, etc. Memo on Conference 17/6/21'. Comments by Dr Wallace.

11 PRO PIN 15/55. Discussion and Correspondence on the Conversion of Hollesley Bay. W.F. Furste to C.F.A. Hore, Ministry of Pensions, 13/4/21.

12 Captain L. Gameson RAMC, Memoirs, unpublished typescript, Imperial War Museum, 82.

13 B.M. Downes, 'Memoria Technica as used in the Treatment of War Torn Comprehension in the War of 1914–18'. Ts., Imperial War Museum, 28.

14 Ibid., 29–30.

15 PRO PIN 15/54. Notes by Sir John Collie on treatment and examination by the Special Medical Board of Neurasthenic cases 11-4-17.

16 See especially Sir A. Keogh, G.C.B., 'The Treatment of the Disabled', *Recalled to Life*, 1 June 1917, 10–11.

17 See, for example, PRO PIN 14/58. Treatment of Cases of Neurasthenia in Special Neurological Hospitals. Investigation of Saltash Cases.

18 *Report of the War Office Committee of Enquiry into 'Shell Shock'*, pp. 21–2.

19 Keogh, 'The Treatment of the Disabled', 8–9.

20 This and following examples of physical disability percentage ratings are taken from Keogh, 'The Treatment of the Disabled', 10–11.

21 'Suicide and War Neurosis', *The Lancet*, 6 August 1921, 311.

22 PRO PIN 15/58. 'Treatment of Cases of Neurasthenia in Special Neurological Hospitals. 1925 Reports, General'.

23 PRO PIN 15/58. Review of Saltash Cases II. Underassessment; G.M. Smith and T.H. Mitchell, *The Official History of the Great War*, vol.17, chart opposite p. 328.

24 PRO PIN 15/58. Review II. Underassessment.

25 Ibid.

26 PRO PIN 15/58. Review I. Hospitalisation.

27 PRO PIN 15/57. 'The Question of Providing an Institution for Certain Types of Incurable Cases'.

28 PRO PIN 15/57. 'Mental and Neurasthenic Cases for Supervision'.

29 PRO PIN 15/58. 1925 Report on Harrowby.

30 PRO PIN 15/58. G. Crystal (Ministry of Pensions) to the Treasury Secretary, Whitehall, 1 May 1923.

31 PRO PIN 15/57. 'The Question of Providing an Institution'; PRO PIN 15/58. 'Treatment of Cases of Neurasthenia in Special Neurological Hospitals. Review of Saltash Cases 1926'; PRO PIN 15/58. Cases at Maghull, 31 August 1931.

32 PRO PIN 15/58. Review II. Underassessment.

33 PRO PIN 15/58. Maghull Review.

34 Ibid.

35 The National Hospital, Queen Square, Medical Notes and Records. Dr Saunders, 1920. Medical Notes and Records on Private A.L.

36 PRO PIN 15/58. Treatment of Cases of Neurasthenia in Special Neurological Hospitals. Review of Saltash Cases 1926.

37 See examples below, and The Cassel Hospital for Nervous Diseases, Yearly Reports 1921–39; The National Hospital, Queen Square, Medical Records and

Notes, 1915–25; PRO PIN 15/54. Neurasthenia Case Reviews; PRO PIN 15/58. Treatment of cases of Neurasthenia in Special Neurological Hospitals. Cases retained in Hospitals for prolonged Periods, 1923–33.

38   Cassel Hospital for Functional Nervous Disorders. Yearly Statistics and Reports, 1921–22, Report on the First Six Months, 1.

39   T.A. Ross, *The Common Neuroses: Their Treatment by Psychotherapy* (London: Edward Arnold, 1923), p. 131. See also T.A. Ross, *An Enquiry into Prognosis into the Neuroses* (Cambridge: Cambridge University Press, 1936), p. 87.

40   Sir J. Purves-Stuart, 'Discussion of Traumatic Neurasthenia and Litigation Neurosis', *Proceeding of the Royal Society of Medicine*, XXI (1928) 359–61; PRO PIN 15/54. War Pensions and Statutory Committee, and Special Medical Board, Neurasthenia Case Reviews.

41   Showlater, *The Female Malady*, p. 179.

42   Bristol Re-survey Board, case notes on Mr E., 27-7-25. Cassel Hospital Sample case notes 1926. For a full explanation of the work of the local pensions boards see below.

43   Dr T.A. Ross to Sir Maurice Craig. Cassel Hospital Sample case notes 1926. Case notes on Mr E. 10 July 1926.

44   D.A. Thom, 'War Neurosis: Experience of 1914–18', *Journal of Laboratory and Clinical Medicine*, XXVIII (1943) 499–508.

45   See, for example, Fenton, *Shellshock and its Aftermath*.

46   K. Figlio, 'How does Illness Mediate Social Relations? Workmen's Compensation and Medico-Legal Practices, 1890–1940', in P. Wright and A. Treacher, eds., *The Problem of Medical Knowledge: Examining the Social Construction of Medicine* (Edinburgh: Edinburgh University Press, 1982), pp. 174–228.

47   Sassoon, *Sherston's Progress*, pp. 71–2.

Chapter 10

1   The following examples are taken from the *Oxford English Dictionary*, XV, second edn (1989), p. 233.

2   E.A. Mackintosh, *War, the Liberator* (London: John Lane, 1918), p. 148.

3   E. Fraser and J. Gibbon, *Sailor and Soldier Words* (London: Routledge, 1925), p. 225.

4   W. Holden, *Shell Shock: The Psychological Impact of War* (London: Channel 4, 1997), p. 80.

5   J.F.C. Fuller, *Generalship* (London: Faber, 1933), p. 20.

6   See especially Shepherd, *A War of Nerves*, pp. 169–297.

7   G. Greene, *The Ministry of Fear* (London: William Heinemann, 1943); Holden, *Shell Shock*, p. xx.

8   S. Kauffman, *The Philanderer* (London: Secker and Warburg, 1953), p. 108.

9   *The Listener*, CLXVIII, 9 February 1978, 2.

10   Holden, *Shell Shock*, p. 158; p. 160.

11   R. Samuel, *Theatres of Memory: Past and Present in Contemporary Culture* (London: Verso, 1994), x.

12   'Shot at Dawn', *John Bull*, 23 February 1918, 6–7, in S. Hynes, *A War Imagined* (London: Macmillan, 1990), p. 213; G. Oram, *Worthless Men* (London: F. Boutle, 1998), pp. 100–1.

13 H. Read, *Naked Warriors* (London: Arts and Letters, 1919); A.P. Herbert, *The Secret Battle* (New York: Knopf, 1920); W. Owen, *Poems*, introduction by S. Sassoon (London: Chatto and Windus, 1920).

14 Read, *Naked Warriors*, p. 43.

15 Winston Churchill, in A.P. Herbert, *The Secret Battle* (New York: Knopf, 1920), p. v.

16 *The Secret Battle*, pp. 215–16.

17 Ibid., pp. 92–3.

18 Ibid., pp. 71–2.

19 Ibid., pp. 164–5.

20 Ibid., pp. 212–13.

21 Ibid., p. 210.

22 On Frankenau, see H. Cecil, 'British War Novelists', in Cecil and Liddle, *Facing Armageddon*, pp. 801–16. D.L. Sayers, *Whose Body?* (London: Gollancz, 1923); D.L. Sayers, *Busman's Honeymoon* (London: Gollancz, 1937). See also R.F. Delderfield, *To Serve Them All My Days* (New York: Pocket Books, 1937).

23 R. West, *The Return of the Soldier* (London: Virago, 1979); J. Van Druton, *The Return of the Soldier* (London: Gollancz, 1928).

24 *The Return of the Soldier*, p. 66.

25 Ibid., p. 67.

26 V. Woolf, *Mrs Dalloway* (New York: Harcourt Brace, 1925); S. Trombley, *'All that Summer She was Mad'* (London: Junction Books, 1981); S. Thomas, 'Virginia Woolf's Septimus Smith and Contemporary Perceptions of Shell Shock', *English Language Notes*, XXV (1987) 49–57.

27 Thomas, 'Virginia Woolf's Septimus Smith', 50.

28 Woolf, *Mrs Dalloway*, pp. 102–3.

29 M. Craig, *Nervous Exhaustion* (London: J.A. Churchill, 1922); G.H. Savage and E. Goodwin, *Insanity and its Allied Neuroses: A Practical and Clinical Manual* (London: Cassell, 1912).

30 W. Owen, *Poems*, introduced by Siegfried Sassoon (London: Chatto and Windus, 1920). See also Box 14: Early Press Cuttings, Wilfred Owen Collection; D. Hibberd, 'The Date of Wilfred Owen's "Exposure"', *Notes and Queries*, New Series, XXIII (1976), 305–8.

31 E.B., 'The Real War', *The Athenaeum*, 10 December 1920. Wilfred Owen Collection, Box 14, piece 10.

32 *The Observer*, 19 December 1920. Wilfred Owen Collection, Box 14, piece 19.

33 B. Bond, 'British War Writing', in Cecil and Liddle, *Facing Armageddon*, p. 820.

34 E.B., 'The Real War'.

35 *The Poems of Wilfred Owen. A new edition including many pieces now first published and notices of his life and work by Edmund Blunden* (New York: Viking, 1931), p. 3.

36 Ibid., pp. 27–8.

37 Ibid., p. 39.

38 Dyer, *The Missing of the Somme*, pp. 31–2.

39 S. Sassoon, *Siegfried's Journey* (New York: Viking, 1946).

40 Ibid., p. 90.

41 Ibid., pp. 93–4.

42 A. Clark, *The Donkeys* (London: Pimlico, 1991); L. Woolf, *In Flanders Field* (Harmondsworth: Penguin, 1979); Theatre Workshop Collective, *Oh What a Lovely War* (London: Methuen, 1965).

43 *Oh What a Lovely War*, pp. 47–8.

44 Clark, *The Donkeys*, p. 11.

45 Ibid., pp. 186–7.

46 C. Carrington, *Soldier From the Wars Returning* (New York: David McKay, 1965), p. 267.

47 Clark, *The Donkeys*, p. 11.

48 R.J. Lifton, *Home from the War* (New York: Simon and Schuster, 1973); American Psychiatric Association, *Diagnostic and Statistical Manual of Mental Disorders*, third edn (Washington: American Psychiatric Association, 1980). On the 'DMS III Revolution', see Young, *The Harmony of Illusions*, pp. 89–142.

49 M. Evans, 'Rehabilitating the Traumatised Veterans: The Case of French Conscripts from the Algerian War, 1954–62', in M. Evans and K. Lunn, eds., *War and Memory in the Twentieth Century* (Oxford: Berg, 1997), p. 81.

50 Holden, *Shell Shock*, p. 165.

51 Ibid., p. 160.

52 P. Nora, 'Between Memory and History: Les Lieux de Mémoire', *Representations*, XXVI (1989) 7–25.

53 E. Hobsbawm, *The Age of Extremes: The Short Twentieth Century, 1914–1991* (London: Abacus, 1995), pp. 2–5. See also Evans and Lunn, eds., *War and Memory in the Twentieth Century*; R. Porter, *Myths of the English* (Cambridge: Polity, 1992).

54 A. Thompson, *Anzac Memories: Living with the Legend* (Oxford: Oxford University Press, 1994).

55 A. Babbington, *Shell-shock: A History of Changing Attitudes to War Neurosis* (London: Leo Cooper, 1997); H. Binneveld, *From Shell Shock to Combat Stress* (Amsterdam: Amsterdam University Press, 1997); W. Holden, *Shell Shock* (London: Channel 4, 1997).

56 P. Barker, *The Regeneration Trilogy* (Harmondsworth: Penguin, 1998).

57 Barker, *The Regeneration Trilogy*, p. 43.

58 Ibid., p. 53.

59 Ibid., p. 160.

60 Ibid., p. 544.

61 For another interpretation of Rivers' contribution, see A. Young, *The Harmony of Illusions: The Invention of Post-Traumatic Stress Disorder* (Princeton: Princeton University Press, 1995).

Chapter 11

1 See, for example, V. Kolocontroni, J. Goldman and O. Taxidou, *Modernism: An Anthology of Sources and Documents* (Edinburgh: Edinburgh University Press, 1998), F. Marinetti, 'The Variety Theatre' (1913), pp. 253–6; 'Preface to *Some Imagist Poets*' (1915), pp. 268–9; T. Tzara, 'Dada Manifesto' (1918), pp. 276–80.

2 P. Conrad, *Modern Times, Modern Places: Life and Art in the 20th Century* (London: Thames and Hudson, 1998), p. 111.

3 See J. Bourke, 'Disciplining the Emotions: Fear, Psychiatry and the Second World War', in R. Cooter et al., eds., *War, Medicine and Modernity* (Stroud: Sutton, 1999), pp. 225–38.
4 See Shepherd, *A War of Nerves*, pp. 165–8.
5 W. Sargant and E. Slater, *An Introduction to Physical Methods of Treatment in Psychiatry* (Edinburgh: Livingstone, 1944); W. Sargant, *The Unquiet Mind* (London: Heinemann, 1967).
6 S.H. Foulkes, *Introduction to Group-Analytic Psychotherapy* (London: Heinemann, 1948).
7 Shepherd, *A War of Nerves*, p. 326.

Bibliographical Note

1 P. Fussell, *The Great War and Modern Memory* (Oxford: Oxford University Press, 1975). E. Leed, *No Man's Land: Combat and Identity in World War One* (Cambridge: Cambridge University Press, 1979).
2 Fussell, *The Great War and Modern Memory*, p. ix.
3 Ibid., pp. 36–74; pp. 279–309.
4 Leed, *No Man's Land*, p. ix.
5 E. Showalter, *The Female Malady: Women, Madness and English Culture, 1830–1980* (London: Virago, 1987), p. 5; p. 6.
6 E. Showalter, 'Rivers and Sassoon: The Inscription of Male Gender Anxieties', in M.R. Higgonnet et al., *Behind the Lines: Gender and the Two World Wars* (New Haven: Yale University Press, 1987), p. 69.
7 Showalter, *The Female Malady*, pp. 18–19.
8 B. Shepherd, *A War of Nerves: Soldiers and Psychiatrists 1914–1994* (London: Jonathan Cape, 2000), p. 184.
9 Showalter, *The Female Malady*, p. 172.
10 D. Pick, *War Machine: The Rationalisation of Slaughter in the Modern Age* (New Haven: Yale University Press, 1993), pp. 165–75.
11 Pick, *War Machine*, p. 168. See also M.R. Trimble, *Post Traumatic Neurosis: From Railway Spine to Whiplash* (Chichester: John Wiley, 1981).
12 L. Smith, 'The French High Command', p. 79; J. Bourne, 'The British Working Man in Arms', p. 336; S. Audoin-Rouzea, 'The French Soldier in the Trenches', p. 221, all in H. Cecil and P. Liddle, eds., *Facing Armageddon: The First World War Experienced* (London: Leo Cooper, 1996).
13 M. Micale and P. Lerner, eds., *Traumatic Pasts*, forthcoming.
14 R. Cooter and S. Sturdy, eds., 'Of War, Medicine and Modernity: Introduction', in R. Cooter, M. Harrison and S. Sturdy, *War, Medicine and Modernity* (Stroud: Sutton, 1999), pp. 1–21.
15 O. Bartov, *The Eastern Front 1941–45, German Troops and the Barbarization of Warfare* (London: Macmillan, 1985).
16 T. Ashworth, *Trench Warfare 1914–18: The Live and Let Live System* (London: Macmillan, 1980); J. Keegan, *The Face of Battle: A Study of Agincourt, Waterloo and the Somme* (London: Jonathan Cape, 1976); T. Wilson, *The Myriad Faces of War, Britain and the Great War 1914–18* (Cambridge: Polity, 1986).
17 J.C. Fuller, *Troop Morale and Popular Culture in the British and Dominion Armies 1914–18* (Oxford: Oxford University Press, 1990); H. Strachan, *The Politics of*

the British Army (Oxford: Oxford University Press, 1997); T.H.E. Traver, *The Killing Ground: The British Army, the Western Front and the Emergence of Modern Warfare* (London: Macmillan, 1987).

18 P.F. Lerner, 'Hysterical Men: War, Neurosis and German Mental Medicine, 1914–21', unpublished PhD thesis, Columbia University, 1996, pp. 325–411. Also R.W. Whalen, *Bitter Wounds: German Victims of the Great War, 1914–1939* (Ithaca: Cornell University Press, 1984); R. Bessell, *Germany after the First World War* (Clarendon: Oxford, 1993).

19 A. Babbington, *Shell-Shock: A History of the Changing Attitudes to War Neurosis* (London: Leo Cooper, 1997); H. Binneveld, *From Shellshock to Combat Stress: A Comparative History of Military Psychiatry* (Amsterdam: Amsterdam University Press, 1997); W. Holden, *Shell Shock: The Psychological Impact of War* (London: Channel 4, 1998).

20 A. Young, *The Harmony of Illusions: Inventing Post-Traumatic Stress Disorder* (Princeton: Princeton University Press, 1995); B. Shepherd, *A War of Nerves: Soldiers and Psychiatrists 1914–1994* (London: Jonathan Cape, 2000).

21 Lerner, 'Hysterical Men'; M.O. Roudebush, 'The Battle of Nerves: Hysteria and its Treatments in France during World War I', unpublished PhD thesis, University of Columbia at Berkeley, 1995.

22 J. Winter, *Sites of Memory, Sites of Mourning* (Cambridge: Cambridge University Press, 1995), pp. 1–11; Fussell, *The Great War and Modern Memory*, pp. 310–35; S. Hynes, *A War Imagined: The First World War and English Culture* (London: Pimlico, 1992).

Bibliography

Archive sources

British Library
Craigleith Hospital Chronicle, 1914–19.
Springfield War Hospital Gazette, 1916–17.

British Psychological Society Archive
Pear, T.H., 'Reminiscences', unpublished MS, 1959.

British Red Cross Archive
The Red Cross Journal, 1914–18.
Joint War Reports of the British Red Cross and St John, 1914–18.

Cambridge University Library War Collection
Barlow, M., *War Pensions, Gratuities, Allowances, Treatment and Training for Officers, N.C.O.s and Men. A Handbook*, sixth edn (London: HMSO, 1918).
Brophy, J. and Partridge, E., *Songs and Slang of the British Soldiers 1914–18*, third edn (London: Eric Partridge, 1931).
Lord Charnwood, ed., *Recalled to Life: A Journal Devoted to the Care, Re-education, and Return to Civil Life of Disabled Soldiers and Sailors*, No. 1–3, 1918.
Galsworthy, J., ed., *Reveille: Devoted to Disabled Sailors and Soldiers*, No. 1–2, 1918.
Gazette of the 3rd London Hospital, 1915–19.

Cassel Hospital
Yearly Reports and Statistics, the Cassel Hospital for Nervous Diseases.

Imperial War Museum
H. Crerar, Second Lieutenant, Letters and Documents.
A.W. Downes, Ts. Manuscript.
L. Gameson, Captain, RAMC, Memoirs from Ts. and Diary.
E. Kay, Recollections.
J.C. Latter, Major-General, Papers relating to 'Shell Shock' and Court Martial Proceedings.
W. McRobb, Ms. And Ts. on Fitness after 'Shell Shock'.
S. Sassoon, Letters and Documents relating to W.H.R. Rivers. (SS7).
E. Sheard, Account by a Medical Orderly.
H. Sturdy, Ms. Account.
Baroness E. de T'Serclaes, Diaries.
W. Tyrell, Box 29 – Shell Shock.

Leeds University Peter Liddle 1914–18 Personal Experience Archive

Written and recorded accounts, letters and diaries.

National Hospital, Queen Square

Medical Records and Notes, 1915–24.

Oxford English Faculty Library Wilfred Owen Collection

The Hydra. The Magazine of the Craiglockhart War Hospital. April 1917–June 1918.
Box 14. Early Press Cuttings 1919–46.
Box 33/2. *Not About Heroes: The Friendship of Siegfried Sassoon and Wilfred Owen: A Play in Two Acts,* by Stephen MacDonald. Revision of 31 March 1986 from the National Theatre Production.

Oxfordshire District Health Authority Archive

Admission and Discharge Records, September 1918–February 1922, the Ashurst War Hospital, Littlemore, Oxford.

Public Record Office

MH 106/ 1887–1890. Admission and Discharge Registers, Craiglockhart War Hospital, October 1916–February 1919.
MH 106/ 2101–2102. Mental Illness/Neurasthenia Sample Case Sheets.
PIN 15/ 4–5. Medical Boards 1917–22 and 1918.
PIN 15/ 8. Medical Boards 1918–20.
PIN 15/ 53–58. Treatment of Neurasthenia.
PIN 15/ 102. Pensions Appeal Tribunal 1919–21.
PIN 15/ 131–2. Ministry Clinics 1918 and 1918–19.
PIN 15/ 292. Revisions of Estimates to Reduce Expenditure 1919–20.
PIN 15/ 421. Unrest Amongst Ex-Soldiers: Administration of Labour Exchanges, etc. 1919–20.
PIN 15/ 570–1. Entitlement to Pensions 1916–20 and 1919–20.
PIN 15/ 1069–70. Tuberculosis: Entitlement to Pensions: Q. of Attribution or Aggravation 1917 and 1918–19.
PIN 15/ 1105–6. Special Medical Boards for the Examination of Neurasthenia and Functional Nervous Disorder Cases 1916 and 1918.
PIN 15/ 1230. Medical Boarding During or Following Treatment 1917–21.
PIN 15/ 1431. Examination of Cases of Suspected Malingering 1917–18.
Ministry of Pensions Files – Soldiers Documents.
WO 32/ 4747. War Office Committee of Enquiry into 'Shell-Shock' – Minutes and Correspondence.
WO 71/ 387–1238. Judge Advocate General's Record of Courts Martial.
WO 95. War Diaries.

Scottish Record Office

GD1/ 677/1. Medical Case Sheets from the Lennel Private Convalescent Home for Officers, Coldstream, Scotland.
GD1/ 677/2. Letters to Lady Clementine, 1915–18.
GD1/ 677/3. Admission and Discharge Register for the Lennel, 1916–17.

Wellcome Library for the History and Understanding of Medicine, RAMC Historical Collection

148. *RAMC Training Manual* (London: HMSO, 1911).
446/ 6. Notes and Observations made by Major H.E.M. Douglas and Captain H. St.M. Carter RAMC during the Serbo-Bulgarian War, 1913.
466/ 9. Fripp, Oyston and Perry, Memorandum on Army Medical Services to December 1915.
466/ 11. 'Shell Shock.' Proceedings of a Court of Enquiry Dealing with the Failure of an Infantry Battalion to Carry Out a Raid. July 1916.
739/ 2/13. Kaye, Capt. H.W. Written Account of a Shell Shock Case.
976. *The Buckle. The Journal of the Craiglockhart College of Education.*

Periodicals and newspapers

American Journal of Insanity.
American Medicine.
Archives of Neurology and Psychiatry.
Brain.
British Journal of Medical Psychology.
British Medical Journal.
Contemporary Review.
Cotswold Field Naturalist Association Journal.
Craigleith Hospital Chronicle.
The Hydra.
International Clinics.
John Bull.
Journal of Abnormal Psychology.
Journal of the American Medical Association.
Journal of Laboratory and Clinical Medicine.
Journal of Mental Science.
Journal of the RAMC.
Journal of State Medicine.
Lancet.
Long Island Medical Journal.
Manchester Guardian.
Medical Annual.
Medical Press and Circular.
Mental Hygiene.
New Statesman.

Medical: books

Abercrombie, J., *Diseases of the Brain and Spinal Cord*, fourth edn (London: Longman, 1828).
Bonhoeffer, K., ed., *Hanbuch Der Arztlichen Erfarung im Weltkrieg 1914–18:* Vol. 4, *Geistes- und Nervenkrankheiten* (Leipzig: J.M. Barth, 1922).
Brereton, F.S., *The Great War and the RAMC* (London: Constable, 1919).
Brock, A.J., *Health and Conduct* (London: Le Play House, 1923).
Clevinger, F.S., *Spinal Concussion* (London: F.A. David, 1889).

Collie, J., *Malingering and Feigning Sickness* (London: E. Arnold, 1917).
Craig, M., *Nervous Exhaustion* (London: J.A. Churchill, 1922).
—— *Psychological Medicine* (London: J.A. Churchill, 1905).
Crichton Miller, H., ed., *Functional Nerve Disease: An Epitome of War Experience for the Practitioner* (London: Hodder and Stoughton, 1920).
Culpin, M., *Psychoneuroses in War and Peace* (Cambridge: Cambridge University Press, 1920).
—— *Recent Advances in the Study of Psychoneuroses* (London: J.A. Churchill, 1931).
Eder, M.D., *War-Shock: The Psycho-Neuroses of War Psychology and Treatment* (London: W. Heinemann, 1917).
Erichson, J.E., *On Concussion of the Spine* (London: Longman, Green, 1882).
Fenton, N., *Shell Shock and its Aftermath* (London: H. Kimpton, 1926).
Ferenczi, S. et al., *Psycho-Analysis and the War Neuroses* (London: Psychoanalytic Press, 1921).
Foulkes, S.H., *Introduction to Group-Analytic Psychotherapy* (London: Heiremann, 1948).
Gavin, H., *On Feigning and Factitious Diseases Chiefly of Soldiers and Sailors* (London: J.A. Churchill, 1843).
Hamilton, A.M., *Railway and Other Accidents* (London: Baillière Tindall, 1906).
Hurst, A.F., *The Psychology of the Special Senses and their Functional Disorders* (Oxford: Oxford University Press, 1920).
Jones, A.B. and Llewellyn, L.J., *Malingering or the Simulation of Disease* (London: Heinemann, 1917).
Leri, A., *Shell Shock, Commotional and Emotional Aspects* (London: University Press, 1919).
MacCurdy, J.T., *War Neurosis* (Cambridge: Cambridge University Press, 1918).
McDougall, W., *Introduction to Social Psychology* (London: Methuen, 1908).
—— *An Outline of Abnormal Psychology* (London: Methuen, 1926).
MacPherson, Major-Gen. Sir W.G. et al., ed., *Medical Services Diseases of War*, Vol. 2, *Medical Aspects of Aviation and Gas Warfare and Gas Poisoning in Tanks and Mines* (London: HMSO, 1923).
Marr, H.C., *Psychoses of the War* (London: H. Froud, 1919).
Maxwell, W.M., *A Psychological Retrospective of the Great War* (London: George Allen and Unwin, 1923).
Mott, F.W., *War Neuroses and Shell Shock* (London: Hodder and Stoughton, 1919).
Myers, C.S., *Present Day Applications of Psychology* (London: Methuen, 1919).
—— *Shell-Shock in France* (Cambridge: Cambridge University Press, 1940).
Oppenheim, H., *Die Traumatischen Neurosen nach den in der Nervenklinik der Charite in den 8 Jahren 1883–1889 gesammelten Beobachtungen* (Berlin: Hirschwald, 1889; revised and updated 1893).
Page, H., *Injuries of the Spine and Spinal Cord Without Apparent Mechanical Lesion* (London: J.A. Churchill, 1885).
Read, C.S., *Military Psychiatry in Peace and War* (London: H.K. Lewis, 1920).
Rivers, W.H.R., *Instinct and the Unconscious* (Cambridge: Cambridge University Press, 1920).
—— *Psychology and Politics* (London: Kegan Paul, Trench and Trubner, 1923).
Ross, T.A., *The Common Neuroses, their Treatment by Psychotherapy* (London: E. Arnold, 1923).

——*An Enquiry into Prognosis in the Neuroses* (Cambridge: Cambridge University Press, 1936).

Salmon, T.W., *The Care and Treatment of Mental Diseases and War Neurosis ('Shell Shock') in the British Army* (New York: War Work Committee of the National Committee for Mental Hygiene, 1917).

——et al., *The Medical Department of the United States Army of the World War, X, Neuropsychiatry* (Washington: Government Printing Office, 1929).

Sargant, W., *The Unquiet Mind* (New York: Atlantic/Little, Brown, 1969).

Sargant, W. and Slater, E., *An Introduction to Physical Methods of Treatment in Psychiatry* (Edinburgh: Edinburgh University Press, 1944).

Savage, G.H. and Goodall, E., *Insanity and Allied Neuroses* (London: Cassell, 1907).

Smith, E. and Pear, T.H., *Shell-shock and its Lessons* (London: Longmans Green, 1917).

Smith, G. and Mitchell, T.H., *History of the Great War*, Vol. 7, *Medical Services* (London: HMSO, 1931).

Sollier, P. and Chartier, M., *La Commotion par explosifs et ses conséquences sur le système nerveux* (Paris: Baillière, 1915).

Southard, E.E., *Shell-Shock and other Neuro-Psychiatric Problems, Presented in Five Hundred and Eighty Case Histories from the War Literature, 1914–18* (New York: Arno, 1973).

Stoddard, W.B.H., *The Mind and Its Disorders* (London: H.K. Lewis, 1908).

Wier Mitchell, S., *Blood and Fat and How to Use Them* (Philadelphia: J.B. Lippincott, 1877).

Yealland, L.R., *Hysterical Disorders of Warfare* (London: Macmillan, 1918).

Medical: articles

Adrian, E.D. and Yealland, L.R., 'Treatment of some Common War Neuroses', *Lancet* (9 June 1917) 867–72.

Ballard, E.F., 'The Psychoneurotic Temperament and Its Reactions to Military Service', *Journal of Mental Science*, LXIV (1919) 152–80.

Bryce, W., 'Some Considerations in Psycho-Therapy', *Journal of Mental Science*, LXVII (1921) 195–205.

Collie, J., 'The Management of Neurasthenia and Allied Disorders Contracted in the Army', *Journal of State Medicine*, XXVI (1918) 2–17.

Cowen, T.P., 'Types of Traumatic Insanity', *Journal of Mental Science*, XLII (1896) 122–9.

Culpin, M., 'The Problems of the Neurasthenic Pensioner', *British Journal of Medical Psychology*, I (1919–20) 316–26.

Eder, M.D., 'An Address on the Psycho-Pathology of the War-Neuroses', *Lancet* (12 August 1916) 264–8.

Fielding, A., 'Loss of Personality from "Shell Shock" ', *Lancet* (19 July 1915) 63–6.

Finucane, M.I., 'General Nervous Shock, Immediate and Remote, After Gunshot and Shell Injuries in the South Africa Campaign', *Lancet* (15 September 1900) 1807–9.

Freud, S., 'Introduction to Psychoanalysis and the War Neuroses', 1919, *Standard Edition of the Complete Works*, XVII, pp. 205–10.

——'Memorandum on the Electrical Treatment of the War Neurotics', *Standard Edition of the Complete Works*, XVII, pp. 211–15.

Good, T.S., 'The Oxford Clinic', *Journal of Mental Science*, LXVIII (1922) 17–23.

Graham, S., 'The Ex-Service Mind of Europe', *Contemporary Review*, CXXIII (1923) 290–300.

Hansard, 'Debate on Setting up of the Enquiry into "Shell Shock"', House of Lords (28 April 1920) 1101.

Hotchkis, R.D., 'Renfrew District Asylum as a War Hospital for Mental Invalids', *Journal of Mental Science*, LXIII (1917) 238–49.

Howland, G.W., 'The Neurosis of Returning Soldiers', *American Medicine* (May 1917) 313–19.

Hurst, A.F., 'Cinematographic Demonstration of War Neurosis', *Proceedings of the Royal Society of Medicine, Neurology Section*, XI (1917–18) 39–42.

——'Observations on the Etiology and Treatment of War Neuroses', *British Medical Journal* (29 September 1917) 409–14.

——'Nerves and the Men (The Mental Factor in the Disabled Soldier)', *Reveille*, II (November 1918) 260–8.

Jeffrey, G.R., 'Heredity and Neuro-Insane Constitution', *Journal of Mental Science*, LVI (1910) 286–96.

Kaufmann, F., 'Die Planmässige Heilung komplizierter psychogener Bewegungsstörungen bei Soldaten in einer Sitzung', *Münchener Medizinische Wochenschift, Feldärztliche Beilage*, LXIII (1916) 802–4.

McDougall, W., 'The Present Position of Clinical Psychology', *Journal of Mental Science*, LXV (1919) 141–52.

——'The Revival of Emotional Memories and Its Therapeutic Value' (III), *British Journal of Psychology, Med. Sec.*, I (1920) 23–9.

Massonneau, G., 'A Social Analysis of a Group of Psychoneurotic Ex-Servicemen', *Mental Hygiene*, VI (1922) 575–91.

Mott, F.W., 'Chadwick Lecture: Mental Hygiene in Shell Shock, during and after the War', *Journal of Mental Science*, LXIII (1917) 467–88.

——'Neurasthenia: The Disorders and Disabilities of Fear', *Lancet* (26 January 1918) 127–9.

——'The Neuropathic Inheritance', *Journal of Mental Science*, LIX (1913) 222–63.

——'The Relation of Head Injuries to Nervous and Mental Disease', *British Medical Journal* (30 September 1911) 733–44.

Myers, C.S., 'A Contribution to the Study of Shell Shock: (1), Being an Account of 3 Cases of Memory, Vision, Smell and Taste, Admitted to the Duchess of Westminster War Hospital, Le Toquet', *Lancet* (13 February 1915) 317–20.

——'Contribution to the Study of Shell Shock: (2), Being an Account of Certain Cases Treated by Hypnosis', *Lancet* (8 January 1916) 642–55.

——'Contribution to the Study of Shell Shock: (3), Being an Account of Certain Disorders of Cutaneous Sensibility', *Lancet* (18 March 1916) 782–97.

Neymann, C.A., 'Some Experiences in the German Red Cross', *Mental Hygiene*, I (1917) 392–6.

Purves-Stewart, J., 'Discussion on Traumatic Neurasthenia and Litigation Neurosis', *Proceedings of the Royal Society of Medicine*, XXI (1928) 359–61.

Remarque, E.M. and Hamilton, I., 'The End of War? A Correspondence between the Author of *All Quiet on the Western Front* and General Sir Ian Hamilton GCB GCMG', MacCarthy, D., ed., *Life and Letters*, III (18 November 1929) 406.

Richards, R.L., 'Mental and Nervous Diseases During the Russo-Japanese War', *Military Surgeon*, XXVI (1910) 177–93.

Rivers, W.H.R., 'The Repression of War Experience', *Lancet*, I (1918) 173–7.

Robinson, W., 'The Future of Patients in Mental Hospitals', *Journal of Mental Science*, LXVII (1921) 40–8.

Rows, R.G., 'Mental Conditions following Strain and Nerve Shock', *British Medical Journal* (25 March 1916) 441–3.

Rudy, C., 'Concerning Tommy', *Contemporary Review* (November 1918) 545–52.

Salmon, T.W., 'The Care and Treatment of Mental Diseases and War Neuroses in the British Army', *Mental Hygiene*, I (4 October 1917) 509–47.

Savage, G.H., 'Moral Insanity', *Journal of Mental Science*, XXVII (1881) 147–55.

—— 'Insanity of Conduct', *Journal of Mental Science*, XLII (1896) 1–17.

—— 'Mental Disabilities for War Service', *Journal of Mental Science*, LXII (1916) 653–7.

Soukhanoff, S., 'On Hypochondriacal Melancholia in Russian Soldiers', *Journal of Abnormal Psychology*, I (1906) 135–42.

Swan, J.M., 'An Analysis of Ninety Cases of Functional Diseases in Soldiers', *Archives of International Medicine*, XXVIII (1921) 586–602.

Thom, D.A., 'War Neurosis: Experience of 1914–18', *Journal of Laboratory and Clinical Medicine*, XXVIII (1943) 499–508.

Thomson, D.G., 'A Descriptive Record of the Conversion of a County Asylum into a War Hospital for Sick and Wounded Soldiers in 1915', *Journal of Mental Science*, LXII (1916) 123–4.

Turner, W.A., 'Arrangements for the Cure and Treatment of Nervous and Mental Shock Coming from Overseas', *Lancet*, I (1916) 1073–5.

—— 'Nervous and Mental Shock – A Survey of Provision', *British Medical Journal* (10 June 1916) 82–3.

Turrell, W.J., 'Electrotherapy at a Base Hospital', *Lancet* (30 January 1915) 229–31.

Vincent, W., 'The Use of Asylums as Military Hospitals', *Journal of Mental Science*, LXII (1916) 174–8.

Wolfson, J.M., 'The Predisposing Factors of War Psycho-Neuroses', *Lancet* (2 February 1918) 177–80.

Wright, H., 'Postbellum Neuroses: A Clinical Review and Discussion of their Mechanism', *Archives of Neurology and Psychiatry*, III (1920) 429–34.

Official reports

Ministry of Labour Report of an Investigation into the Personal Circumstances and Industrial History of 10,000 Claimants to Unemployment Benefit (London: HMSO, 1924).

Annual Reports of the Minister of Pensions (London: HMSO, 1917–39).

Report of the War Office Committee of Enquiry into 'Shell-Shock' (London: HMSO, 1922).

Historical: books

Babbington, A., *Shell-Shock: A History of the Changing Attitudes to War Neurosis* (London: Leo Cooper, 1997).

Binneveld, H., *From Shellshock to Combat Stress: A Comparative History of Military Psychiatry* (Amsterdam: Amsterdam University Press, 1997).

Eissler, K.R., *Freud as an Expert Witness: The Discussion of War Neurosis between Freud and Wagner-Jauregg* (Madison: International University Press, 1986).

Holden, W., *Shell Shock: The Psychological Impact of War* (London: Channel 4, 1998).

Shephard, B., *A War of Nerves: Soldiers and Psychiatrists 1914–1994* (London: J. Cape, 2000).

Showalter, E., *The Female Malady: Women, Madness and English Culture, 1830–1980* (Harmondsworth: Penguin, 1985).

Young, A., *The Harmony of Illusions: Inventing Post-traumatic Stress Disorder* (Princeton: Princeton University Press, 1995).

Historical: articles

Bogacz, T., 'War Neurosis and Cultural Change in England 1914–22: The Work of the War Office Committee of Enquiry into "Shell-Shock"', *Journal of Contemporary History*, XXIV (1989) 227–56.

Feudtner, C., '"Minds the Dead have Ravished". Shell Shock, History and the Ecology of Disease-Systems', *History of Science*, XXXI (1993) 377–420.

Leese, P.J., 'Problems Returning Home: The British Psychological Casualties of the Great War', *The Historical Journal*, XL (1997) 1055–67.

Lerner, P., 'Hysterical Cures: Hypnosis, Gender and Performance in World War One and Weimar Germany', *History Workshop*, XLV (1998) 79–101.

Shephard, B., '"The Early Treatment of Mental Disorders": R.G. Rows and Maghull 1914–18', in Freeman, H. and Berrios, G.E., eds., *150 Years of British Psychiatry*. Vol. 2: *The Aftermath* (London: Athlone, 1996), pp. 434–64.

Showalter, E., 'Hysteria, Feminism and Gender', in Gilman, S. et al., *Hysteria beyond Freud* (Berkeley: University of California, 1993), pp. 286–345.

Stone, M., 'Shellshock and the Psychologists', in Bynum, W.F., Porter, R. and Shepherd, M., eds., *The Anatomy of Madness*, vol. 2 (London: Tavistock, 1985), pp. 242–71.

Historical: unpublished

Brent, Wilson J., 'The Morale and Discipline of the B.E.F. 1914–18', MA thesis, University of New Brunswick, Canada, 1978.

Crampton, C., 'The Cambridge School: The Life, Work and Influence of James Ward, W.H.R. Rivers, C.S. Myers, and Sir Frederick Bartlett', PhD thesis, University of Edinburgh, 1978.

Herrick, C., 'Of War and Wounds. The Propaganda, Politics and Experience of Medicine in World War One', PhD thesis, University of Manchester, 1996.

Hiebert, D.M., 'The Psychological Consequences of War and Demobilization in Germany 1914–29', 1985.

——'Social History on the Magic Mountain: German Psychiatric Records as a Source for Historians', n.d.

Leed, E., 'Haunting Memories: How Holocaust Becomes History', 1996.

Lerner, P.F., 'Hysterical Men: War, Neurosis and German Mental Medicine, 1914–21', PhD thesis, Columbia University, 1996.

Lynch, P.J., 'The Exploitation of Courage: Psychiatric Care in the British Army 1914–18', MPhil thesis, University of London, 1977.

Richie, R.D., 'One History of "Shellshock"', PhD thesis, University of California, San Diego, 1986.

Roudebush, M.O., 'The Battle of Nerves: Hysteria and its Treatments in France during World War I', PhD thesis, University of California at Berkeley, 1995.

—— 'Battle of Nerves: Hysteria and its Treatments in France during World War One', 1997.

Rowlands, J.K., 'A Mental Hospital at War', 1985.

Shephard, B., 'Shell-Shock on the Somme', 1998.

Stone, M., 'The Military and Industrial Roots of Clinical Psychology in Britain, 1900–45', PhD thesis, University of London, 1985.

Medical/military: books

American Psychiatric Association, *Diagnostic and Statistical Manual of Mental Disorder*, third edn (Washington: American Psychiatric Association, 1980).

Bartov, O., *The Eastern Front 1941–45: German Troops and the Barbarization of Warfare* (London: Macmillan, 1985).

Cooter, R. et al., eds., *War, Medicine and Modernity* (Stroud: Sutton, 1999).

Dowbiggin, I.R., *Inheriting Madness: Professionalization and Psychiatric Knowledge in Nineteenth-Century France* (Berkeley: University of California, 1991).

Evans, M. and Lunn, P., eds., *Memory and War in the Twentieth Century* (Oxford: Berg, 1997).

Evans, M.N., *Fits and Starts: Genealogy of Hysteria in Modern France* (London: Cornell University Press, 1991).

Goldstein, J., *Console and Classify: The French Psychiatric Profession in the Nineteenth Century* (Cambridge: Cambridge University Press, 1987).

Haymaker, W. and Schiller, F., *Founders of Neurology* (Springfield, Illinois: C.C. Thomas, 1970).

Hearnshaw, L.S., *A Short History of British Psychology 1840–1940* (London: Methuen, 1964).

Holmes, G., *The National Hospital Queen's Square, 1860–1948* (Edinburgh: Livingstone, 1954).

Lifton, R.J., *Home from the War* (New York: Simon and Schuster, 1973).

Micale, M.S., *Approaching Hysteria: Disease and its Interpretations* (Princeton: Princeton University Press, 1995).

Miller, E., ed., *The Neuroses of War* (New York: Macmillan, 1940).

Rosenberg, C.E. and Golden, J., *Framing Disease: Studies in Cultural History* (New Brunswick: Rutgers University Press, 1992).

Slobodin, R., *W.H.R. Rivers* (New York: Columbia University Press, 1978).

Trimble, M.R., *Post-Traumatic Neurosis: From Railway Spine to Whiplash* (Chichester: John Wiley, 1981).

Trombley, S., *'All That Summer She Was Mad'*: Virginia Woolf and Her Doctors (New York: Junction, 1981).

Verin-Bora, R. and Lotari, L., with McDougall, W., *William McDougall: Explorer of the Mind* (New York: Gerret, 1967).

Weldon, R.W., *Bitter Wounds: German Victims of the Great War 1914–39* (London: Cornell University Press, 1984).

Medical/military: articles

Appel, J. et al., 'Comparative Incidence of Neuro-Psychiatric Casualties in World War One and World War Two', *American Journal of Psychiatry*, CIII (1946–7) 196.

Bourke, J., 'Disciplining the Emotions: Fear, Psychiatry and the Second World War', in R. Cooter et al., eds., *War, Medicine and Modernity* (Stroud: Sutton, 1999), pp. 225–38.

Clark, M.J., 'The Rejection of Psychological Approaches to Mental Disorders in Late Nineteenth-Century British Psychiatry', in Scull, A., ed., *Madhouses, Mad-Doctors and Madmen: A Social History of Psychiatry in the Victorian Era* (Pennsylvania: Pennsylvania University Press, 1981), pp. 271–312.

Evans, M., 'Rehabilitating the Traumatized Veteran: The Case of French Conscripts from the Algerian War, 1954–1962', in Evans, M. and Lunn, P., eds., *Memory and War in the Twentieth Century* (Oxford: Berg, 1997), pp. 73–83.

Figlio, C., 'How Does Illness Mediate Social Relations? Workmen's Compensation and Medico-Legal Practices 1890–1940', in Wright, P. and Treacher, A., eds., *The Problem of Medical Knowledge: Examining the Social Construction of Medicine* (Edinburgh: Edinburgh University Press, 1982), pp. 174–228.

Henry, W.D., 'The Case of Captain Colthurst', *Practitioner*, CCV (1981) 418–20.

Karpe, R. and Schnap, I., 'Nostopathy – A Study of Pathogenic Homecoming', *American Journal of Psychiatry*, CIX (1952–3) 46–51.

Porter, R., 'The Body and the Mind, The Doctor and the Patient: Negotiating Hysteria', in Gilman, S. et al., *Hysteria beyond Freud* (Berkeley: University of California Press, 1993), pp. 225–85.

Sicherman, B., 'The Uses of a Diagnosis: Doctors, Patients, and Neurasthenia', *Journal of the History of Medicine*, XXXII (1977) 33–54.

Memoirs and letters

Campbell, P.J., *In the Cannon's Mouth* (London: Hamish Hamilton, 1979).

Carrington, C., *Soldier from the Wars Returning* (New York: David McKay, 1965).

Coppard, G., *With a Machine Gun to Cambrai* (London: Imperial War Museum, 1969).

Cushing, H., *From a Surgeon's Journal 1915–18* (Boston: Little, Brown and Cushing, 1938).

Dunham, F., *The Long Carry – The Journal of Stretcher Bearer Frank Dunham*, ed. Haigh, R.H. and Turner, P.W. (Oxford: Pergamon, 1970).

Edmonds, C., *A Subaltern's War* (London: P. Daines, 1929).

Junger, E., *The Storm of Steel: From the Diary of a German Storm-Troop Officer on the Western Front* (London: Chatto and Windus, 1929).

O'Prey, P., *In Broken Images: Selected Letters of Robert Graves 1914–16* (London: Hutchinson, 1982).

Owen, W., *Collected Letters*, ed. Owen, H. and Bell, J. (Oxford: Oxford University Press, 1967).

Seymour-Smith, M., *Robert Graves: His Life and Works* (London: Hutchinson, 1982).

Stallworthy, J., *Wilfred Owen* (London: Chatto and Windus, 1974).

Stuart Dolden, A., *Cannon Fodder: An Infantryman's Life on the Western Front, 1914–18* (Poole: Blandford, 1980).

Fiction/poetry: books

Aldington, R., *Death of a Hero* (London: Chatto and Windus, 1929).
Barker, P., *Regeneration Trilogy* (Harmondsworth: Penguin, 1998).
Caesar, A., *Taking it Like a Man: Suffering, Sexuality and the War Poets: Brooke, Sassoon, Owen, Graves* (Manchester: Manchester University Press, 1993).
Carr, J.L., *A Month in the Country* (Harmondsworth: Penguin, 1980).
Delderfield, R.F., *To Serve Them All My Days* (New York: Pocket, 1973).
Dowling, D., *Mrs Dalloway: Mapping Streams of Consciousness* (Boston: Twayne, 1991).
Fussell, P., *Siegfried Sassoon's Long Journey* (Oxford: Oxford University Press, 1983).
Graves, R., *Goodbye to all That* (London: Cassell, 1930).
Herbert, A.P., *The Secret Battle* (New York: Knopf, 1920).
Klein, H., ed., *The First World War in Fiction* (London: Macmillan, 1976).
MacDonald, A.G., *England, Their England* (London: Macmillan, 1936).
Owen, W., *Poems*, introduced by S. Sassoon (London: Chatto and Windus, 1920).
——*The Poems of Wilfred Owen. A New Edition Including Many Pieces now First Published and Notices of his Life and Work by Edmund Blunden* (New York: Viking, 1931).
Read, H., *Naked Warriors* (London: Arts and Letters, 1919).
Sassoon, S., *The Complete Memoirs of George Sherston* (London: Faber, 1937).
——*Memoirs of an Infantry Officer* (London: Faber, 1931).
——*Selected Poems* (London: William Heinemann, 1927).
Sayers, D.L., *Busman's Honeymoon* (London: V. Gollancz, 1937).
——*Whose Body?* (London: V. Gollancz, 1923).
Schauwecker, F., *The Fiery Way*, trans. Holland, T. (London: J.W. Dent, 1929).
Theatre Workshop, *Oh What a Lovely War* (London: Methuen, 1965).
West, R., *Return of the Soldier*, 1918 (London: Virago, 1979).
Woolf, V., *Mrs Dalloway* (New York: Harcourt Brace, 1925).

Fiction/poetry: articles

Breen, J., 'Wilfred Owen (1893–1918): His Recovery from "Shell Shock"', *Notes and Queries*, New Series, XXVII (1976) 301–5.
Hibberd, D., 'A Sociological Cure for Shellshock: Dr Brock and Wilfred Owen', *Sociological Review*, XXV (1977) 377–86.

The Great War: books

Ashworth, T., *Trench Warfare 1914–18: The Live and Let Live System* (London: Macmillan, 1980).
Beckett, I. and Simpson, K., *A Nation in Arms* (Manchester: Manchester University Press, 1985).
Boraston, Lieut.-Col. J.H., ed., *Sir Douglas Haig's Despatches* (London: J.M. Dent, 1919).
Bourke, J., *Dismembering the Male: Men's Bodies, Britain and the Great War* (London: Reaktion, 1996).

Brophy, J. and Partridge, E., *The Long Trail: Soldiers' Songs and Slang 1914–18* (London: A. Deutsch, 1963).

Cecil, H. and Liddle, P., *Facing Armageddon: The First World War Experienced* (London: Leo Cooper, 1996).

Clark, A., *The Donkeys* (London: Pimlico, 1991).

Crutwell, C., *A History of the Great War 1914–18*, second edn (Oxford: Clarendon, 1936).

Dunn, J.C., *The War the Infantry Knew* (London: Cardinal, 1989).

Dyer, G., *The Missing of the Somme* (Harmondsworth: Penguin, 1994).

Eksteins, M., *Rites of Spring: The Great War and the Birth of the Modern Age* (Boston: Houghton Mifflin, 1989).

Ellis, J., *Eye-Deep in Hell* (London: Croom Helm, 1976).

Fussell, P., *The Great War and Modern Memory* (Oxford: Oxford University Press, 1975).

Holmes, R., *Firing Line* (London: Jonathan Cape, 1985).

Hynes, S., *A War Imagined: The First World War and English Culture* (London: Macmillan, 1990).

James, Brig. E.A., *British Regiments 1914–18* (London: Samson, 1978).

——*A Record of the Battles and Engagements of the British Armies in France and Flanders 1914–18* (London: Gale and Polden, 1924).

Keegan, J., *The Face of Battle: Study of Agincourt, Waterloo and the Somme* (London: J. Cape, 1985).

Leed, E.J., *No Man's Land: Combat and Identity in World War One* (Cambridge: Cambridge University Press, 1981).

Macdonald, L., *They Called in Passchendaele* (London: M. Joseph, 1987).

——*The Roses of No Man's Land* (London: Papermac, 1984).

McLaughlin, R., *The R.A.M.C.* (London: Leo Cooper, 1971).

Oram, G., *Death Sentences Passed by Military Courts of the British Army 1914–1924* (London: F. Boutle, 1998).

——*Worthless Men: Race, Eugenics and the Death Penalty in the British Army during the First World War* (London: F. Boutle, 1998).

Terrain, J., *Impact of War 1914 and 1918* (London: Hutchinson, 1970).

——*White Heat: The New Warfare 1914–1918* (London: Sidgewick and Jackson, 1982).

Thompson, A., *Anzac Memories: Living with the Legend* (Oxford: Oxford University Press, 1994).

The Times History of the War, VII (London: Times Publishing, 1916).

Ward, S.E., ed., *The War Generation: Veterans of World War One* (New York: Kennikat/Port Washington, 1975).

Wilson, T., *The Myriad Faces of War: Britain and the Great War, 1914–1918* (Cambridge: Polity, 1986).

Winter, D., *Death's Men: Soldiers of the Great War* (London: Allen Lane, 1978).

Winter, J.M., *The Experience of World War One* (Oxford: Oxford University Press, 1989).

——*The Great War and the British People* (London: Macmillan, 1986).

——*Sites of Memory, Sites of Mourning: The Great War in European Cultural History* (Cambridge: Cambridge University Press, 1995).

Wohl, R., *The Generation of 1914* (London: Weidenfeld and Nicolson, 1980).

Woodward, Sir Ll., *Great Britain and the War of 1914–18* (London: Methuen, 1967).
Woolf, L., *In Flanders Field* (Harmondsworth: Penguin, 1979).

The Great War: articles

Ashworth, T., 'The Sociology of Trench Warfare', *British Journal of Sociology*, XXI (1968) 407–20.
Bessel, R. and Englander, D., 'Up from the Trenches: Some Recent Writing on the Soldiers of the Great War', *European Studies Review*, II (1981) 387–95.
French, D., 'The Meaning of Attrition, 1914–16', *English Historical Review*, CIII (1988) 385–405.
—— 'Total War 1: The Great War', in C. Townsend, ed., *The Oxford Illustrated History of Modern War* (Oxford: Oxford University Press, 1997), pp. 99–119.
Habeck, M.R., 'Technology and the First World War: The View from Below', in J. Winter et al., eds., *The Great War and the Twentieth Century* (New Haven: Yale University Press, 2000), pp. 99–131.
Leese, P.J., 'The Memory and Mythology of the Great War in Contemporary Britain', in K. Kujawińska-Courtney and R. Machnikowski, eds., *The Role of Britain in the Modern World* (Łódz University Press, 1999), pp. 165–76.
Thomson, A., 'The Anzac Legend: Exploring National Myth and Memory in Australia', in Samuel, R. and Thompson, P., *Myths We Live By* (London: Routledge, 1990), pp. 74–82.
Travers, T., 'The Hidden Army: Structural Problems in the British Officer Corps, 1900–1918', *Journal of Contemporary History*, XVII (1982) 523–44.
van Creveld, M., 'Technology and War to 1945', in Townsend, C., ed., *The Oxford Illustrated History of Modern War* (Oxford: Oxford University Press, 1997), pp. 175–93.
Winter, J.M., 'Military Fitness and Civilian Health in Britain During the First World War', *Journal of Contemporary History*, XV (1980) 211–44.

Culture/society: books

Conrad, P., *Modern Times, Modern Places: Life and Art in the 20th Century* (London: Thames and Hudson, 1998).
Grayling, C., *A Land Fit for Heroes: British Life After the Great War* (London: Buchan and Enright, 1987).
Hobsbawm, E., *The Age of Extremes: The Short Twentieth Century* (London: Abacus, 1995).
Holmes, G., *The National Hospital Queen's Square, 1860–1948* (Edinburgh: Livingstone, 1954).
Kern, S., *The Culture of Time and Space 1880–1918* (Cambridge, Mass.: Harvard University Press, 1983).
Pick, D., *War Machine: The Rationalization of Slaughter in the Modern Age* (New Haven: Yale University Press, 1993).
Porter, R., *Myths of the English* (Cambridge: Polity, 1992).
Rabinbach, A., *The Human Motor: Energy, Fatigue and the Origins of Modernity* (New York: Basic Books, 1990).

Samuel, R., *Theatres of Memory: Past and Present in Contemporary Culture* (London: Verso, 1994).

Samuel, R. and Thompson, P., *Myths We Live By* (London: Routledge, 1990).

Schivelbusch, W., *The Railway Journey: The Industrialization of Time and Space in the 19th Century* (Berkeley: University of California, 1986).

Skelley, A.R., *The Victorian Army at Home* (London: Croom Helm, 1977).

Summers, A., *Angels and Citizens: British Women as Military Nurses, 1854–1914* (London: Routledge and Kegan Paul, 1988).

Culture/society: articles

Nora, P., 'Between Memory and History: Les Lieux de Memoire', *Representations*, XXVI (1989) 7–25.

Simmel, G., 'The Metropolis and Mental Life', in Harrison, C. and Wood, P., *Art in Theory 1900–1990* (Oxford: Blackwell, 1992), pp. 323–4.

Index